Initiatives in Strategic S

Series Editor
James J. Wirtz
Department of National Security Affairs
Naval Postgraduate School
Monterey, CA, USA

This important series on topical and timeless issues relating to strategy studies provides a link between the scholarly and policy communities. The focus is on conceptually sophisticated analyses of political objectives and military means. Strategy, the focus of strategic studies, revolves around core and perennial concerns: protecting the country and people, influencing friends and opponents, using a variety of military tools in various ways, including to deter or coerce other actors. Strategy deals with problems of national policy and the nexus of political, diplomatic, psychological, economic, cultural, historic and military affairs. Central to strategic studies is an understanding of the environment, including increased comprehension of other strategic actors.

More information about this series at
http://www.palgrave.com/gp/series/14854

Jeannie L. Johnson
Kerry M. Kartchner
Marilyn J. Maines
Editors

Crossing Nuclear Thresholds

Leveraging Sociocultural Insights into Nuclear
Decisionmaking

Editors
Jeannie L. Johnson
Department of Political Science
Utah State University
Logan, UT, USA

Kerry M. Kartchner
Department of Political Science
Brigham Young University
Provo, UT, USA

Marilyn J. Maines
Center for Advanced Study of
Language
University of Maryland
College Park, MD, USA

Initiatives in Strategic Studies: Issues and Policies
ISBN 978-3-030-10247-0   ISBN 978-3-319-72670-0   (eBook)
https://doi.org/10.1007/978-3-319-72670-0

This Palgrave Macmillan imprint is published by the registered company Springer International Publishing AG part of Springer Nature.
The registered company address is: Gewerbestrasse 11, 6330 Cham, Switzerland

Jeannie dedicates this book to Steve, Benjamin, Sam, and Jess, who light up her world and remind her what it is all about.

Kerry dedicates his modest contributions to this book to his Samoan brother, Tracy William Kauaheahe Spencer, lifelong friend, companion, and role model. His steadfast courage, selfless compassion, infectious humor, and unwavering grace in the face of every twist and turn life has thrown at him have been a source of strength and inspiration not only to me, but to our mutual family members, and to Tracy's many friends and extended Samoan family as well.—Alofa tele.

Marilyn dedicates this book to husband David, children Sonya, Sasha, and Bobby, and grandson Rene, in hope of a nuclear-free future. Having family is what enables me to get up each morning and face new challenges and inspires me to write and share ideas. Thank you for all the love and support and all the joy you bring to my life.

Preface and Acknowledgments

In the near- and medium-term future, the United States will face a wide range of over-the-horizon nuclear challenges including ensuring state adherence to the terms of existing nuclear treaties and nonproliferation agreements; dealing with a menacing number of potential nuclear aspirants seeking to join the nuclear club; engaging with friends and allies bent on unilateral military action to protect regional nuclear monopolies; and deterring increasingly alarming prospects of nuclear use. The case studies included in this volume tackle a number of nuclear challenges—termed "nuclear thresholds"—likely to be faced by the United States, its friends, and allies, and identify the most promising points of leverage available to American policymakers in confronting these threats.

Nuclear decisionmaking scholars have long recognized that nuclear aspirations and planning are often instigated within elite circles, but once put in motion come to fruition only through co-opting or keeping at bay or circumventing key competing constituencies within domestic populations and critical and opposed foreign governments (whether ally or adversary). A major premise of this volume is that for policymakers and analysts to more accurately anticipate the likelihood of successful nuclear acquisition, or other critical nuclear decisions, identifying those key constituencies within a polity of concern and assessing the internal socio-cultural drivers which shape their thinking and decisionmaking on weapons of mass destruction (WMD) issues is essential. Distilling leverage points within the internal dynamics of those groups who may facilitate acquisition, or if properly motivated may act to oppose or constrain acquisition, is key to understanding options that can be engaged by policymakers when confronted with a leadership cadre bent on nuclear acquisition and norm violation.

With decades of US engagement on WMD issues on display, the next generation of WMD aspirants will likely hedge against traditional US mechanisms for thwarting nuclear advances and potentially prepare to absorb an anticipated level of sanctioning. US counterproliferation efforts must become increasingly clever, tailored, and focused. Those efforts require an analytical tool which yields a high degree of granularity concerning salient rewards and effective coercive measures applied in sometimes starkly diverse contexts. The United States may find itself confronting both an ally and a serious adversary seeking nuclear ownership within the same time frame. Such a situation would render generic sanctioning approaches difficult and likely counterproductive. These moments will require an analytical approach designed to yield individualized solutions with contours that fit each discrete situation with maximum impact. Providing this policy-relevant analysis will require an intimate knowledge of the national, sub-national, or transnational actor sets likely to weigh in, or with the potential to weigh in, on a country's WMD decisionmaking and action.

This volume advances the strategic cultural research program we previously surveyed in a book titled *Strategic Culture and Weapons of Mass Destruction: Culturally Based Insights into Comparative National Security Policymaking*, published by Palgrave Macmillan in 2009. The present volume showcases insights made possible by rigorously applying key elements of the cutting-edge socio-cultural model (Cultural Topography Analytic Framework—CTAF) pioneered by our team. The CTAF model draws from the research paradigm of strategic culture employed in our earlier volume which was refined for use within the intelligence community as well as by academicians and regional experts seeking solutions to these nuclear challenges. Our authors employed the basic principles of that model here with an eye toward isolating those vectors of nuclear decisionmaking on which the United States might exert influence within a foreign state. The US response will require strategies tailored to the perception of threat experienced by the actors in question, the value the actors place on their relationship with the United States, and the domestic context driving decisionmaking. Our volume offers a nuanced look at each actor's identity, national norms, values, and perceptual lens in order to offer culturally focused insights into behavior and intentions. Additionally, each case study includes a set of recommendations specifically tailored for use with that actor. As long-time regional experts, our authors offer an honest and often self-critical assessment of what is likely to work within the US deterrence, assurance, and dissuasion toolkit and what is not.

Given these considerations, this volume explicitly sets out to do the following:

- To identify and consolidate recent developments in socio-cultural modeling and analysis, especially those related to strategic cultural analysis and country personality profiling;
- To develop and articulate terms of reference for validating and applying those analytical developments and scholarly research to the challenge of scoping emerging nuclear proliferation risks;
- To apply these new analytical frameworks to defining the emerging nuclear proliferation landscape, with particular emphasis on identifying target decisionmaking vectors and narratives in countries of potential future nuclear proliferation concern, identified in this study as WMD aspirants;
- To provide novel and innovative insights to communities seeking to reduce WMD threats through deterrence, mitigation, and consequence management, as well as through new arms control and nonproliferation initiatives focused on those countries and leadership cadres at greatest risk of crossing the nuclear threshold.

This volume targets three wide audiences: students and scholars of international relations whose research and coursework touches on strategic threats and nuclear decisionmaking, policymakers who must navigate the precarious and complex nuclear arena, and the intelligence analysts who must deliver timely new insights and hedge against surprise on the world's deadliest question.

To scholars interested in growing and refining methodologies within the strategic culture paradigm, we offer novel treatment of the methodological conundrum that has long beset scholars of strategic culture and introduce an approach certain to provoke discussion.

The editors wish to gratefully acknowledge the support and encouragement provided by the Naval Postgraduate School's Project on Advanced Systems and Concepts for Countering Weapons of Mass Destruction (PASCC) via Assistance Grant No. N00244-15-1-0033 awarded by the NAVSUP Fleet Logistics Center San Diego (NAVSUP FLC San Diego).

The views expressed in written materials or publications, and/or made by speakers, moderators, and presenters, in connection with the workshops and other contributions to this project, do not necessarily reflect the official policies of the Naval Postgraduate School nor does mention of trade names, commercial practices, or organizations imply endorsement by the US government.

Jeannie, Kerry, and Marilyn would also like to acknowledge the major contribution to the preparation of this book by our friend, colleague, and editorial assistant Briana Bowen. Without her ardent support, supreme organizational skills, and keen editorial talents, this book would never have reached publication. We are so proud of Briana's recent graduation from Oxford and are happy she has returned to our team. We expect to see Briana make significant contributions to, among other things, the emerging generation of strategic culture scholarship.

We would also like to acknowledge the Center for Advanced Study of Language at University of Maryland for supporting research on the Cultural Topography Analytic Framework as well as its predecessor version, the Cultural Analytic Framework. Many thanks to colleagues and codevelopers of the CAF, Joe Danks, John Walker, Kathy Faleris, and Anne Wright and to CASL research director Mike Bunting.

Logan, UT	Jeannie L. Johnson
Provo, UT	Kerry M. Kartchner
College Park, MD	Marilyn J. Maines

CONTENTS

5   **Israeli Strategic Culture and the Iran "Preemption Scare"**
    of 2009–2013   141
    Gregory F. Giles

NOTES ON CONTRIBUTORS

Dmitry (Dima) Adamsky is an associate professor within the School of Government, Diplomacy, and Strategy, IDC Herzliya. He is the author of *Operation Kavkaz: Soviet Intervention and Intelligence Failure in the War of Attrition*, and *The Culture of Military Innovation*. He is currently working on a book about religion and strategy in Russia.

Nima Gerami is Director of the Program for Emerging Leaders and a Research Fellow in the Center for the Study of Weapons of Mass Destruction at the National Defense University (NDU), where he specializes in Iranian foreign and security policy, WMD nonproliferation, and Persian Gulf security affairs. He teaches at NDU and is a regular guest instructor at other US senior service schools.

Gregory F. Giles serves as Senior Director of the Science Applications International Corporation and President of Giles Consulting LLC. Mr. Giles advises US government decisionmakers on issues pertaining to the Middle East, nonproliferation, and deterrence. He has published widely and testified before Congress on these subjects and has guest lectured at United States, Saudi, and NATO Defense Colleges.

Jeannie L. Johnson is an assistant professor within the Political Science Department at Utah State University. Her primary research interest, strategic culture, examines the impact of national and organizational cultures on the formation of security policy. Dr. Johnson co-edited the volume *Strategic Culture and Weapons of Mass Destruction: Culturally Based Insights into Comparative National Security Policymaking* published with

Palgrave Macmillan in 2009. Her second book explores the internal culture of the US Marine Corps and its impact across 100 years of counterinsurgency operations: *The Marines, Counterinsurgency, and Strategic Culture: Lessons Learned and Lost in America's Wars* (2018).

Dr. Johnson worked within the CIA's Directorate of Intelligence as a member of the Balkan Task Force from 1998 to 1999 and served with the US State Department in Embassies Paris and Zagreb. Her current academic work includes ongoing efforts with members of the intelligence community, State Department, and Department of Defense to improve cultural research methods and analysis. The cultural research methodology she pioneered with co-author Matt Berrett was featured in CIA's June 2011 edition of *Studies in Intelligence*. She received her PhD from the University of Reading (UK) in 2013.

Kerry M. Kartchner has more than 25 years of experience analyzing, implementing, negotiating, and teaching the theory and practice of American diplomacy, especially as it relates to national security strategy, weapons of mass destruction, strategic arms control, and nuclear nonproliferation.

He has served on the faculty of the Naval Postgraduate School, as well as Missouri State University, and has been a visiting lecturer at the Bush School of Government and Public Service at Texas A&M University. Dr. Kartchner has served on the staffs of the US Arms Control and Disarmament Agency, and since 1999, the US Department of State, where he was responsible for negotiating resolutions to complex compliance and inspection issues with counterparts from Russia, Ukraine, Belarus, and Kazakhstan, in the context of the Joint Compliance and Inspection Commission (for the START Treaty) and formulating diplomatic strategy for pursuing missile defenses (in the context of the ABM Treaty's Standing Consultative Commission).

He has also served two extended assignments with the Department of Defense's Defense Threat Reduction Agency, as Senior Foreign Policy Advisor, and as Chief of the Division of Strategy and Policy Studies, where he was responsible for developing and managing so-called Track II diplomatic engagements with experts from Russia, China, India, Pakistan, Japan, South Korea, Brazil, Australia, South Africa, and Israel. Dr. Kartchner is the author of *Negotiating START: Strategic Arms Reduction Talks and the Quest for Strategic Stability* and co-editor of

Strategic Culture and Weapons of Mass Destruction (Palgrave Macmillan, 2009). His most recent book, co-edited with Jeffrey Larsen, titled *On Limited Nuclear War in the 21st Century*, was published by Stanford University Press in 2014, and he is the recipient of the Chief Scientist of the Air Force's Award for Outstanding Research. He holds a PhD and MA in International Relations from the University of Southern California. His BA is from Brigham Young University.

Jeffrey A. Larsen is Director of the Research Division at the NATO Defense College in Rome. A retired US Air Force Lieutenant Colonel, he served as a Senior Policy Analyst for Science Applications International and has taught as an adjunct professor in the graduate programs of Denver, Northwestern, and Texas A&M Universities. He holds a PhD in Politics from Princeton University.

Marilyn J. Maines education includes BA, MA, and ABD degrees from Rutgers University and University of Chicago in Russian Language and Russian Area Studies. Her experience includes over 30 years of government service in the Intelligence Community working on a wide range of issues as an analyst, linguist, manager, and senior executive. Her assignments include support to the National Intelligence Council, management of a large Proliferation Office, and leading the Nuclear Negotiations Section on the Arms Control Intelligence Staff. While on the Arms Control Staff, she participated in US delegations to Russia, Ukraine, Belarus, and Kazakhstan as part of the Nunn-Lugar Cooperative Threat Reduction initiatives.

Following government service, Ms. Maines moved to University of Maryland's Center for Advanced Study of Language (CASL) to conduct research in socio-cultural analysis and modeling, exploring how social and cultural variables in foreign countries impact WMD decisionmaking. She has also conducted studies on how cultural factors and values impact social unrest and political instability, examining data in social media and using techniques for sentiment analysis developed at CASL. Ms. Maines has collaborated with Johnson on the development of the Cultural Topography Analytic Framework (CTAF) used in this volume and is currently working with Johnson and Kartchner on a joint UMD–USU research project on using the CTAF to examine nuclear intentions of over-the-horizon countries.

J.E. Peterson is a political analyst and historian specializing in the con-temporary Arabian Peninsula and Gulf and the author of a dozen books and nearly 40 scholarly articles on the region. He is affiliated with the Center for Middle Eastern Studies at the University of Arizona and has been a fellow and visiting professor at the University of Durham (UK) and the Paris School of International Affairs of SciencesPo (France).

Shane Smith a senior research fellow at the Center for the Study of Weapons of Mass Destruction, National Defense University (NDU), has been a nuclear policy adviser in the US Office of the Secretary of Defense and at the Defense Threat Reduction Agency. He has taught at NDU, the University of Colorado at Boulder, and Johns Hopkins University.

Ekaterina Svyatets is an assistant professor (Teaching) at the University of Southern California (USC) and an expert on international energy security and environmental policy. She is the author of *Energy Security and Cooperation in Eurasia: Power, Profits and Politics* (2016). She holds a PhD in International Relations and Political Science from USC.

LIST OF FIGURES AND TABLES

Figures

CHAPTER 1

Introduction: Sociocultural Approaches to Understanding Nuclear Thresholds

Kerry M. Kartchner

The phrase "nuclear threshold" has always referred primarily to that moment in a conflict when nuclear weapons are first used, when a conventional war becomes a nuclear war.[1] Beginning with the earliest literature on the advent of nuclear weapons, it was that instant when one side or the other, verging on the precipice of abject military and political collapse and in desperate fear for survival, and having exhausted all other options, commits the "unthinkable," and introduces nuclear weapons in order to radically alter the calculus of victory and defeat, thus instantly changing the terms of conflict even if it meant placing the future of humanity in jeopardy.[2] This literature assumed that this threshold would be crossed only in the midst of a conflict, and it sought to establish the normative conviction that nuclear weapons are somehow special and distinct from "conventional" weapons, and their employment must be reserved for only the most dire and catastrophic circumstances, as a last resort. Extensive political, doctrinal, and diplomatic efforts have been engaged to reinforce this distinction, and to perpetuate the presumption against crossing the threshold of nuclear use, a prohibition sometimes referred to as the "nuclear taboo."[3]

As nations beyond the United States and the Soviet Union acquired nuclear weapons, the attention of the international community turned

K. M. Kartchner (✉)
Department of Political Science, Brigham Young University, Provo, UT, USA

© The Author(s) 2018
J. L. Johnson et al. (eds.), *Crossing Nuclear Thresholds*,
Initiatives in Strategic Studies: Issues and Policies,
https://doi.org/10.1007/978-3-319-72670-0_1

1

increasingly to the task of preventing, slowing, or rolling back horizontal nuclear proliferation, and the phrase took on a second connotation, referring to the decision to acquire nuclear weapons, or at least a nuclear weapons capability.[4] As an example of the use of this meaning in a nonproliferation context, Israel was widely assumed to have "crossed the threshold" of nuclear acquisition as early as 1966,[5] and successive nuclear tests by India and Pakistan in 1998 were interpreted to mean that those countries had crossed a "nuclear threshold." More pertinent to the present era, North Korea's nuclear tests have decisively established that it too has crossed the threshold of nuclear acquisition. Here the meaning, as indicated by the context, is clearly the acquisition of nuclear weapons capability (demonstrated unambiguously in the case of India, Pakistan, and North Korea through the testing of nuclear devices, more ambiguously in the case of Israel). Nevertheless, now that India, Pakistan, North Korea, and presumably Israel, have crossed the threshold of nuclear acquisition, further discussions of crossing nuclear thresholds in those regions plainly refer to the original meaning of crossing the threshold of nuclear use.[6]

The existing literature on nuclear decisionmaking has therefore focused largely on this second meaning, the issue of nuclear acquisition—on what factors contribute to or constrain a nation's consideration of embarking on a program to acquire nuclear weapons, or, as Jim Walsh phrased it, "the process tucked between wanting and making a bomb."[7] Yet, the decision to acquire nuclear weapons may not be made in a single moment, and the path to such a decision is replete with other thresholds that must be crossed and re-crossed. The leaders of any given nation in these situations will have to consider crossing or not crossing many key thresholds; whether to develop peaceful nuclear energy capabilities, whether or not to join with the rest of the international community in complying with global nonproliferation norms, whether to establish and operationalize a deployed nuclear deterrent, whether to preemptively counter a regional rival's nascent nuclear program, and, possibly in extreme cases, whether to break the taboo against actual use of nuclear weapons and launch a nuclear attack. Each of these thresholds will test a nation's determination, organizational prowess, and resources. But they will also be manifestations of that nation's discursive constitution of its own identity, its own values, and its own place in the world of states.

Not only does the context convey the particular connotation meant by the phrase "crossing the nuclear threshold," but usage of the two alternate meanings also depends on which community of scholars is employing the term. Understandably, the meaning of threshold as nuclear acquisition is most widely used within the nonproliferation community, while the first meaning described above, to actually use nuclear weapons, is the province of the deterrence and strategic stability communities. In fact, within the nuclear nonproliferation community, a key issue at the foundation of any analysis of nuclear thresholds is the question of what exactly constitutes acquiring a "nuclear weapons capability," and has been the subject of some dispute. It can mean either when a country has tested a nuclear device, or when it has accumulated sufficient fissile material (or "significant quantity") through transfer or indigenous manufacture, to assemble a functional nuclear weapon.[8]

This chapter has five objectives. First, going beyond and supplementing the definitions given above, I introduce additional possible meanings of the concept of "crossing nuclear thresholds," that supplement the original notion associated with both the cataclysmic decision to use nuclear weapons and the decision to acquire nuclear weapons. The following chapters further develop these other possible meanings as well, including the threshold of using military force to preemptively counter the prospective nuclear acquisition of a regional rival, the threshold of the "culminating point of deterrence," and the threshold of deploying operational nuclear weapons capability (often conflated with the nuclear weapons acquisition threshold).

Second, I discuss six types of nuclear thresholds that the authors in this volume have assessed from a sociocultural perspective. The idea and terminology of "nuclear thresholds" are central to long-standing debates over the causes of nuclear weapons proliferation, but some of the meanings of these different uses of the phrase "crossing nuclear thresholds" have not been the subject of substantive definitional discourse, and therefore the ways these terms have been used is not always clear or consistent.[9] This book is an attempt to provide more explicit definitions and examples for six different potential meanings of the phrase.

Third, I present a preliminary discussion of the notion that identity, values, norms, and perceptual lens can shape and contextualize a given country's decisions regarding crossing nuclear thresholds, as will be further developed by the contributing authors. Our approach is intended to employ these four dimensions to craft tailored policy options based upon the cultural profile of a given country's nuclear decisionmaking culture.

Fourth, I briefly situate the approach taken by this book's editors and authors within the context of other recent literature and concepts that engage and explore ideational factors at play in nuclear decisionmaking.

Fifth, I preview the subsequent chapters and outline the overall structure of the book.

CROSSING NUCLEAR THRESHOLDS

For states pondering their nuclear future, nuclear thresholds can come in many forms. Invariably, the first threshold is acquiring some modicum of nuclear energy producing capability, to generate power or to produce medical isotopes, or to conduct fission experiments. But even this apparently modest threshold poses daunting, time-consuming, and expensive technical, material, experiential, and institutional hurdles. No country that has crossed, or considered crossing, the threshold of nuclear acquisition since the Nuclear Nonproliferation Treaty (NPT) entered into force in 1970, has done so without first building at least a modest civil nuclear power or research infrastructure with the assistance of some other established nuclear power.[10] Since Eisenhower's "Atoms for Peace" initiative in the 1950s, crossing the threshold of civilian nuclear power has had the consensual endorsement and support of the international community, and was enshrined in the NPT as an "inalienable right."[11] It has even taken on the symbology of modernity—it often seems that no country can consider itself truly modern if it has not partaken of the nuclear fruit. And, importantly, for those who chose to pursue this capability under the auspices of membership in the NPT, it has not required violating any international norm, so long as the pursuit of such capability was kept within the regulatory bounds of the international nuclear regime, closely monitored by the International Atomic Energy Agency. Indeed, membership in the NPT brings with it the benefits of technology transfer and assistance, training and experience, a knowledge of safety procedures, and other forms of material and managerial aid.[12]

So, taking into account our sociocultural focus, I offer this definition of the phrase "crossing the nuclear threshold": it refers to that point in time where both constitutive sociocultural and political psychological factors converge with objective or structural military, institutional, diplomatic, and economic factors to lead a given state to choose one course of action over another (or, to choose inaction) with respect to its nuclear weapons aspirations. As used in this volume, "crossing the nuclear threshold" can refer to any of several culminating moments in a state's nuclear decision-making process. These include whether to establish a latent civilian nuclear hedge against a future decision to develop nuclear weapons; to comply with or transgress international nuclear nonproliferation norms; to proliferate or accept the transfer of sensitive dual-use nuclear technology; to preemptively attack or counter another state's nascent nuclear program; to accept or extend nuclear assurances toward another state or state collective; or, in extremis, to break the nuclear taboo and use nuclear weapons. The editors and authors of the present volume understand that both situational (material) and dispositional (ideational) factors will bear on any such decision, but the emphasis of the following chapters is on the ideational and contextual dynamics of identity, values, norms, and perceptual lens, and how these factors can sometimes transcend purely objective considerations to decisively promote and shape nuclear weapons aspirations. After all, as another analyst concluded, "if a country has the political will, not even poverty or underdevelopment can keep it from building a nuclear weapons program."[13]

Such thresholds might be approached quietly and covertly so as not to provoke a public outcry or diplomatic backlash, or with much fanfare, celebration, and national holidays. Crossing a given threshold does not necessarily imply irreversibility. Nearly any given decision can be undone, for purely domestic reasons, for resource constraints, through international diplomacy and economic pressure, or bombing. Neither should it be assumed that these thresholds are mutually exclusive. A state may enter into the development of civil nuclear energy infrastructure for a host of reasons, including to implicitly pursue a hedging strategy. Of particular relevance to the subject of this book, this meaning is often reflected in the contemporary discourse over Iranian nuclear aspirations, specifically to whether or not Iran will acquire nuclear weapons.[14] Intent here is crucial, and the elaboration and explication of intent is a major sub-theme of this volume.

For countries which contemplate crossing the first threshold by acquiring nuclear weapons and contemplate going beyond the operation of a peaceful nuclear energy program, either to embark full throttle on a program to acquire a nuclear weapons capability (as in the case of North Korea) or to establish a latent capacity to acquire nuclear weapons in the future (as prospectively in the case of Saudi Arabia, among others), a second threshold must be confronted: whether to breach commitments under the NPT; or, if not already a member of the NPT, to defy the well-established norms and accepted practices governing peaceful nuclear energy generation and normative presumption of nuclear nonproliferation, and thus to assume the role of a renegade, inviting the collective opprobrium of the entire international community. The obstacles and powerful disincentives to defying these broadly upheld international norms in pursuit of an illicit nuclear weapons program have sometimes been underestimated by the academic and policy communities, but additional scholarship has clarified and expounded the enormous hurdles and disincentives that confront the prospective nuclear norm-breaking state.[15] Here, the aspiring nuclear weapons state must surmount not only formidable technical, material, and programmatic challenges but also political and diplomatic impediments, that have proven far more daunting in more instances than is sometimes realized. As noted above, the international community has expended considerable effort to establish and reinforce a series of global norms against nuclear proliferation, under the rubric of the nuclear nonproliferation regime.

The 1970 NPT is considered the cornerstone of this regime, with its endorsement of nuclear weapons possession by the so-called P-5, or Nuclear Weapon States, and its prohibition on acquiring such weapons by all other states party to the treaty, designated as Non-Nuclear Weapon States. Nuclear scholar Maria Rost Rublee has underscored the powerful effect of this normative regime on promoting "nuclear forbearance." As one possible answer to the mystery of why so few states have developed nuclear weapons. Rublee finds that a strong systemic impetus to accept and comply with the nuclear nonproliferation was created by the establishment of the NPT and its antinuclear norm. "The emerging antinuclear norm led to the development of the nuclear nonproliferation regime, which set forth a clear injunctive norm against nuclear proliferation; and then as states acceded to the treaty, the expanding regime established a descriptive norm against nuclear proliferation as well. The negotiations to create the regime, and the regime itself, communicated that a nuclear weapons program was a violation of international norms, instead of an act of national pride." Rublee posits that "states complied with the nonproliferation regime because the benefits (technology transfer and assistance with nuclear energy programs) outweighed the perceived benefits of a costly nuclear weapons program."[16] She further notes that "once states accede to the regime, they are tethered to it in a number of ways: a domestic bureaucracy is created and empowered to advocate for the NPT, nuclear decisionmaking becomes no longer solely a function of security advisors but also involves those in the foreign ministry, and elites fear that backing out of the NPT would result in a loss of international credibility and legitimacy."[17]

Six Nuclear Thresholds

While many thresholds and hypothetical sub-thresholds, such as those described above, have been mentioned in the discourse of nuclear nonproliferation in addition to the two meanings of use or acquisition of nuclear weapons, the chapter in this book address six specific thresholds, which are summarized below for the reader's convenience, together with the central analytical question to be addressed with respect to each particular threshold.[18]

- *Acquisition of Nuclear Weapons, or Nuclear Weapons Capability.* This is what is most commonly meant when using the phrase "crossing the nuclear threshold." It can entail either embarking on an effort to acquire nuclear weapons capability short of assembling operational weapons, or it can refer to actually acquiring deployable nuclear weapons. Our concern in this book is to ask, how do sociocultural factors inform or shape incentives for acquiring nuclear weapons or nuclear weapons capability?
- *Nuclear Norm Violation.* To cross the threshold of cheating on an arms control agreement, or of choosing to violate existing commitments with international norms. This begins with decisions related to whether or not to sacrifice some degree of national autonomy by entering into and adhering to international nonproliferation regimes and norms, and then to whether to maintain that adherence by complying with the terms of the regime, including those related to transparency and verification. How do sociocultural factors reinforce or mitigate against international or domestic norm-adherence policies and behavior?
- *Nuclear Counter-Proliferation.* This threshold is taken by a state to actively deny acquisition of nuclear weapons to others through preemptive attack. We ask what role do sociocultural factors play in strategic decisions to actively deny or counter the acquisition of nuclear weapons by neighboring states?
- *Proliferation and Transfer of Nuclear Weapons.* To cross the threshold of transferring nuclear capability to another state or nonstate actor. How do sociocultural factors promote or inhibit motivations,

tendencies, or incentives to proliferate or transfer nuclear weapons or sensitive nuclear weapons technology?

- *Operational Deployment of Nuclear Weapons.* How do sociocultural factors help determine whether to proceed with overt deployment of nuclear weapons, or to deploy covertly (as presumably in Israel's case)?
- *Use of Nuclear Weapons.* To cross the threshold of operationally deploying functional nuclear explosive devices, usually on ballistic missiles. This is the other most common use of the phrase "to cross the nuclear threshold." In these so-far hypothetical situations, how do sociocultural factors influence decisions to use nuclear weapons, either in the sense of wielding nuclear weapons for deterrence and coercive purposes or in the sense of actually conducting attacks with nuclear weapons?

SOCIOCULTURAL ANALYSIS OF NUCLEAR PROLIFERATION

Scholarship on the dynamics of nuclear proliferation has come a long way since the classical dual notions of a security imperative coupled with a technological imperative.[19] In an oft-cited categorization of the field of nonproliferation studies, Scott Sagan proposed grouping theories of nonproliferation into three models. The first is the security model, "according to which states build nuclear weapons to increase national security against foreign threats, especially nuclear threats." According to this model, "states will seek to develop nuclear weapons when they face a significant military threat to their security that cannot be met through alternative means," and that "nations will seek to enhance their security through acquiring nuclear weapons if they are technologically capable of procuring such weapons."[20] Second is the domestic politics model, "which envisions nuclear weapons as political tools used to advance parochial domestic and bureaucratic interests." According to the third model, termed the norms model, "nuclear weapons decisions are made because weapons acquisition, or restraint in weapons development, provides an important normative symbol of a state's modernity and identity."[21]

In the intervening years, the field has grown to encompass a multiplicity of additional theories, including:

- Supply-side and demand-side theories;
- Theories that incorporate the dichotomy between capability and willingness, or willingness and opportunity;

- Normative theories, focusing on identity, prestige, and national pride;
- Psychological theories, addressing individual leadership predispositions and national identity conceptions;
- Theories of institutional capacity and organizational ability to manage large engineering projects;
- Pragmatist theories, addressing a state's socially constructed political, historical, and cultural contexts; and
- Constructivist sociocultural theories addressing a state's internal discursive narratives.

These theories may be roughly divided between those that address objective factors (capacities and resources) and those that focus on ideational factors (psychological predispositions and identity constructs). It is fair to say that while the majority of traditional scholarly research has been grounded in the security model, this list demonstrates the increasing attention to the ideational side of the research equation. The present volume does not necessarily set out to provide a critique of this literature, nor does it focus solely on nuclear proliferation per se, but is squarely situated in the ideational category with an emphasis on sociocultural factors that shape and inform nuclear aspirations, whether those aspirations are to acquire, use, or prevent the use of nuclear weapons.

FOUR PERSPECTIVES FOR SOCIOCULTURAL ANALYSIS

The chapters in this book contain case studies of selected countries, designed to illustrate the ways in which identity, values, norms, and perceptions can shape and contextualize key nuclear decisions.[22] We define each of these sociocultural concepts in the following terms, followed by a fuller discussion of each:

- **Identity:** The character traits a given group assigns to itself, the reputation it pursues, the individual roles and statuses it designates to members, and the distinctions it makes between those people who are considered members of the group ("us") and those who are not members of the group ("them").
- **Values:** Deeply held beliefs about what is desirable, proper, and good that serve as broad guidelines for social life. Values include material or ideational goods that are honored or confer increased

status to individual actors or members of groups. These include both secular and sacred values.

- **Norms:** Accepted, expected, or customary behaviors within a society or group. Norms can be explicit or implicit; prescriptive or proscriptive.
- **Perceptual Lens:** Filters through which individual actors or members of a group determine "facts" about themselves and others.

I discuss each of these in turn below.

Identity

The concept of identity has received a great deal of attention in the IR theory literature, especially with the need to better understand newly emergent post-Cold War state actors.[23] One of our editors has defined identity as a "nation's view of itself, comprising the traits of its national character, its intended regional and global roles, and its perceptions of its eventual destiny."[24] Our sociocultural approach "assumes that states form their interests, and their views of other actors, based on a normative understanding of who they are, and what role they should be playing."[25] And it holds identity to be the predominant cultural trait, from which is derived the other three core analytical constructs in our framework—values, norms, and perceptual lens.

Collective identities should not be understood as fixed or invariant, but may shift in agreement and disagreement about the meanings and priorities they confer on alternative national goals and role conceptions. To give one example, Greg Giles, in his survey of Israeli strategic culture, notes the presence of three "sub-cultures," each competing for their own respective policy preferences and notions of Israel's national sense of purpose. The *security subculture* "believes that Israel is locked in a battle for survival with its Arab neighbors, and that a major Israeli military defeat would mean annihilation of Israeli Jews." The *conflict subculture* "assumes that the Jewish-Arab conflict is just another incarnation of historic anti-Semitism." The *peace subculture* "sees the Jewish-Arab conflict as no different from any other negotiable dispute and is unconnected to the persecution of Jews in the past."[26]

Identity can be a powerful factor in a state's deliberations over whether to pursue nuclear weapons. One recent study of factors underlying nuclear proliferation places identity at the center of its analysis. According to author Ursala Jasper, "nuclear decision-making of states follows from the intersubjectively shared beliefs and narratives regarding the country's identity, its self-perception or its position vis-à-vis significant others."[27] Status is an important element of a state's identity. State identity conceptions are, in part, a function of self-perceived status, relative to others in the region and on the world stage. For some states, nuclear weapons are the ultimate status symbol. Historian Beatrice Heuser confirms this view, and argues that nuclear weapons:

> are the ultimate guarantee that a traumatising [sic] historical experience they have had will not repeat itself; to some, they serve important domestic purposes; to some, they are the magic that keeps wars at bay; to some, they symbolise [sic], or indeed incarnate, ultimate evil. In the 1950s and early 1960s, nuclear weapons were symbols of modernity, and successful nuclear tests were celebrated with naïveté, champagne and celebration cakes much like successful space-rocket launches even more recently than that. Nuclear weapons have a certain cachet which other WMD lack; they are political as well as military instruments, and can be made to convey a series of political signals, from *noli me tangere* ("touch me not") to a claim to superpower status which no other existing weapons system presently confers.[28]

This theme of nuclear weapons as symbols of a nation's status and reflective of its own conception of national identity is developed in Jacques E.C. Hymans' book, *The Psychology of Nuclear Proliferation: Identity, Emotions, and Foreign Policy*.[29] In this book, Hymans develops a concept of "National Identity Conception," or NIC. According to Hymans, what sets leaders with "definite nuclear weapons ambitions apart from the many who do not harbor such ambitions" "...is a deeply held conception of their nation's identity," which Hymans terms "oppositional nationalist." Hymans inserts an emotional element into his framework. Leaders who adhere to or reflect this identity "see their nation as both naturally at odds with an external enemy, and as naturally its equal if not its superior. Such a conception tends to generate the emotions of fear and pride—an explosive psychological cocktail." Hymans believes that leaders driven by fear and pride "develop a desire for nuclear weapons that goes beyond calculation to self-expression."[30] Thus, an individual's understanding of the nation's 'true' identity—his or her sense of what the nation naturally stands for and its rightful status in comparison to others in its regional or international arena—has a powerful influence on the decision to cross the threshold of nuclear acquisition.

Values

The second component of our basic analytical framework involves those sorts of goods—both material and immaterial—that society values more highly than others.[31] Values can include protecting and defending territory, or pursuing "life, liberty, and the pursuit of happiness." Values can be ascertained from studying foundational or canonical texts and narratives. Leaders' explicit endorsement of key national values can strengthen their legitimacy to rule.

A study of values includes those ideational or material values which confer increased status on members of the group. Ideational goods may be thought of in terms of those personal or state characteristics that are considered "honorable" and are therefore status enhancing. Highly valued material goods may confer the same status-enhancing benefit. Identifying these sorts of "values" within a society is key for the development of salient foreign policy levers. The discovery of highly valued ideational "goods," for instance, provides a window into the sort of public political praise that would effectively "reward" a state or substate actor for cooperative behavior. A lack of understanding on this front can lead to counterproductive mirror imaging: concepts that constitute high praise in one culture (e.g., willingness to compromise) may backfire when applied as an attempt at public compliment for another. The same may be said of threats: unless threats target key ideational or material values, they are unlikely to alter behavior. A nuanced understanding of material values aids the design of foreign policy levers in the same way. Salient material rewards are those that are tailored to the specific value orientation of the society or actor set targeted. Threats to highly valued material components of the society ("smart sanctions") capture attention in ways that generalized and sweeping threats may not.

Recent work in social and cognitive psychology finds that not all values have equal trade-off value and that certain values termed "sacred values," or sometimes called "protected values," are so deeply held and revered, and constitute such strong moral obligations, that they transcend normal, secular reasoning, and are therefore highly resistant to exogenous pressure. That is, holders of sacred values are strongly averse to using traditional utility-based models to reason about these values.[32] In fact, analysts have found that when holders of such sacred values are pressured to compromise or surrender these values, it can result in a "backlash" effect that causes the holder of the value to become further entrenched in clinging to that value, and less likely to be willing to resolve disputes based on that value. According to two important social psychologists, "while a secular value can easily be substituted with another value, tradeoffs involving sacred values result in strong negative emotions and moral outrage."[33] Research into the decisionmaking dynamics of these sacred values has found the following:

- Sacred values may be critically involved in sustaining seemingly intractable cultural and political conflicts;
- Sacred values appear to be intimately bound up with sentiments of personal and collective identity;
- Sacred values resist material tradeoffs;
- Sacred values show insensitivity to quantity and calculations of loss versus gain;
- Protected values were more likely to be associated with moral obligations to act rather than moral prohibitions against action; and
- People motivated by protected values appear to show "quantitative insensitivity," that is, in tradeoffs situations they are less sensitive to the consequences of their choices than people without protected values.[34]

Sacred values can include the pursuit of nuclear weapons possession, or the development of a latent capacity for creating nuclear weapons, or simply the desire to establish a civilian nuclear power infrastructure, wherein such programs are deemed "inalienable rights," and are resistant to international pressures for restraint. In a 1997 study of Iranian public opinion, a team of social psychologists found that "a relatively small but politically significant portion of the Iranian population believes that acquiring nuclear energy has become a sacred value, in the sense that proposed economic incentives and disincentives result in a 'backfire effect' in which offers of material rewards or punishment lead to increased anger and greater disapproval. This pattern was specific to nuclear energy and did not hold for acquiring nuclear weapons."[35]

Norms

Norms are a third component of our basic sociocultural framework, and have been generically defined as "accepted and expected modes of behavior."[36] These are rules, or laws, that govern proper behavior of actors within a given identity group. Norms and identity can be closely related. Norms can be "constitutive" of identity by defining actions that either enable members of the group to relate to each other or cause members of other groups to recognize a particular identity. Or norms can be "regulative" and specify boundaries of proper behavior within a given rule system, including, for example, standard operating procedures.[37] Norms can constrain elite behavior by delimiting the range of acceptable behavior necessary to maintain ruling legitimacy. Again, contrasting a political realist perspective with a sociocultural constructivist approach, Theo Farrell states:

> What matters most for realists is the material structure of world politics. States do what they have the power to do. For constructivists, states do what they think most appropriate. In so doing, states are guided by norms that define the identities of the main actors in world politics (i.e. modern, bureaucratic, sovereign states) and define the formal rules and accepted practices of the international game. When culturalists look at the impact of domestic norms on state form and action, they invariably find norms producing differences in what states do. Thus, norms peculiar to national communities and organization are seen as shaping uniquely national military styles and organizational ways of war.[38]

It is these norms that shape "uniquely national military styles" that we are most concerned with here, especially those norms that shape unique styles in nuclear decisionmaking. It can be argued that the most important nuclear norms are the following:

1. The nonproliferation norm: avoiding and preventing the horizontal proliferation of nuclear weapons.
2. The disarmament norm: the commitment to engage in good faith negotiations leading toward the complete elimination of nuclear weapons.
3. The right to civil nuclear energy norm: the freedom to pursue the benefits of nuclear energy for economic or other uses.
4. The non-use norm, or "nuclear taboo": the presumption that nuclear weapons will never be used, or will only be used as a last resort, and never in a first-strike or preemptive manner.
5. The responsible nuclear stewards' norm: the notion that Nuclear Weapon States have a duty to ensure the safety, security, and reliability of their nuclear arsenals.

6. The extended deterrence norm: the expectation that a nuclear-armed state will provide nuclear assurances to its allies.
7. The nuclear safety culture norm: the requirement to ensure the safety and reliability of civilian nuclear power operations.

Another specific manifestation of norms in the international arena will figure prominently in the chapters of this book—the normative presumption against the use of nuclear, chemical, or biological weapons. According to social scientists Richard Price and Nina Tannenwald, "the reluctance manifested by states in employing these weapons [nuclear and chemical] is a product of normative boundaries on action—in this case, global norms adopted at the domestic level."[39]

Perceptual Lens

The fourth component of our basic sociocultural framework is the perceptual lens through which cultures interpret the world around them. One of our editors has earlier defined and explained perceptual lens as "beliefs (true or misinformed) and experiences or the lack of experience that color the way the world is viewed." She further explained that "behavior is based on the *perception* of reality, not reality itself. Perceptions of 'fact,' of our own histories, of our image abroad, of what motivates others, of the capabilities of our leadership and our national resources, and other security-related ideas, all play a strong role in forming what each regime believes to be rational policy."[40]

Several factors have been shown to color, or distort, perceptions of national security issues. First, the perceptions of virtually every country are subject to some form of ethnocentrism. Each views itself as the center of the universe in some aspect or character trait, or superior in some way to all other countries, or as the source of ancient wisdom available for dispatching to other less wise countries, or as the vanguard of the "true" religion or the "final" ideological paradigm, or as the champion of human rights, or the guardian of the sacred places. Second, each country sees what other countries say or do through the prism of its own self-interest, and its own presumed universal centrality, and will tend to see the statements or actions of other countries, no matter how proximate or distant, as aimed at them, even if the offending state had no intention of directing those declarations or actions against that state. Third, virtually all states will believe that their own perceptions and threat assessments are peremptorily the most valid.

Fourth, national myths will represent the perceptual lenses through which members of a nation will process their own values and status. Nations tend to culturally process what constitutes "victory" or "defeat."[41]

Noted international relations and social psychology scholar Robert Jervis has summed up several of the most important key aspects of image and perception in international relations.[42] Jervis has been largely responsible for promoting the notion among international relations theorists, as well as in social and political psychology circles, that decisionmakers' perceptions of the world and of other actors diverge from reality in detectable patterns referred to as perceptual biases. Jervis has further argued that serious potential instabilities arise if an aggressor believes that the status quo powers are weak in capability or resolve, so therefore states must often go to extremes in policy or polemic declarations because moderation or conciliation will be seen as weakness. What cultures or nations learn from key events in international history is an important factor in determining images that shape the interpretation of incoming information. It is a common misperception to see the actions of others as more centralized, planned, and coordinated than they really are. Additionally, actors exaggerate the degree to which they play a central role in others' policies. More recently Jervis has compiled his professional observations in a new book, titled *How Statesmen Think: The Psychology of International Politics.*[43] Jervis opens by saying that "[m]any consequential foreign policy decisions—including ones that shape the world, such as Britain's decision to fight on after the fall of France in 1940 ... are deeply contested, and knowing only the external situation does not tell us why different individuals came to different conclusions, let alone who prevailed. We need to look inside the 'black box' of the state to study the goals, beliefs, and perceptions of the decisionmakers."[44]

COMPLEMENTARY APPROACHES IN RECENT LITERATURE

The present volume joins a small but growing number of other recent academic efforts to promote and explore the impact of ideas, beliefs, values, norms, perceptions, rituals, narratives, practices, and other ideational phenomena on the nuclear decisionmaking of the state. While the contributions of this emerging body of literature do not necessarily all share a common analytical framework, they do share three common premises.

First, they all entail a certain dissatisfaction with the adequacy of the dominant realist paradigm in the study of international relations. As one author puts it, certain dominant assumptions of this school of thought have led to the "consolidation of a realist orthodoxy in security studies that has left little room for alternative approaches."[45] Second, they all focus on the situational, nonlinear, and interactional dynamics at play in a state's discursive formulation of policy goals, motivations, preferences, and outcomes. Third, they all recognize the constitutive importance of some form or combination of identity, values, norms, and perceptual lenses.

In *The Politics of Nuclear Nonproliferation*, Swiss scholar Ursala Jasper is primarily concerned with the question of nuclear restraint, or why certain states elected to forgo nuclear weapons, despite the realist tenet which assumes that, faced with an anarchical international system prowling with existential threats, states will automatically and reflexively seek to increase their objective means of security. Her primary premise is that "nuclear decisionmaking of states follows from the intersubjectively shared beliefs and narratives regarding the country's identity, its self-perception or its position vis-à-vis significant others."[46] Her two main case studies are Switzerland and Libya, two states that consciously embarked on nuclear weapons development efforts, only to choose to reverse that decision, under widely varying circumstances. She sets out to open the 'black box' of state decisionmaking, and to try to understand how "in a deeply political process—narratives and frames regarding its identity, threat perception, preferences or position in the international system emerge and shift... These narratives embody the cognitive-ideational basis for state action." In Jasper's analytical construct, the state's "place in the world" is discursively constructed, and "state action—and a state's security and nuclear policies—is shaped by socially shared political, historical and cultural imaginaries and narratives."[47] Jasper's analytical approach is to identify key participants and their major contributions to the nuclear discourse, and to outline the broader sociopolitical and cultural environment in which the nuclear discourse is embedded. She further urges analysts "to pay tribute to human agency, reflexivity and historical contingency, rather than parsimony, causality, and universality."[48]

The theme of stressing ideational factors is also taken up in a recently published book by John Baylis and Kristan Stoddart, *The British Nuclear Experience: The Role of Beliefs, Culture, and Identity.*[49] Baylis and Stoddart consider that although traditional approaches that states seek to enhance their security and prestige "have some merit, they are somewhat limited in their explanatory power, and that much more can be gleaned from looking at beliefs, culture and identity factors which lay at the heart of the British nuclear experience from the Second World War until today."[50] They hold that "[n]uclear weapons are seen as part of a broader self-identity of Britain playing a vital role in maintaining international peace and protecting universal values."[51] These authors find that nuclear weapons possession has underpinned Britain's "core identity as a 'force for good' in the international system, and nuclear weapons reinforce an interventionist foreign policy that supports universal values of peace and freedom and the Rule of Law." Possession of nuclear weapons enables Britain to maintain credibility with its regional peers and to underwrite its special relationship with the United States. It also supports Britain's aspirations to be seen as "a responsible and leading defender of Western Europe."[52] However, while Baylis and Stoddart support Hymans' thesis relating to National Identity Conceptions that were held by key individuals in historically decisive leadership positions, they argue that with respect to the British case, "[h]igh-level decisions relating to the acquisition of atomic and thermonuclear weapons were taken by small ad hoc groups of ministers and not by prime ministers on their own."[53] In other words, the relevant and pivotal national identity conceptions were shared by groups of decisionmakers acting in concert, and not necessarily by individuals acting in their sole capacity.

Middle East scholar Norman Cigar, in a recent publication titled *Saudi Arabia and Nuclear Weapons: How Do Countries Think about the Bomb?*, examines the cultural mindsets and social discourses that would be relevant to a possible Saudi Arabian decision in the future to pursue a nuclear weapons capability. His main thesis is that "should Iran at any time decide on a nuclear breakout, then Saudi Arabia would very likely follow suit."[54] Cigar surveys leading theories of motivations for acquiring nuclear weapons, and concludes that none of them in and of themselves adequately explains those factors that would impact Saudi Arabia's potential nuclear aspirations, or the sociocultural and intersubjective processes that would be necessary to formulate and promulgate a Saudi decision to cross the threshold of nuclear acquisition. Cigar asserts that "[t]he case of Saudi Arabia, in particular, confirms the significance of a country's identity, political, and ideological foundation, and national interests, in shaping threat perceptions, objectives, and policy and, in particular in stimulating and legitimizing the need to acquire nuclear weapons."[55] As long as Iran restrains from crossing the threshold of nuclear acquisition, so will Saudi Arabia. Nevertheless, Cigar holds that Saudi Arabia has been developing the basic justifications, institutional components, and political conditions for a potential nuclear capability, and that these preparations and their potential future culmination can only be fully understood through a sociocultural perspective that takes into account factors of identity, values, norms, and perceptual lens.

OVERVIEW OF THE VOLUME

The remainder of this book is organized as follows. In Chap. 2, "The Cultural Topography Analytic Framework," Jeannie Johnson and Marilyn Maines walk the reader through the development of the Cultural Topography Analytic Framework, describe the sociocultural analytical shortcomings it is meant to remedy, and explain the process of employing it as a research method. At the core of the Cultural Topography Analytic Framework is the goal of explicating the key identity factors, values, norms, and perceptual lens of the state contemplating crossing a nuclear threshold, and then designing a tailored set of traditional and nontraditional foreign policy levers for interlocutors to use to impact that decision. The chapter briefly introduces the reader to the field of strategic culture and its early contributions to the nuclear policy literature. The authors highlight continuing deficiencies within this methodological field, including failures to account for shifts in national behavior over time, and an inability to reconcile or anticipate which of the several and often competing national security narratives within a particular regime will dominate decisionmaking on the nuclear issue. The authors' model is designed both to remedy deficiencies and to illuminate new, untapped or underutilized sources of information for identifying and understanding emerging threats.

Chapter 3, "Iran's Strategic Culture: Implications for Nuclear Policy," Nima Gerami, addresses the threshold of norm compliance. Gerami strikes a note of caution in his chapter concerning the prospects for preserving compliance with the 2015 nuclear agreement—the Joint Comprehensive Plan of Action (JCPOA)—between Iran and the P5+1. He explains that Iran sees itself as "a great civilization on par with global superpowers" with "a legitimate interest in scientific development"; two aspects of national narrative which "fuel its sense of entitlement to advanced nuclear fuel cycle technologies." In theory, as JCPOA restrictions begin to expire, Iran could "scale up its enrichment program to the point where it would have sufficient capacity to produce nuclear weapons in the span of a few weeks, should it choose to do so." Thus, Gerami emphasizes, "[d]espite robust monitoring and verification measures in place to detect such a breakout, the question of Iran's *nuclear intent* will grow increasingly important over the next decade" [emphasis added]. Gerami affirms the salience of examining cultural context in any assessment of nuclear intent: "cultural factors are likely to play a significant and complementary role alongside other indicators in determining Iran's propensity to cheat on the JCPOA and its ability to overcome longstanding ideological hostilities with the West."

In Chapter 4, "Prospects for Proliferation in Saudi Arabia," J. E. Peterson examines the Saudi deliberations over crossing the threshold of acquiring a latent nuclear capability, as a prelude to a possible future nuclear acquisition. He reviews complex narratives, historic culture, and decisionmaking processes inside Saudi Arabia and assesses a low probability that the Kingdom will act to acquire nuclear arms in the near term. His assessment is based on an operational cultural narrative that combines both push and pull factors concerning nuclear acquisition and hinges to a significant extent on the Kingdom's relationship with the United States. Triggers within the security threat matrix that may flare Saudi motivation to acquire nuclear capability include concern over regional disintegration, Israeli provocation, continued Iranian belligerence and involvement in regional crises, and deterioration of the JCPOA or evidence of direct Iranian provocation or interference in Gulf States' domestic affairs. Peterson argues, however, that the Saudi reaction will likely hinge primarily on perceptions of the United States as a reliable security partner and its valuing of this relationship.

Chapter 5, "Israeli Strategic Culture and the Iran 'Preemption Scare' of 2009–2013," by Greg Giles, illustrates how the threshold of counter-proliferation can take many forms, from enacting and imposing sanctions and other penalties designed to dissuade a country from crossing the nuclear threshold, to more decisive military action. Giles offers a useful and unconventional take on the Israeli nuclear question by focusing on its commitment to protecting its ostensible regional nuclear monopoly— with unilateral acts of military force if necessary—and US efforts to steer and moderate potential Israeli action. Giles succinctly captures the basic elements of Israel's operational cultural narrative as they relate to the Begin Doctrine: support within Israel for the use, if necessary, of military force to preemptively destroy enemy nuclear facilities. Giles highlights a specific set of critical cultural factors which have consistently functioned within Israel's operational cultural narrative on nuclear issues. To demonstrate these crucial cultural points, Giles details the decisionmaking process behind the military strike on nuclear facilities in Syria and Iraq—showing that each of the criteria within Israel's operational cultural narrative for nuclear issues was met. Giles draws a sharp line of contrast with Netanyahu's proposed military action against Iran (2009–2013) in which these criteria were not met. Israel's decisionmaking process on nuclear action provides a number of leverage points for US policymakers given the prominent role of the US-Israel alliance within its strategic culture.

In Chapter 6, "Cultural Underpinnings of Current Russian Nuclear and Security Strategy," noted Israeli scholar Dima Adamsky addresses aspects of deterrence thresholds. He contextualizes this analysis by tracking Russian strategic culture from the Soviet period through the current day. His argument is that this culture is marked more by continuity than discontinuity. His chapter captures several specific categories of Russian security thinking: the balance of moral-psychological and material factors in the culture of war, a holistic approach to strategy, theory-driven military innovations, the Russian management and learning style, and Russia's historic siege mentality. Adamsky's chapter interweaves an analysis of Russian strategic culture with descriptions of the current Russian geopolitical threat perception, the architecture of its nuclear community, and the evolution of Russian nuclear and cross-domain coercion strategies over the last two decades. He cautions that Russia's siege mentality and inclination to accept conspiratorial theories color its perceptual lens. Imagined threat perceptions may encourage Moscow to interpret particular events through the lens of past associations, draw flawed conclusions from connecting unrelated events, attribute nonexistent aggressive intentions and capabilities to its adversaries and consequently result in overreaction.

In Chapter 7, "Ukraine's Nuclear Culture: Past, Present, and Future," Ekaterina Svyatets maps Ukraine's social circles and values in order to explain Ukrainian restraint regarding crossing the threshold of seeking a nuclear weapons option, despite its inheritance at the breakup of the Soviet Union of facilities and residual (or latent) capabilities to do so. Ukraine's nuclear decisionmaking posture has historically been caught between desires to act as a team player and to position itself as a "Western" state, alongside realities requiring a sufficient defense against Russia on its border. Svyatets examines the aspects of Ukrainian identity, social and security norms, values, and public memory of its nuclear age to identify those cultural factors which are likely to strengthen Ukraine's nonproliferation stance and those that are likely to push against it. As Ukraine's security woes continue to flame, so too will its wistful narratives of nuclear capability. Svyatets makes clear where the United States and the West at large have a critical window of opportunity to intervene by providing Ukraine the incentives it is looking for to remain a "team player" and to forgo a trip down the nuclear path.

In Chapter 8, "North Korea's Strategic Culture and Its Evolving Nuclear Strategy," Shane Smith, unenviably tasked with addressing one of the most opaque and inaccessible regimes on the planet, acknowledges that North Korea has crossed the nuclear acquisition threshold and now possesses enough fissile material to build "anywhere from six to about thirty weapons" and that its leader, Kim Jung Un, has declared his intention to "ceaselessly develop nuclear weapons technology to actively develop more powerful and advanced nuclear weapons." Over the horizon projections indicate that "sooner or later it will be able to target South Korea, Japan and the United States" with the United States as its "primary nuclear target." The question of acquisition has already been answered. The critical decisions ahead for North Korea are "the shape, size, and character of its arsenal" and scenarios for nuclear use. Smith examines North Korea's identity narratives which have increasingly featured nuclear weapons in a dominant role as well as North Korean perceptions of threat which hold that the United States is bent on destroying North Korea and the distinct Korean identity. The result for Pyongyang is an inclination toward exaggerating its nuclear accomplishments and capabilities, a scenario made more dangerous by an extreme authoritarian system which cedes unconstrained nuclear power to Kim Jung Un himself. The mindset within North Korea is consistently conditioned to expect "a final war against imperialism" and has been imbued with the notion that "their military is more courageous, spirited, and resilient than that of their opponents and that using nuclear weapons is the surest way to defeat its enemies." Smith warns that consistent exposure to this narrative may mean that North Koreans actually come to believe it, and "become emotionally committed to an irrational optimism about the prospects of waging and prevailing in a nuclear conflict." With these warnings as backdrop, Smith offers carefully constructed advice to would-be interlocutors on the nuclear question.

Finally, in Chapter 9, Jeffrey Larsen examines the outlook and implications of the varied case studies and nuclear thresholds contained in this volume, with a focus on how understanding the cultural factors involved in nuclear decisionmaking adds to the analytic process. Decisions on whether the identified nuclear thresholds will be crossed depend to a large extent on US understanding of the decisionmaking process of states involved and US ability to craft creative diplomatic strategies to influence that process.

NOTES

1. In fact, this is the definition of the phrase given in two popular modern dictionaries. The *Oxford Dictionary* defines "nuclear threshold" as "a point in a conflict at which nuclear weapons are or would be brought into use." A similar definition is provided in the *Collins English Dictionary*. Available at https://www.collinsdictionary.com/us/dictionary/english/nuclear-threshold, accessed 26 August 2017.
2. This distinction dates from the very dawn of the nuclear age. See Bernard Brodie, et al., *The Absolute Weapon: Atomic Power and World Order* (New York: Harcourt, Brace, 1946).
3. See, for example, the thorough treatments of this taboo threshold in Nina Tannenwald, *The Nuclear Taboo: The United States and the Non-Use of Nuclear Weapons Since 1945* (Cambridge: Cambridge University Press, 2007); and T.V. Paul, *The Tradition of Non-Use of Nuclear Weapons* (Stanford University Press, 2009). An excellent essay on US nuclear trends that may jeopardize this taboo is given in George H. Quester, "The End of the Nuclear Taboo?" in Jeffrey A. Larsen and Kerry M. Kartchner, eds., *Limited Nuclear War in the Twenty-First Century* (Stanford University Press, 2014), pp. 172–190.
4. A third meaning, used in the phrase "to raise or lower the nuclear threshold," refers to actions and rhetoric exchanged during a crisis for the purpose of escalation management intended to make the use of nuclear weapons either easier and more likely to be undertaken, or to make that use less likely. This meaning, while it has important nuclear policy implications, is outside the scope of this book.
5. Avner Cohen, "Crossing the Threshold: The Untold Nuclear Dimension of the 1967 Arab-Israeli War and Its Contemporary Lessons," *Arms Control Today*, June 2007. Available at: https://www.armscontrol.org/act/2007_06/Cohen, accessed 26 August 2017.
6. This is the clear meaning in, for example, "Pakistan Seen Ready to Cross Nuclear Threshold." Available at https://www.theatlantic.com/international/archive/2011/06/pakistan-seen-readying-to-cross-nuclear-threshold/239817/, accessed 26 August 2017.
7. Jim Walsh, "Surprise Down Under: The Secret History of Australia's Nuclear Ambitions," *The Nonproliferation Review* (Fall 1997), p. 14.

8. Jacques E.C. Hymans, "When Does a State Become a 'Nuclear Weapon State'? An Exercise in Measurement Validation," *Nonproliferation Review*, Vol. 17, No. 1 (March 2010), pp. 161–180. Available at https://www.nonproliferation.org/wp-content/uploads/npr/npr_17-1_hymans.pdf, accessed 26 August 2017. See also, Jacques E.C. Hymans and Matthew S. Gratias, "Iran and the Nuclear Threshold," *The Nonproliferation Review*, Vol. 20, No. 1 (2013), pp. 13–38. Available at: http://www-bcf.usc.edu/~hymans/Hymans%20and%20Gratias%20Nonproliferation%20Review%20FINAL-1.pdf, accessed 26 August 2017. Hymans and Gratias argue that ballistic missile testing is a proxy for nuclear weapons testing, and that the two often go hand-in-hand, and therefore assert that such testing should be considered the definitive "threshold" of nuclear weapons acquisition.

9. One exception is the excellent discussion of alternative metrics for crossing nuclear thresholds in Jacques E.C. Hymans and Matthew S. Gratias, "Iran and the Nuclear Threshold," *The Nonproliferation Review*, Vol. 20, No. 1 (2013), pp. 13–38. Available at http://www-bcf.usc.edu/~hymans/Hymans%20and%20Gratias%20Nonproliferation%20Review%20FINAL-1.pdf, accessed 13 August 2017. Hymans and Gratias make a case for using the occurrence of a nuclear test as the point at which the nuclear "rubicon" has been crossed, as opposed to the accumulation by a state of a "significant quantity" of bomb-making material.

10. Matthew Kroenig, *Exporting the Bomb: Technology Transfer and the Spread of Nuclear Weapons* (Ithaca, NY: Cornell University Press, 2010); and Matthew Fuhrmann, "Taking a Walk on the Supply Side," *Journal of Conflict Resolution*, Vol. 53, Issue 2 (January 2009), pp. 181–208.

11. Article IV, para. 1. The term is used in the secular sense of irrevocable, not in the US Constitutional sense of "God given," although some countries may be tempted to invoke that connotation.

12. Maria Rost Rublee, *Nonproliferation Norms: Why States Choose Nuclear Restraint* (Athens: University of Georgia Press, 2009), p. 202.

13. Ibid., p. 201. See also Feroz Hassan Khan's story of the extreme sacrifices nations can make in pursuing nuclear weapons in *Eating Grass: The Making of the Pakistani Bomb* (Stanford University Press, 2012).

14. Note the reference to "a subtle debate going on [in Iranian elite circles] regarding the wisdom of crossing the nuclear threshold" in Ray Takeyh, "Iran's Nuclear Calculations," *World Policy Journal*, Vol. 20, No. 2 (2003), p. 21. See also Jael Espinoza, "North Korea and Iran: Crossing the Nuclear Threshold," 26 April 2017, Western Free Press. Available at: http://www.westernfreepress.com/2017/04/26/north-korea-iran-crossing-nuclear-threshold/, accessed 26 August 2017.

15. In addition to Maria Rost Rublee's *Nonproliferation Norms*, see also Mitchell Reiss, *Bridled Ambition: Why Countries Constrain Their Nuclear Capabilities* (Washington, DC: Woodrow Wilson Center Press, 1995).

16. Rublee, *Nonproliferation Norms*, p. 10.

17. Ibid., p. 202.

18. These thresholds utilize and expand on the four key WMD decision areas originally identified and discussed in Kerry Kartchner, "Strategic Culture and WMD Decision Making," in Jeannie L. Johnson, Kerry M. Kartchner, and Jeffrey A. Larsen, eds., *Strategic Culture and WMD Decision Making* (New York: Palgrave Macmillan, 2009), pp. 55–67.

19. The literature has benefited from several essays that survey the state of the field, and compare the several theories of proliferation that have been advanced. Among the most helpful are the following: Dong-Joon Jo and Erik Gartzke. "Determinants of Nuclear Weapons Proliferation," *Journal of Conflict Resolution*, Vol. 51, No. 1 (February 2007), pp. 167–194; Harald Müller and Andreas Schmidt, "The Little Known Story of Deproliferation: Why States Give Up Nuclear Weapon Activities," in *Forecasting Nuclear Proliferation in the Twenty-First Century: The Role of Theory*, edited by William C. Potter and Gaukhar Mukhatzhanova (Stanford, CA: Stanford University Press, 2010); Tanya Ogilvie-White, "Is There a Theory of Nuclear Proliferation? An Analysis of the Contemporary Debate," *The Nonproliferation Review*, Vol. 4 (1996), pp. 43–60; William C. Potter and Gaukhar Mukhatzhanova, "Divining Nuclear Intentions: A Review Essay," *International Security*, Vol. 33, No. 1 (Summer 2008), pp. 139–169; Jacques E. C. Hymans, "Theories of Nuclear Proliferation," *The Nonproliferation Review*, Vol. 13, No. 3 (2006), pp. 455–465; and, Alexander H. Montgomery and Scott D. Sagan, "The Perils of Predicting Proliferation," *Journal of Conflict Resolution*, Vol. 53 (2009), pp. 302–328.

See also the extensive literature review and critique in a series of online commentaries and responses that were part of an *International Studies Quarterly* online symposium, headlined by the essay from Todd S. Sechser, "A Pivotal Moment in Proliferation Research," *International Studies Quarterly*, posted 9 February 2016. Available at www.isanet.org/Publications/ISQ/Posts/ID/5012/A-Pivotal-Moment-in-Proliferation-Research, accessed 27 August 2017.

Excellent reviews of the literature on nuclear proliferation can also be found in the following books: Alexandre Debs and Nuno P. Monteiro, *Nuclear Politics: The Strategic Causes of Proliferation* (Cambridge University Press, 2017); Jacques C. Hymans, *The Psychology of Nuclear Proliferation: Identity, Emotions, and Foreign Policy* (Cambridge: Cambridge University Press, 2006); K. P. O'Reilly, *Nuclear Proliferation and the Psychology of Political Leadership: Beliefs, Motivations, and Perceptions* (New York: Routledge, 2015); Ursula Jasper, *The Politics of Nuclear Non-Proliferation: A Pragmatist Framework for Analysis* (London: Routledge, 2014); Robert Rauchhaus, Matthew Kroenig, and Erik Gartzke, eds., *Causes and Consequences of Nuclear Proliferation* (London: Routledge, 2011); and Etel Solingen, *Nuclear Logics: Contrasting Paths in East Asia & The Middle East* (Princeton: Princeton University Press, 2007).

20. Scott Sagan, "Why Do States Build Nuclear Weapons?: Three Models in Search of a Bomb, *International Security*, Vol. 21, No. 3 (Winter, 1996–1997), pp. 54–86. Available at: https://fsi.stanford.edu/sites/default/files/Why_Do_States_Build_Nuclear_Weapons.pdf, accessed 27 August 2017.

21. Scott Sagan, "Three Models in Search of a Bomb."

22. This section draws on and supplements the excellent discussion of identity, values, norms, and perceptual lens in Jeannie L. Johnson, "Conclusion: Toward a Standard Methodological Approach," in Jeannie L. Johnson, Kerry M. Kartchner, and Jeffrey A. Larsen, eds. *Strategic Culture and Weapons of Mass Destruction: Culturally Based Insights into Comparative National Security Policymaking* (London, New York: Palgrave Macmillan, 2009), pp. 243–257.

23. See especially William Bloom, *Personal Identity, National Identity and International Relations* (Cambridge University Press, 1990); Yosef Lapid and Friedrich Kratochwil, eds., *The Return of Culture and Identity in IR Theory* (Boulder, CO: Lynne Rienner, 1996); and Part 2: Identity, in Peter Katzenstein, ed., *The Culture of National Security: Norms and Identity in World Politics* (New York: Columbia University Press, 1996), pp. 271–447.

24. Jeannie L. Johnson, "Conclusion: Toward a Standard Methodological Approach," in Jeannie L. Johnson, Kerry M. Kartchner, and Jeffrey A. Larsen, eds. *Strategic Culture and Weapons of Mass Destruction: Culturally Based Insights into Comparative National Security Policymaking* (London, New York: Palgrave Macmillan, 2009), pp. 245.

25. Johnson, "Conclusion: Toward a Standard Methodological Approach," p. 246.

26. Gregory F. Giles, "Continuity and Change in Israel's Strategic Culture," in Jeannie L. Johnson, Kerry M. Kartchner, and Jeffrey A. Larsen, eds. *Strategic Culture and Weapons of Mass Destruction: Culturally Based Insights into Comparative National Security Policymaking* (London, New York: Palgrave Macmillan, 2009), pp. 100–101. Giles, in turn, derives his description of these subcultures from Baruch Kimmerling, *The Invention and Decline of Israeliness: State, Society, and the Military* (Berkeley, CA: University of California Press, 2001).

27. Ursula Jasper, *The Politics of Nuclear Non-Proliferation: A Pragmatist Framework for Analysis* (London: Routledge, 2014), p. 4.
28. Beatrice Heuser, "Beliefs, Culture, Proliferation and Use of Nuclear Weapons," *Journal of Strategic Studies: Special Issue on Preventing the Use of Weapons of Mass Destruction,*" Vol. 23, No. 1 (March 2000), p. 75.
29. Jacques E.C. Hymans, *The Psychology of Nuclear Proliferation: Identity, Emotions, and Foreign Policy* (Cambridge: Cambridge University Press, 2006).
30. Ibid., p. 2.
31. Johnson, "Conclusion: Toward a Standard Methodological Approach," p. 247.
32. The most important recent exploration of sacred values can be found in Scott Atran, *Talking to the Enemy: Violent Extremism, Sacred Values, and What it Means to be Human* (London: Allen Lane, 2010). For a sampling of other relevant literature, see Scott Atran, "Genesis of Suicide Terrorism," *Science*, Vol. 299 (2003), pp. 1534–1539; Scott Atran, "Sacred Values, Terrorism and the Limits of Rational Choice," in J. McMillan, ed., *In The Same Light As Slavery: Building A Global Antiterrorist Consensus* (Washington, DC: Institute for National Strategic Studies, National Defense University Press, 2007); S. Atran, R. Axelrod, and R. Davis, "Sacred Barriers to Conflict Resolution," *Science*, 317 (2007), pp. 1039–1040; Baron, J. and M. Spranca. "Protected Values," *Organizational Behavioral and Human Decision Processes*, Vol. 70 (1997), pp. 1–16; H. Bazerman, A. Tebrunsel, and K. Wade-Benzoni, "When Sacred Issues are at Stake," *Negotiation Journal*, Vol. 24, No. 1 (2008), pp. 113–117; and, J. Ginges, S. Atran, D. Medin, and K. Shikaki, "Sacred Bounds on Rational Resolution of Violent Political Conflict," *Proceedings of the National Academy of Sciences*, Vol. 104 (2007), pp. 7357–7360.
33. Philip E. Tetlock, "Thinking the Unthinkable: Sacred Values and Taboo Cognitions," *Trends in Cognitive Sciences*, Vol. 7, No. 7 (July 2003), pp. 320–324; Atran, 2010.
34. Daniel M. Bartels and Douglas L. Medin, "Are Morally-Motivated Decision Makers Insensitive to the Consequences of their Choices?" Northwestern University, *Psychological Science*, Vol. 18, No. 1 (2007), pp. 24–28. Available at http://home.uchicago.edu/bartels/papers/Bartels-Medin-2007-PsychSci.pdf, accessed 9 September 2017.
35. See Morteza Dehghani, Scott Atran, Rumen Iliev, Sonya Sachdeva, Douglas Medinand Jeremy Ginges, "Sacred Values and Conflict over Iran's Nuclear Program," *Judgment and Decision Making*, Vol. 5, No. 7, December 2010, pp. 540–546. Available at http://journal.sjdm.org/10/101203/jdm101203.pdf, accessed 9 September 2017.

36. Johnson, "Conclusion: Toward a Standard Methodological Approach," p. 248.
37. Peter J. Katzenstein, "Introduction: Alternative Perspectives on National Security," in Peter J. Katzenstein, ed., *The Culture of National Security: Norms and Identity in World Politics* (New York: Columbia University Press, 1996), p. 5.
38. Theo Farrell, "Constructivist Security Studies: Portrait of a Research Program," *International Studies Review*, Vol. 4, No. 1 (Spring 2002), p. 54.
39. Richard Price and Nina Tannenwald, "Norms and Deterrence: The Nuclear and Chemical Weapons Taboos," in Peter J. Katzenstein, ed., *The Culture of National Security: Norms and Identity in World Politics* (New York: Columbia University Press, 1996), pp. 114–152.
40. Johnson, "Conclusion: Toward a Standard Methodological Approach," p. 252.
41. Dominic D. P. Johnson, and Dominic Tierney, *Failing to Win: Perceptions of Victory and Defeat in International Politics* (Cambridge: Harvard University Press, 2006).
42. Robert Jervis, *Perception and Misperception in International Politics* (Princeton: Princeton University Press, 1976).
43. Robert Jervis, *How Statesmen Think: The Psychology of International Politics* (Princeton: Princeton University Press, 2017).
44. Jervis, *How Statesmen Think*, p. 3.
45. Ursala Jasper, *The Politics of Nuclear Non-Proliferation: A Pragmatist Framework for Analysis* (London: Routledge, 2014), p. 2.
46. Ibid., p. 6.
47. Ibid., p. 4.
48. Ibid., p. 6.
49. John Baylis and Kristan Stoddart, *The British Nuclear Experience: The Role of Beliefs, Culture, and Identity* (Oxford: Oxford University Press, 2015).
50. Ibid., p. 207.
51. Ibid., p. 9.
52. Ibid., p. 208.
53. Ibid., p. 209.
54. Norman Cigar, *Saudi Arabia and Nuclear Weapons: How Do Countries Think about the Bomb?* (New York: Routledge, 2016), p. 1.
55. Ibid., p. 215.

CHAPTER 2

The Cultural Topography Analytic Framework

Jeannie L. Johnson and Marilyn J. Maines

This chapter walks the reader through the development of the Cultural Topography Analytic Framework (CTAF), describes the analytical shortcomings it is meant to remedy, and explains the process of employing it as a research method. At the core of the CTAF is the goal of isolating the key identity factors, norms, values, and perceptions of state actors contemplating crossing a nuclear threshold, and then designing a tailored set of foreign policy levers for interlocutors to use to impact or influence that decision. Perhaps the most significant contribution of the CTAF is the guard it provides against dangerous mirror imaging in our policy forecasting and concomitant nuclear counterproliferation and deterrence strategy. The CTAF allows users to examine nuclear decisionmaking by countries of concern from a non-US, non-Western perspective and then to craft a diplomatic approach effectively tailored to that country's identity, values, beliefs, and norms.

This chapter briefly introduces the reader to the field of strategic culture and its early contributions to the nuclear policy literature. We

J. L. Johnson (✉)
Department of Political Science, Utah State University, Logan, UT, USA

M. J. Maines (✉)
Center for Advanced Study of Language, University of Maryland,
College Park, MD, USA

© The Author(s) 2018
J. L. Johnson et al. (eds.), *Crossing Nuclear Thresholds*,
Initiatives in Strategic Studies: Issues and Policies,
https://doi.org/10.1007/978-3-319-72670-0_2

highlight continuing deficiencies within this methodological field, including failures to account for shifts in national behavior over time, and an
inability to reconcile or anticipate which of the several and often competing national security narratives within a particular regime will dominate
decisionmaking on the nuclear issue. Our model is designed both to remedy deficiencies and to unearth new, untapped or underutilized sources of
information for identifying and understanding emerging threats.

The CTAF approach, which was used to conduct research for the case
studies in this volume, was developed by combining two cutting-edge
models in sociocultural analysis that were both originally designed to support intelligence analysts in the US Intelligence Community. The first
model, the Cultural Topography Framework (CTops), was designed by
Jeannie Johnson and Matthew Berrett at the CIA to isolate and assess
primary sociocultural influences impacting the decisionmaking and behavior of a key actor on a selected policy issue.[1] The second model, the
Cultural Analytic Framework (CAF), was developed for the National
Counterproliferation Center by the Center for Advanced Study of
Language (CASL) at the University of Maryland (Joseph Danks, Marilyn
Maines, John Walker, Kathy Faleris, and Anne Wright) in 2011, to specifically assess nuclear decisionmaking. The CTAF draws elements from each,
integrating the cultural mapping approach from CTops with a weapons of
mass destruction (WMD) focus and a new process for development of
tailored policy responses to the proliferation behavior of over-the-horizon
states from the CAF. In order to understand the methodological advantages offered by this combined approach, it is useful to briefly examine the
growing pains of the strategic culture paradigm from which the models
were drawn.

Growing Pains in the Strategic Culture Paradigm

Conceptualizing and operationalizing the study of strategic culture continues to be a complex undertaking, and scholarship has produced several
divergent veins for carrying out the task.[2] Contrasting methodological
approaches are one notable outgrowth of this plurality of thought; a point
criticized by some[3] but defended by the field's proponents as an inevitable
stage of "big concept" development—one similar to that faced by the
traditional fields of international theory in grappling with empirical means
of measuring and assessing such indispensable concepts as "power" and
"wealth."[4]

The term "strategic culture" was first coined by nuclear scholars in the 1970s. The concept came about as a theoretical supplement to, and improvement upon, the international relations theories of realism and neorealism. Its first operational definition was generated by Jack Snyder, who captured it as *the sum total of ideas, conditioned emotional responses, and patterns of habitual behavior that members of a national strategic community have acquired through instruction or imitation with each other with regard to nuclear strategy.*[5] Ken Booth, a first-generation strategic culture scholar, outpaced Snyder's enthusiasm for his own concept and carried the idea forward, arguing that it represented a more historically accurate explanation of nations' nuclear and security policy than that of the rational actor and game theory constructs proposed by neorealism. The central theoretical argument posited by Booth and contemporary first-generation strategic culturalists took issue with neorealism's foundational presumption of states as "black box" actors whose actions could be mapped and projected simply by applying the formulaic parameters of a universal rationality. The claim that any state presented with the same stimuli in the security decisionmaking sphere, *ceteris paribus*, will come to the same conclusions and follow the same course of action clearly dismisses the significance of any internal state dynamics, privileging instead the belief that all states and their security apparatuses operate on a predictable calculus of cost-benefit analysis geared toward a ubiquitous goal of shoring up relative security and power.[6] Booth argued that the neorealist assumption of a "universal rationality" tread dangerously into ethnocentric mirror imaging, likely to lead to critical misperceptions and a failure to understand another nation's behavior in its own terms, including those "irrationalities" of action that did not fit into the observer's rational code.[7]

Not all strategic culture scholars find their discipline incompatible with the core tenet of realism and realpolitik. First-generation strategic culture scholar Colin Gray insists that the basic assumption of realism—that the world is occupied by rational actors pursuing their own interests—is not at odds with a strategic culture approach. It is the notion that rational decisionmaking takes on the same universal character, measuring costs and benefits in similar ways regardless of domestic politics, history, and culture, that strategic culture scholars take to task. Scholars pursuing strategic culture employ an alternative assumption: that rationality—the weighing of costs and benefits—be understood as culturally encoded. As this volume will demonstrate, what is desired and valued by one national group may be dismissed out of hand by another; a strategic ploy or operational tactic seen as advantageous to one actor may be taboo or a weapon of last resort for another. Nuclear decisionmaking at every stage of the cycle may be influenced by culturally bounded realities which set initial acquisition motives, development thresholds, and rationale for expanding or renouncing nuclear ambitions at different points for differing actors. As a consequence, the foreign policy levers available to influence a state's nuclear decisionmaking are not likely to be received in identical ways across cases. Impacting the rational calculus of another state requires understanding the identities, mindsets, traditions, and outlook that underpin their nuclear decisionmaking.

The study of culture's place in influencing the security process may be theoretically applied at any level of the decisionmaking chain, including key security institutions and subnational groups, but strategic culture scholarship has notably concentrated on state-based analysis.[8] Critics of national strategic culture profiles have pointed out that attempts to provide a comprehensive portrait of an enduring national strategic culture may lead to unhelpful overgeneralizations and mask important undercurrents.[9] They are right. The strategic culture of any nation state comprises competing narratives. Strategic culture, then, is best understood as a bundle of narratives, some held at the national level and some cultivated within particular organizations. Which of these is dominant at any point in time and for any particular issue is driven by a number of impacting factors including the nation's most recent formative events, the sway of particularly charismatic political figures, popular perceptions of the nation's future security, and a national sense of status and role on the world stage.

The field of strategic culture has done much to illuminate both the influence of national culture and the influence of the bureaucratic cultures within a nation's strategic community on its security policy decisionmaking. Noted deficiencies within this field of work are failures to account for shifts in national behavior over time or to anticipate which of the several layers of sometimes contradictory cultural narratives within a security community will influence actor decisionmaking on any particular issue.[10] In order to provide policymakers with enhanced clarity on the range of likely behaviors within a regime, sociocultural analysis must not only identify the variety of subcultures within any particular polity, it must enable assessments of their interplay in order to identify the operative—or dominant—cultural narrative for any particular issue.[11]

At the end of our last volume, *Strategic Culture and Weapons of Mass Destruction: Culturally Based Insights into Comparative National Security*

Policymaking, our team began to develop a practical framework for refining strategic culture research toward these ends. This volume further develops that framework, which has been applied and tested by case-study drafters in several workshops. The advances made since that time have improved the methodological tool set of the strategic culture approach with an eye toward higher utility for policymakers.

In addition to identifying and understanding national and subnational nuclear narratives, a policymaker must have some sense of where his or her nation might wield influence along another actor's nuclear decisionmaking timeline in order to craft and apply effective policy. Toward that end, the CTAF includes focused analysis of a national actor's internal decisionmaking processes with specific focus on identifying those decision vectors most open to influence by the United States or US partners. Intrinsic to the research process is an evaluation of key actors with potential to influence nuclear decisionmaking: individuals as well as group actors such as the nation's scientific community, or key components of its military, that are positioned to act as enablers or important obstructers to a nuclear threshold decision. Based on this intimate look at the national and subnational narratives surrounding the nuclear issue, the decisionmaking pathways a nuclear decision is likely to travel, and the subnational actors most likely to exert influence, analysts are prepared to offer pointed and evidence-based policy recommendations. With these in hand, a policymaker is better positioned to craft an assurance, dissuasion, or deterrence strategy tailored to effectively engage the identity, values, norms, and perceptual lens of key actors within the state of concern. Nuclear threshold decisions in the near and medium term are likely to involve attempts to influence the nuclear decisions of both allies and adversaries simultaneously. The blanket counterproliferation and deterrence strategies pursued in the past will not suffice.

THE CULTURAL TOPOGRAPHY ANALYTIC FRAMEWORK

The CTAF focuses on "moving to the left" in examining nuclear decisionmaking. The methodology strives to discover cultural factors that pertain to foreign decisions on nuclear weapons development as early as possible on the weapons development timeline. The intent is to allow analysts to concentrate their efforts chronologically *earlier* ("move to the left") in the nuclear weapons development or acquisition cycle, potentially recognizing movement toward proliferation or other nuclear activity at the plans and intentions stage. The analytic goal is to provide US policymakers with maximum time and flexibility to apply appropriate levers to deter or dissuade such activity. Cultural information on the identity (including role conception), values, norms, and perceptual lens of the country of concern may provide the key to selecting salient levers before a nuclear threshold is crossed (see Fig. 2.1).

The CTAF process consists of five interconnected steps that take researchers through the analytic process of (1) identifying an issue of strategic interest, (2) identifying key actors in the nuclear weapons decision process, (3) identifying and exploring cultural influences impacting the thinking and behavior of those actors from four research angles: identity, norms, values, and perceptual lens, (4) evaluating and assessing the strength and impact of the identified cultural factors in relation to key actors to determine which factors are most critical to the nuclear threshold decision, and (5) based on these findings, developing a robust set of traditional and nontraditional foreign policy levers, selected and tailored to have maximum influence on the key nuclear decisionmakers within the country of concern (see Fig. 2.2).

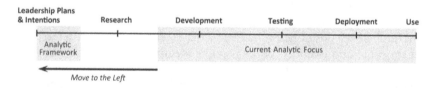

Fig. 2.1 Nuclear weapons development or acquisition timeline. Used with permission of the University of Maryland

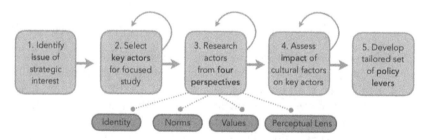

Fig. 2.2 Basic steps of the Cultural Topography Analytic Framework

Step 1: Identify an Issue of Strategic Interest

In order to provide higher utility to policymakers than that offered by the often "portrait-like" national profiles sometimes found within the strategic culture literature, the CTAF process begins sociocultural research with a policy question. By identifying a particular issue of strategic interest or concern, analysts are better able to isolate *relevant* cultural data and provide clearer forecasting about the ways in which cultural influences are likely to weigh in on decisionmaking. The narrower the issue, the more targeted the cultural research, and the more likely it will yield actionable data. The issue selected may reflect a frequently asked question that needs examination from a new angle, or a question that policymakers are not asking—perhaps due to ethnocentric blinders, habit, or limited knowledge of the region—but should be.

For the purposes of this volume, our authors were asked to examine a particular strategic interest: the range of possible nuclear actions in the state they covered. Their preliminary research for Step 1 created a field of both plausible near- and medium-term nuclear actions and unearthed the range of nuclear narratives found in national discourse.

In proliferation studies of nuclear intentions, the most commonly asked questions, which are also those of greatest strategic importance, are focused on the specific stage of the nuclear weapons development timeline a country of concern has already reached or the next specific nuclear threshold(s) to be crossed. This is the challenge that is most urgently facing the policymaker, and why the CTAF methodology is designed to move this assessment as much to the left on the nuclear weapons development timeline as possible, while a country is in very early stages or still considering a nuclear program. Chances to influence that decision and ensure that the state remains compliant with the Nonproliferation Treaty (NPT) are greatest before the state has invested substantially in beginning a weapons program or has actually crossed significant nuclear thresholds.

As basic research is done into the existing history of the nuclear program within the country of concern at this first stage, the CTAF approach focuses on identifying key nuclear narratives that have been used across time within the country in promoting or debating taking initial nuclear steps. Of greater interest, however, are the current or emerging narratives used by key decisionmakers for gaining support for nuclear development from both key stakeholders and the general population, as well as any competing nuclear narratives held by various individuals and groups within the program. These narratives are often rich sources of cultural elements that are used to justify why a desired nuclear step is necessary for a particular state at this time in history. Nuclear narratives also may serve as basic signposts that identify the goals of the nuclear program from a sociocultural perspective. In identifying these nuclear narratives, it is also critical to identify which individuals or groups hold or support that narrative.

From this field of both plausible nuclear intentions and key nuclear narratives, analysts are asked to select a potential nuclear threshold for focused study. The selection process may be driven by diverse concerns: that a particular nuclear threshold is the most likely next step along an acquisition timeline, because it is the threshold most dangerous for US policy and therefore of peak concern, or because it is an understudied "wild card" that deserves further attention.

As presented in Chap. 1, a "nuclear threshold" is that point in time when a given state chooses one course of action over another (or, chooses inaction) with respect to its nuclear weapons aspirations, including whether to establish a latent civilian nuclear hedge against a future decision to develop nuclear weapons, to comply with or transgress international nuclear nonproliferation norms, to proliferate or accept the transfer of sensitive dual-use nuclear technology, to preemptively attack another state's nascent nuclear program, to accept or extend nuclear assurances to another state or state collective, or in extremis, to break the nuclear taboo and militarily employ nuclear weapons.

Figuring out the specific "nuclear threshold" under consideration by the county of concern in each case study is the essential goal of Step 1. This decision provides the basis for narrowing the focus of the approach in Step 2 where decisions are made by authors on directing research toward particular actors or groups within the state. The inverse might also occur. As researchers get deeper into understanding nuclear narratives emanating from various groups within the state, they may determine that the original "nuclear threshold" selected is not actually the primary concern and switch to a different emphasis based on the insights which have surfaced during their research process.

This brings us to a critical point that we wish to emphasize about use of our methodology. The CTAF is meant to be a looping method—circling back to earlier steps in order to refine the issue under consideration. For example, it may be necessary to refine or change an issue of strategic interest (nuclear threshold), narrow focus to a few key actors or expand it to new ones, or redirect research to include some previously understudied narratives. This process should continue so long as it is productive in refining the forecasting utility of the cultural data available.

Step 2: Select Key Actors (Individuals or Groups) for Focused Study

In order to identify the nuclear narratives likely to dominate in the decisionmaking process and isolate decision vectors which may present opportunities for US influence, analysts must catalog and assess the likely role of actors and groups involved in national security decisionmaking for the country of concern. The term "actor" includes individuals, government organizations, nongovernmental groups, or other sub-elements of a society that play a role in policy processes. This would include the primary decisionmakers related to the initiation of a nuclear weapons development program or some other nuclear threshold, as well as their inner circle of trusted advisors, family members, key scientists, and military and political leaders. Of particular concern are any sub-state actors who may be open to US or allied influence and are positioned to act as enablers to a nuclear agenda, or conversely, any potential obstructers who may delay or prevent achievement of nuclear goals.

Analysts or academic researchers using the CTAF methodology are encouraged to first examine the overall structure of influential individuals and organizations operating within a country's nuclear program and then, after some basic research, to focus in on a select number of individuals or groups that seem to be most central to the decisionmaking process and apply the deeper sociocultural analysis techniques to those actors and groups. It is useful to keep in mind that as more data is identified through research, initial selections may change or new individuals or groups of importance may be revealed, changing the original presumed outline or structure of the nuclear program.

In exploring the sociocultural factors that impact the most significant individuals and groups, analysts may wish to look at both (1) primary actors and (2) secondary actors engaged in the nuclear development process. Primary actors are the key decisionmakers related to the initiation of a nuclear weapons development program, as well as their inner circle of trusted advisers, key scientists, and critical military and political leaders. For most over-the-horizon or threshold nuclear states, as well as for states with existing nuclear weapons programs, this is the level where most decisions are made. Secondary actors are those supporting actors that impact the primary decisionmakers in either a positive or negative way. While secondary actors do not usually have actual decisionmaking authority, they can significantly accelerate or delay a chosen course of action and at times prevent a country of concern from crossing a nuclear threshold. In countries with strong dictators, such as the Soviet Union under Stalin or North Korea under Kim Jong Un, secondary actors may have little impact on nuclear decisionmaking, with the political leader and only a very few trusted advisors having any real authority.

There is also a set of distinct roles related to the nuclear development process that actors may perform. This division is based upon the individual's position, responsibilities, expertise, and tasks. These roles were originally developed in the Follow-the-People approach, which is widely used within the Intelligence Community.[12] Analysts may find these subcategories useful in thinking through how a particular actor or group fits into the decisionmaking process relevant to the specific nuclear threshold.

- **Decisionmakers.** National-level leaders and other actors who determine WMD-related strategic requirements, policies, threat perceptions, goals, and resource allocations.
- **Influencers.** Actors who can affect choices made by decisionmakers on WMD-related strategic requirements, policies, threat perceptions, goals, and resource allocations.
- **Doers.** Technical, managerial, and nontechnical actors involved in the research, development, testing, and evaluation (RDT&E), and production of WMD, to include associated materials, technologies, equipment, and processes.
- **Enablers.** Actors who support the intentions of the primary decisionmaker(s) and can impact choices made in regard to nuclear-related strategic requirements, policies, threat perceptions, goals, and resource allocations. Enablers may also have control over some critical aspect of nuclear program support or logistics.
- **Users.** Actors who are involved in the doctrine, planning, use, and security of WMD.
- **Obstructers.** Actors who might exert influence to prevent or delay decision or actions by the primary decisionmaker(s). These actors might include political or scientific opponents or rivals, individuals or groups that oppose nuclear weapons for ethical or religious reasons, or actors who were previously part of the inner circle and were later excluded.
- **Latents.** Actors who possess the expertise, experience, and personal connections to support a WMD program, but for a variety of reasons (such as retirement, illness, falling out of favor) are not currently doing so.

In applying a culturally based analytic model, it is important for the analyst to examine the interaction among the various actors, sub-groups, and organizations within the country of interest and to develop insights into what cultural influences may be underlying or driving actions surrounding a nuclear threshold decision. This applies both to countries just starting down the nuclear path and to countries with threshold or established programs. The many competing currents operating at the subnational level may have a significant impact on the direction and pace of a nuclear program, a nation's willingness to disband, freeze, or roll back a nuclear program or the willingness of weapons-capable states to assist over-the-horizon states in acquiring nuclear capabilities. As each nuclear threshold is approached, there are discernable cultural factors that determine whether or not that threshold will be crossed (see Fig. 2.3).

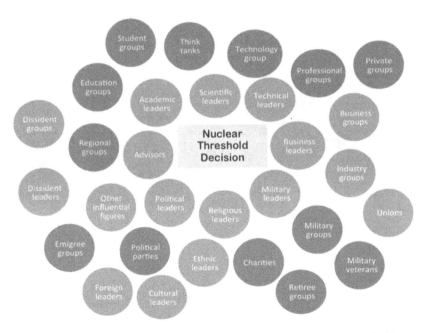

Fig. 2.3 Types of actors potentially involved in nuclear weapons decisions. Circles in light gray depict actors in traditional official roles or positions. Circles in dark grey represent actors in nontraditional roles or positions. Used with the permission of the University of Maryland

Step 3: Research Key Actors from Four Perspectives—Identity, Norms, Values, and Perceptual Lens

After selecting a few key actors for focused study, analysts gather cultural data by exploring four distinct veins of research: identity, norms, values, and perceptual lens. These four categories do not represent an exhaustive list of important cultural factors but are useful as a starting point in examining culture from four policy-relevant perspectives (see Fig. 2.4). The categories each inspire a distinct set of research questions and represent reoccurring conceptual themes across the sociocultural analytic field. We will first introduce the definition employed for each of the four conceptual categories followed by a set of "research prompts" we found useful as starting points. We will then offer a set of sourcing ideas recommended by the CTAF design and employed by our authors to unearth data in the four research categories.

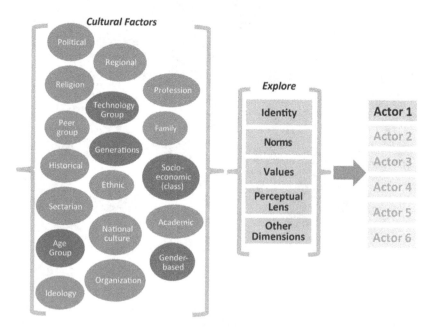

Fig. 2.4   Explore the cultural data from four perspectives. Used with the permission of the University of Maryland

Category 1: Identity. The character traits a given group assigns to itself, the reputation it pursues, the individual roles and statuses it designates to members, and the distinctions it makes between those people who are considered members of the group ("us"), and those who are not members of the group ("them").

Research Prompts Related to Identity:

- Which factors surrounding this issue would cause this actor's identity to be threatened? Alternatively, which might provide the United States common ground for co-option?
- Is group cohesion strong along identity lines in response to this issue? What would cause the group to fracture or to unite behind a common front?
- What individual roles and statuses might group members seek to protect?

Category 2: Norms. Accepted, expected, or customary behaviors within a society or group. Norms can be explicit or implicit, prescriptive or proscriptive.

Research Prompts Related to Norms:

- Does this issue place social institutions or common practices under threat?
- To what extent are national norms and preferences in sync with prevailing global norms on this issue?
- Which practices are likely to be pursued from habit, or bureaucratic inertia, even if seemingly out of step with current security realities?
- Which practices are compatible with US interests on this issue?
- Would US proposed changes in this policy area offer group members a way out of increasingly unpopular normative practices? Which members?

Category 3: Values. Deeply held beliefs about what is desirable, proper, and good that serve as broad guidelines for social life. Values include material or ideational goods that are honored or confer increased status to individual actors or members of groups. These include both secular and sacred values.

Research Prompts Related to Values:

- What is considered "honorable" behavior at the national or subnational level in this issue area?
- Which local values may be in conflict with the US approach to this issue?
- Which values might be coopted in moving US interests forward?
- Where might value differences between target groups present an opportunity to exploit cleavages?

Category 4: Perceptual Lens. Filters through which individual actors or members of a group determine "facts" about themselves and others.

Research Prompts Related to Perceptual Lens:

- What are the preconceived notions of this group concerning the behavior and character of the United States?
- What are the group's beliefs about the future?
- What hurdles must US policymakers overcome in messaging to this group on this issue?

Research Strategies

Identifying and isolating cultural factors is not a simple process. They are rarely expressed overtly and instead must often be inferred from statements, decisions, actions, or inactions of actors or by their responses or reactions to specific information, situations, or events. Identifying cultural factors can require a significant time investment spent sifting and cycling through existing source material as well as identifying gaps or new leads that require the development and review of additional sources. The question of which sources will yield reliable data and which are available for analysis is dependent on the country of concern. In their initial article on the Cultural Topography method, Jeannie Johnson and Matthew Berrett offer a number of innovative research strategies for identifying cultural factors, which are discussed below.[13]

Examine Historical Narratives. To identify cultural influences of historical importance to individuals or groups, the analyst should pay close attention to specific references made when the issues relevant to the analytic charge are addressed, whether in political rhetoric, private conversations, lessons used in school, or expressions from the artistic community.

Physical manifestations such as architecture, street names, statues, and memorials demonstrate which aspects of a nation's history it chooses to preserve and celebrate. Finding and understanding the selection of heroes allows insight into national values. Of particular interest are those symbols that people voluntarily display in their homes.

Tap into the Population. Cultural influences can be identified in interviews or surveys with targeted focus groups. "Key informants" or sources with extensive knowledge of local culture are often interviewed by ethnographers and anthropologists. Looking for the conventional wisdom of a group or "the things everyone knows" is another way of seeking out cultural factors. Examining local newspapers and publications can also reveal issues of concern to the population. Tracking rumors or gossip networks in local areas as well as online discussions and blogs are windows into cultural narratives.

Examples in Case Studies. Author Nima Gerami highlights the social media output of national hero and Iranian Qods Force Commander Soleimani, for instance—one of the most influential voices within Khameni's inner circle— and offers analysis of his recently published memoirs.

Analyze Content of Texts. Key texts within the nuclear domain include doctrinal manuals as well as legends, songs, rhymes, fables, and anecdotes from a country's history. Military texts are essential sources of information on the values, identity, and acceptable methods of achieving security within a regime. Other doctrinal texts, including telegrams, military orders, descriptions of training regimes, diaries, memoirs, and communications between military leaders, may reveal national aspirations over time as well as accepted norms for achieving them.

Examples in Case Studies. Dima Adamsky's meticulous analysis of Russian military texts, both formal and informal, yields profound insights into the Russian cognitive style in national security decisionmaking and draws out the way in which nuclear use norms have been integrated into regular military practice.

Track Political Rhetoric. The key to utilizing political rhetoric effectively is understanding, in local context, the role it plays in communicating with the population. A first step in weighing the value of political rhetoric within a nation is to track its correlation with actual behavior in the past.

Tracking across time and across politicians may yield useful generalizations about government speeches as indicators of sincere goals and security objectives.

> *Examples in Case Studies.* Nearly all authors within this volume place appropriate emphasis on political rhetoric as a key indicator of potential nuclear narratives. Nima Gerami is careful to make the point that Iran's adherence to the Islamic doctrine of *taqiyya*—a Shiite practice of deliberately disguising one's genuine beliefs in order to protect the Shia sect from adversaries—permits Iranian leaders to lie when faced with existential threats, including potentially the nuclear program. Shane Smith dissects political speeches produced by the Kim regime within North Korea with the same care, and warns that given the cultural identity cultivated in the North as the "sole vessel" of the true Korea, rhetorical threats to turn Seoul into a "sea of fire," now commonplace, cannot be dismissed out of hand.

Observe Public Behavior. Public reactions to state leaders' actions and decisions may highlight areas of agreement or congruence between the populace and leaders based on shared beliefs, values, and ideals. Disaffection may be demonstrated in the form of protest, local complaints, or biting humor directed at political officials. Support may be manifested through strong turnout for state events and parades, voluntary display of state insignia, or robust membership in state-related organizations. To understand identity distinctions within large regions, analysts might systematically note patterns in social ceremonies and rituals. Humor can also serve as a direct source of cultural concerns, and analysts are encouraged to note what an individual or group finds funny and who or what is consistently ridiculed. Language is also an indispensable source of cultural information and even rudimentary knowledge of the language of the country of interest can provide insights into what a population values as well as provide linguistic signposts for public opinion.

> *Examples in Case Studies.* Gregory Giles offers close observation of Israeli political norms across time in order to distill a set of indispensable practices for security action. He posits these as a "litmus test" of sorts, a set of criteria that must be met in order for Israel to pursue military action. J.E. Peterson examines the role of public opinion in Saudi decisionmaking and identifies where tracking public opinion on this issue may prove useful, and where it will not.

Evaluate the Output of the Media and the Artistic Community.
Depending on the level of freedom enjoyed by news, entertainment, and artistic producers within a nation, these three sources may yield significant insights into the core identity, norms, and values of actors or actor sets. Controlled media may still offer material for cultural analysis, as state propaganda illuminates the identity, norms, values, beliefs, ideals, and attitudes that the state hopes to achieve and the narrative that it hopes the populace will accept. In a free state, the content of political debates and assessments in the press can identify cleavages in the strategic and political culture. A free press can also serve as a reliable watchdog for norms violations within a state. As a commercial organization, the media must present a worldview that is comfortable to its audience and in agreement with societal values. Entertainment media—including plays, television comedies, and dramas—can also reveal much about the values, ideals, and beliefs of the populace and attitudes toward changes underway in society.

Examples in Case Studies. Ekaterina Svyatets tracks national mythmaking of the Chernobyl disaster across multiple popular mediums including novels, movies, and video games targeting Ukraine's youth, and examines the way in which these narratives impact public thinking on nuclear issues today.

Step 4: Assess Impact of Cultural Factors on Key Actors

In Step 4, the analyst must determine which factors within an actor's identity, norms, values, and perceptual lens are likely to weigh in on the nuclear threshold decision of concern. The approach to data gathering and analysis recommended by the CTAF is rooted in interpretivist research methods and Grounded Theory: seeking an "insider" understanding of a particular group through the collection of "rich data."[14] Data collection and analysis occur simultaneously in order to identify cultural traits and catalog the emergence of patterns. Categories become "saturated" when the exploration of new data sources consistently validates previous findings rather than offering surprises or new insights. Analysts and researchers assess the range of cultural factors which surfaced in the research process in order to identify patterns which emerged across multiple sources and featured as prominent themes within the four research categories. Those cultural traits that consistently surfaced across multiple datasets and coalesced into narratives that interwove aspects of identity, norms, values, and/or perceptual lens will have achieved three key thresholds: *relevance* vis-à-vis the nuclear threshold issue, *robustness*—weightiness in the decisionmaking of a selection of key actors—and, perhaps most important, the likelihood of a cultural factor or trait to provoke a behavioral *response* (cooperative or conflictual) to US policy on this issue. The robustness and salience of a particular cultural factor may be manifest by its frequent appearance across multiple data sources, by its prominence within the discourse of key decisionmakers, by the multiple ways it is manifest across the four categories of research, or by a strong path dependency born of bureaucratic habit that shows little sign of being interrupted. Analysts are asked to provide a sense of robustness for each cultural factor highlighted and examine the scenarios under which it is likely to play a particularly influential role in a nuclear threshold decision.

Having accumulated a large amount of cultural data, analysts must now evaluate that body of data and set some of it aside, honing the data down to those cultural factors that are considered most significant. Assessment of cultural factors that are significant is based upon how likely these factors are to impact key actors in regard to the nuclear decisionmaking process, and how heavily these factors can contribute to a profile of the actor or group in terms of behavioral patterns and primary or sacred values held by that individual or group. Understanding these factors is critical groundwork for the development of a tailored set of levers or diplomatic approach in the next step of the methodology.

Assessment of Cultural Factors in Case Studies

Emerging from this analytical process, our authors offered compelling insights across each of the four research categories. For instance, Nima Gerami identifies "regional aspirations" as a feature of Iran's identity and one which is critical to understanding its nuclear posture. Iran perceives itself as both the vanguard of Shia and Sunni Islam and culturally superior to its Arab neighbors, resulting in "an intrinsic right to regional hegemony." This sense of destiny and superiority has led Iran to engage in revisionist policy. Indeed, it is part of its identity role conception that Iran "play[s] a transformative role in regional and world affairs" and leads the "axis of resistance." Such an identity means that Iran will place limited stake in the status quo, likely including international norms on nuclear behavior, especially where those are seen as cementing unjust and unequal global relationships. In fact, Gerami argues, Iran possesses a strong sense of role regarding the need to restore equality between powerful and weak countries, both to obtain justice and to defeat the arrogance of foreign interventionist powers.

This is starkly juxtaposed with Ekaterina Svyatets' assessment of cultural factors that influence Ukraine's identity as diplomatic, norms-abiding, and Western-leaning; "a young state striving to become a Western state." Ukraine's desire to solidify identity credentials as a Western state means that it is predisposed toward cooperation in Western-led institutions such as the NPT. Not only do national identity narratives reinforce this theme, critical subnational narratives do as well. Ukraine's scientific community prides itself on its leadership in the nonproliferation movement. Svyatets concludes that only a clear and present threat to Ukrainian sovereignty from its Russian neighbor will likely have sufficient force to displace norms-abiding and Western-leaning Ukrainian narratives on this issue.

The case study which perhaps highlights most effectively the centrality of cultural factors (from both identity and perceptual lens categories) in nuclear decisionmaking is Shane Smith's work on North Korea. Nuclear weapons have come to play an indispensable role in Pyongyang's identity narrative which casts North Korea as "the decisive element in the world system, if not the center of the universe." This extraordinary perceptual lens, founded largely on state-born constructions, cannot be dismissed for its delusionary qualities. The belief in the singularity and ancientness of the North Korean people is inextricably linked with the way the state perceives its right to nuclear weapons and its relationship to their use. Nuclear weapons hold special acclaim in the national narratives of the Kim regime. Referred to as the "nation's life" and a "national treasure," there is little doubt that these are inexorably intertwined with North Korean sense of self. Nuclear weapons have become the crown jewel of Pyongyang's defense system and a fulfillment of both *Juche*—North Korea's political ideology—and *Songun*—Kim Jong Il's military first policies. With pride, North Korea openly celebrates its status as a "nuclear state." Smith's assessment of the North Korean identity and security narratives and their congruence with the possession of nuclear weapons leads to a strong note of caution regarding any hope of rolling the program back.

Smith points out that the strong tie between nuclear capacity and national identity has impact on the North Korean perceptual lens. The centrality of nuclear success to the North Korean narrative is likely to lead the regime to "exaggerate nuclear accomplishments and capabilities." This may not be confined to overstatement and braggadocio for foreign consumption, but may be a form of exaggeration that creates internal delusion about actual capabilities. Smith provides evidence of an ill-informed perceptual lens resulting from the internal dissembling endemic to communication norms necessary to survive in North Korea, noting that the regime's "brand of personal despotism likely exceeds that of Stalin's Soviet Union and any other country in modern times" resulting in "no dissent, no loyal opposition, and no 'conversation' with the Supreme Leader in North Korea." The outcome is that nuclear narratives, even those held by the regime's foremost decisionmaker, may be divorced in significant and important ways from reality.

Smith explores the nuclear threshold of "use" through these North Korean lenses, but the North Korean case is not the only one which provides pause regarding the "use" threshold. Dima Adamsky provides careful analysis of military norms and notes that, for Russia, nuclear strategy is not in a class by itself, but is an integrated component across military domains. Strategic and nonstrategic nuclear weapons are treated in mindset and practice as a unified arsenal. Russian military exercises incorporate nuclear and non-nuclear aspects of strategy in an integrated effort to shape the decisionmaking process of an adversary. Despite "practice" with such strategies, Russia lacks "a set of norms or explicit methodology ... for identifying when to cross the nuclear use threshold."

Gregory Giles' assessment of cultural factors also pays special attention to norms, examining those Israel has come to espouse as critical prerequisites to military action. These include demonstrating that an existential threat exists, satisfying a last resort/no choice threshold for military action, correct constitutional processing of the deliberation and decisionmaking, and a persuasive case that the security problem can indeed be solved militarily. Giles demonstrates that by carefully tracking the success or failure of an issue in meeting the built-in requirements of these norms, one might reasonably project the likelihood of unilateral military action. Giles shows that Israel's unilateral attacks on Iraqi and Syrian nuclear facilities were validated through this process and the proposed attack on Iran's nuclear facilities was not.

Giles also points to the high value Israeli leaders place on the special relationship with the United States. This particular value acts as a "deal breaker" in the deliberation process if unilateral military action to protect Israel's nuclear monopoly would do the relationship with the United States serious harm. J.E. Peterson notes the same value playing a role in Saudi deliberations about nuclear acquisition. The Saudi Kingdom places great value on its relationship with the United States but little inherent value on the nuclear nonproliferation regime as an inviolable global norm.

Peterson argues that international law would lose in a clash of wills with Saudi self-conceptions of identity, including its sense of divine mission and self-image as a major power in the Middle East and Islamic world. Within this integrated profile of cultural factors (values and identity), "a nuclear policy might be regarded as an assertion of the KSA's national right," alongside "an inability to comprehend why the nonproliferation regime should apply to the KSA."

This brief synopsis of highlights from across case study chapters demonstrates the ways in which cultural factors unearthed within the four categories during the research process offer insights into the nuclear deliberation process and helps anticipate tipping factors which may compel one narrative on nuclear matters to displace another. Offering policymakers an anticipatory look at scenarios which may plausibly play out within countries of critical interest is the necessary antecedent to crafting salient policy levers.

Step 5: Develop a Tailored Set of Policy Levers to Impact Nuclear Decisionmaking

The objective of Step 5 of the CTAF is to examine the most significant cultural factors identified and assessed for each key actor and then create a tailored set of foreign policy levers that could be effectively applied to deter or dissuade a nuclear threshold decision. To impact or influence foreign actors involved in nuclear weapons decisions, we need to try to understand what these actors are thinking and, as much as possible, to think as they do, outside our traditional Western understanding of decisions and responses. Analysts often fail to ask "Why?" in regard to understanding cultural motivation of foreign actors. This question should be of primary concern when trying to understand culture's influence on decisionmaking. Historically, the United States has been less successful in understanding other nations' cultures and leadership intentions because of the challenges involved in taking on the cultural perspectives of foreign decisionmakers. The underlying purpose for understanding the cultural influences that shape actors' behavior within a state behavior in regard to nuclear decisionmaking is to be able to design a tailored set of levers and a foreign policy approach that will prevent the country of concern from crossing a specific nuclear threshold—dissuading state actors from nuclear aspirations, freezing the progress of that state at a particular level, or rolling back the program to an earlier or more limited level.

What Is a Lever?

Webster's Dictionary provides a succinct and ultimately useful definition of a lever as "an inducing or compelling force or tool." Another definition of lever might include the traditional references to the application of "carrots and sticks" in an effort to bring about desired political decisions or behavior. Our authors were asked to consider a wide range of possible lever "types," some traditional and some less so.

The use of less traditional levers is often coined *soft power*, a term defined by Joe Nye as "the ability to get what you want through attraction rather that coercion or payments."[15] Soft power is based on the attractiveness of a country's culture, political ideas, and policies and is often contrasted with *hard power*, which is the more traditional, established use of inducements (carrots) and threats (sticks). With the emergence of the concept of *smart power* in the aftermath of the US invasion of Iraq in 2003, ideas concerning the mixed application of many different types of levers were explored further.[16] Proponents of smart power prefer that international organizations play a major role, as opposed to reliance on unilateral state actions. Smart power also includes the strategic use of diplomacy, persuasion, and capacity building, alongside the hard power of coercion in order to project power and influence, resulting in a rich baseline set of possible levers to influence political behavior. Smart power gained further endorsement as a political approach from Hillary Clinton during her confirmation hearing for Secretary of State when she stressed that "We must use what has been called smart power—the full range of tools at our disposal—diplomatic, economic, military, political, legal, and cultural—picking the right tool, or combination of tools, for each situation. With smart power, diplomacy will be the vanguard of foreign policy."[17] As part of the soft power discussion, Nye also calls out *cultural diplomacy* as a prime example of soft power or "the ability to persuade through culture, value, and ideas."[18] Cultural diplomacy is based on the recognition and understanding of cultural dynamics and specifically includes the exchange of ideas, information, art, lifestyles, value systems, tradition, beliefs, and other aspects of culture. Cultural diplomacy is a very important concept in relationship to the CTAF, as it brings into practice a strategic diplomatic approach that is built on identification of cultural factors that impact an individual decisionmaker.

Foreign policy levers are most often located across three categories: (1) diplomatic, (2) economic, and (3) military, each of which offers a range of options to policymakers seeking to prevent or delay nuclear development.

Traditional levers of foreign policy are well known and typically applied at the state level against the leadership elite, who generally have nuclear decisionmaking authority. Unlike traditional foreign policy levers, less traditional or unofficial levers may be applied against many different levels of social strata within the country of concern and are more likely to involve nongovernmental, private organizations.

Although the actual decision to cross a nuclear threshold is normally made by small, selective groups of political elites behind closed doors, other groups or social strata can also have significant influence on the primary actors or decisionmakers. Even when a solitary actor or decisionmaker is positioned to make the final nuclear decision, that individual will usually need the support and buy-in of other elite decisionmakers, as well as of other supporting actors in order to be able to carry out the decision. Additionally, the primary actor or decisionmaker at some point will usually want the support of the general population of the country. In a nominally democratic society, moving nuclear decisions to fruition will require skillful political maneuvering. In a more authoritarian society, the buy-in and support can be co-opted or coerced. Historically there are some obvious cases where strong, authoritarian leaders have almost total control of the nuclear decisionmaking process—Stalin in Russia, Qaddafi in Libya, and Kim Jong Il and his son Kin Jong Un in North Korea. In most cases, however, the primary decisionmaker operates under the influence of a close circle of advisors. Regardless of regime type or who makes the final nuclear decision—single actor or small group—there are nontraditional culture-based levers which can be applied at various levels of society. These will be included primarily in the "diplomatic" section, but may be found in the other two categories as well.

Levers can be positive or negative and are designed to either reward or punish a state for its nuclear behavior. Table 2.1 provides a baseline list of potential foreign policy levers, some fairly standard and some more innovative. This list is not intended to be all-inclusive but provides a starting point for consideration and analysis.[19] Our authors were asked to consider which of these levers might be effectively employed against the nuclear threshold issue of concern, and which, given the cultural predisposition of the actors in question, may backfire.

Using Less Direct Approaches to Influence Nuclear Decisions

Many of the less traditional levers suggested in this list fall under the category of "messaging," which the authors define as "using multiple forms

Table 2.1   Foreign policy levers

Diplomatic levers

1. Promises of strategic security or protection offered to a country or group in exchange for desired decisions or behavior.
2. Public diplomatic recognition in an international forum of a country or group as a respected, responsible state adhering to norms of international behavior.
3. Diplomatic alliances or bilateral agreements that provide unique diplomatic support or recognition as a US ally or diplomatic partner in some key initiatives.
4. Assistance in obtaining leadership positions in multinational organizations such as the United Nations.
5. Unusual honor or respect afforded during a state visit, including visits by the US president, Secretary of State, or other high officials to that country and attendance at state dinners/joint speeches and press conferences with country leaders during visits to the United States.
6. Opening or expansion of a US Embassy or diplomatic mission within a country.
7. Provision of humanitarian aid or assistance in nation building and/or democratization.
8. Key speeches or visits by admired and popular US nonofficial figures, such as doctors, social leaders, and philanthropists. In some cases, visits or performances of US artists and musicians who are known to be admired by the actor or his society could have impact.
9. Use of Internet websites, wikis, and chat rooms to inspire discussion around issues of concern, including religion, governance, environmental issues, and antinuclear/global security.
10. Use of online social networking capabilities to identify key individuals likely to support US goals and development of these online networks.
11. Targeted e-mail campaigns designed to reach key segments within the society of concern that may be sympathetic to US goals.
12. Offers of educational opportunities and training within the country of concern targeting particular groups. These may be better received if offered by private groups or NGOs.
13. Holding international technology and nonproliferation conventions and conferences in countries that appear to be supportive of US, UN, and IAEA nonproliferation goals or are countries in which support needs to be shored up.
14. Foreign exchange programs, including trips and visits to the United States for actors or groups that appear to be supportive of US nonproliferation goals.
15. Praising and shaming. Nonofficial articles or publications from widely recognized journalists, authors, or technical experts openly praising positive actions taken by a group or country of concern or criticizing that group or country for undesirable negative actions.
16. Establishment of long-term educational opportunities in the United States for individuals selected by the key decisionmaker(s) within the country of concern.

(continued)

Table 2.1   (continued)

17. Inclusion of selected key leaders from the country of concern in US conferences, working groups, or other international efforts to combat proliferation as a method of strengthening the relationship.

18. Work with trusted partners within the NPT regime to include the country of concern in various NPT initiatives and committees, with frequent outreach by other NPT supporters, making them part of the global solution.

19. Threats to cut off or suspend diplomatic alliance or bilateral agreements.

20. Exertion of diplomatic pressure on other countries to prevent or deter those countries from supplying needed equipment or material to a country.

21. Cut-off or suspension of humanitarian aid or assistance in nation building or democratization.

22. Closing of US Embassy or diplomatic mission within a country.

23. Suspension of all diplomatic relations with a country.

Economic levers

1. Promises of economic assistance or internal development within a country in exchange for desired decisions or behavior.

2. Accordance of "most favored nation" status in regard to trade agreements.

3. Encouragement of US businesses and companies to invest or open offices or begin operation within a country.

4. Provision of desired information technology or advanced scientific equipment that will advance a country's level of development.

5. Provision of cash payments or financial incentives to ensure desired behavior.

6. Provision of desired popular culture and/or luxury items to key actors or decisionmakers, through nonofficial channels.

7. Technical and financial support in regard to alternative energy sources and internal environmental concerns. This will probably be best received if provided by private organizations rather than directly from the US government.

8. Threats of application of economic sanctions if undesirable behavior of a country continues or expands.

9. Efforts to secure multinational economic sanctions through UN resolutions sponsored by the United States and its allies against the country.

10. Cut-off or cessation of specific trade agreements or suspension of sales of desired information technology or advanced scientific equipment to a country.

11. Enactment of economic sanctions unilaterally by the United States against the country.

12. Freezing financial assets of a country.

Military levers

1. Bilateral military alliance with the United States or guarantee of military support if the county is attacked.

2. Sales of conventional military equipment that is deemed significant or necessary to the country for national protection.

3. Military-to-military exchange meetings and agreements between US and foreign military forces (e.g., US naval ship visits).

(*continued*)

Table 2.1   (continued)

4. Training and education of foreign military personnel at US national war colleges, other military training facilities, or in country by US officials.
5. Nomination or US support for entry into multinational military alliance such as NATO or other appropriate alliance.
6. Provision of US peacekeeping forces or military personnel functioning in an advisory role to the country to secure internal stability.
7. Threat of preemptive military action against specific facilities existing or being constructed within a country.
8. Military interdictions of shipments of equipment or material during delivery or transshipment of the equipment or material to a country.
9. Cut-off or suspension of supply or sales of US military equipment to the country.
10. US enactment of military blockade or no-fly-zone restrictions against the country.
11. US invasion of the country or use of kinetic force/military attack.

Used with the permission of the University of Maryland

of communications media—including press, radio and television, music, films, and various Internet applications (websites, e-mail, chat rooms, wikis, blogs, social networks, games, and alternative reality sites)—to convey messages that the US wants heard." Nearly all US foreign and security policy institutions are currently engaged in attempts at public diplomacy—targeting messages toward the population of a particular state in addition to, or rather than, its elite. Whether termed "strategic messaging," "public affairs," "outreach," or "information operations," these efforts tend to employ multiple forms of communications media in an attempt to shape narratives within foreign populations.

The recent explosion in communications technology offers a wide range of options for conveying messages that the United States wants heard. Regardless of a nation's political, economic, religious, or cultural perspective, US popular culture has gradually worked its way into almost every corner of the world to become firmly established as a global phenomenon. Due to this widespread awareness of US culture, many opportunities exist to send messages on desired behavior through existing public and private media. Exploiting such a huge window of opportunity will require careful focus of effort to ensure effective use of limited resources.

Key questions to consider in regard to crafting messages designed to reach members of the state of concern, including key decisionmakers:

1. What media outlets are most likely to impact desired segments or strata of society within the country of concern?

2. Based on identified cultural factors, who could best deliver a message?
3. Through what types of media should the message be conveyed?
4. What individuals and organizations do each strata of the society admire?
5. What are the major cultural factors currently valued by the society, both internal and foreign?
6. What is the *zeitgeist* of popular culture in the society of concern? Can this be used to convey a US message?
7. How do various strata of society perceive the United States?
8. Could the message be better delivered by a proxy rather than directly by the United States?

One aim of messaging is to establish a relationship that scholars within the social psychology field have termed "identification." As discussed by Maria Rost Rublee in *Nonproliferation Norms*, identification takes place when an individual actor or small group responds positively to attempts at influence because the actor or group wants to establish or maintain a satisfying relationship with the influencer.[20] As the actor or group identifies with the admired other, the behavior desired by the other is adopted because it is associated with the desired relationship. The original actor may not personally believe in the new behavior but adopts it to ensure the continuation of the relationship.

In proliferation theory and literature, this concept is particularly relevant when evaluating the motives of various states that have adopted the norms and expected behaviors of the NPT. Nations or actors seeking friendship or advantageous relationships with the United States—alliances or security guarantees, financial or technical support, or social rewards—may outwardly take desired nonproliferation steps at a level Rublee calls "social conformity," while still secretly harboring nuclear or WMD intentions. This type of behavior could apply to other areas of international security as well, where actors or states follow the lead and expected behavior of a strong economic or political state, without actually subscribing to underlying beliefs and goals.

Key questions to consider in regard to whether an actor or group is complying with expected behavior norms due to identification, while still holding other beliefs and motivations, include:

1. What is the default position of the actor or group along the proliferation timeline?
2. Does the actor or group face an immediate threat to survival? A regional threat?

3. How far can security guarantees or other desired support objectives move the actor or group to the left in terms of nuclear/WMD goals?
4. What individuals and organizations within the country are most like to be open and receptive to US overtures?
5. Is the actor or group operating in a country that is relatively homogeneous on this issue? Are there exploitable cleavages between groups?
6. Are there attitudes held by the general public in the country that are compatible with US goals? Antagonistic to US goals?
7. To what extent is this state initiating nonproliferation and counterproliferation measures within the global community? Do effective nonproliferation measures require nudging from external actors?

Identification, over time, may lead to internalized acceptance of nuclear norms advocated by the influencer state, a transformation that constructivist scholars term "persuasion."[21] Persuasion is achieved when the preference of an actor or group in nuclear decisionmaking has been altered at an intrinsic level. The actor, group, or state has become convinced that the desired behavior is in the nation's best interest and makes a genuine change in preference. In the case of our subject matter, decisionmakers' beliefs are transformed to the extent that they are persuaded of the inherent value in stepping back from a nuclear threshold. Therefore, the actor or group is no longer demonstrating desired behavior merely to secure continued acceptance by the influencer state, but because the actor or group genuinely believes the behavior to be a higher order principle and/or in the nation's best interest. From our case studies in this volume, Ukraine is the state that best exemplifies successful persuasion, and is farthest along the path of fully buying in to the NPT nonproliferation goals. Israel and Saudi Arabia, both close allies of the United States, demonstrate strong identification with the United States, but maintain their own independent beliefs and intentions.

Key questions to consider in regard to whether an actor or group is complying with expected behavioral norms due to persuasion and internal acceptance of influencer norms include:

1. What is the current position of the actor or group along the proliferation timeline? Has the actor or group made recent progress to the right or has it been frozen for some time in its current position?
2. What individuals and organizations within the country advocate, of their own accord, public positions aligned with US nonproliferation policy goals?

3. Is the actor or group operating in a country that is socially and culturally ready to forgo nuclear weapons development?
4. Does this actor or group express public disappointment, even in
   admired others, when they perceive failures in living up to NPT
   standards?
5. Are there remaining oppositional elements of society that would wish
   to continue development of a nuclear weapons capability?
6. What are the "sacred values" of the population in the country? How do
   nuclear weapons feature within this set of "sacred values"?
7. Are state or sub-state actors initiating nonproliferation measures on
   their own without external prodding?
8. Have critical state actors adopted identities founded in nonproliferation or nonuse narratives or institutions?

Where specific actors reside along the "identification" and "persuasion" spectrum when the United States is cast as the key influencer proves
critical in an evaluation of which decision vectors are most promising for
US intervention and which policy levers are most likely to prove fruitful.
Attempts to evaluate the efficacy of certain lever "types" (i.e., economic
sanctions or threats to close diplomatic channels such as embassies) without reference to the character of the relationship between the state in
question and the United States can lead to misguided notions about the
potential effectiveness of some frequently employed diplomatic, economic, and military tools.

As our case studies demonstrate, an effective US response to near- and
medium-term nuclear threshold issues requires understanding the perceptions of threat experienced by the actors in question, the value the actors
place on their relationship with the United States, and the domestic sociocultural context driving decisionmaking.

Conclusion

The CTAF represents a new addition to the methodological tool set of the
strategic culture approach with a focus on creating greater utility for policymakers by identifying and understanding national and subnational
nuclear narratives, and providing a sociocultural window into another
country's nuclear decisionmaking process. Additionally, the CTAF places
specific focus on identifying those decision vectors most open to influence
by the United States or US partners.

First, the CTAF focuses on examining nuclear decisions of countries of concern, chronologically *earlier* ("move to the left") on the nuclear weapons development timeline, potentially recognizing movement toward nuclear thresholds at the plans and intentions stage. The authors of this volume believe that the plans and intentions stage is the part of the nuclear weapons decisionmaking process that is most impacted by cultural influences. Focusing on this early stage, therefore, provides US policymakers with maximum time and flexibility to apply appropriate levers to deter or dissuade such activity. Providing cultural insights into plans and intentions is also an area of proliferation theory where sociocultural analysis or strategic culture can best supplement existing approaches to decisionmaking.

Second, intrinsic to the research process of our methodology is a focus on key actors—both individuals and groups—with potential to influence nuclear decisions. Rather than defaulting to the state-based approach favored by most authors writing within the strategic culture paradigm, the CTAF approach looks beyond the state leader to secondary actors, including trusted advisors, inner circle members, military comrades, or scientific partners—those with the ability to influence the primary decisionmaker. Emphasis is placed on identifying critical influencers or obstructers with the ability to advance, delay, or thwart nuclear ambitions.

Third, looking at cultural data across the four categories brings a holistic approach to understanding the full scope of forces that influence nuclear decisionmaking within the state of concern. Understanding the identity, norms, values, and perceptual lenses that shape the thinking and behavior of key decisionmakers opens a new vantage point to policymakers and allows them to look beyond the traditional western frame of reference in interpreting actions and narratives of state actors in regard to nuclear thresholds.

Fourth, based on this intimate look at the national and subnational narratives surrounding the nuclear issue, including pathways a nuclear decision is likely to travel, CTAF users are able to offer pointed and evidence-based policy recommendations. With a tailored set of levers and policy options in hand, a policymaker is better positioned to craft an assurance, dissuasion, or deterrence strategy specifically designed to engage foreign leaders on the diplomatic level.

As noted at the outset of this chapter, the United States faces a near- and medium-term global nuclear landscape in which it is attempting to influence the nuclear threshold decisions of allies and adversaries simultaneously. The blanket counterproliferation and deterrence strategies pursued in the past will be insufficient to deal with very different types of diplomatic challenges posed by the two groups. On the one hand, the United States will be confronting adversary states, such as Iran with a fairly advanced nuclear program currently put on hold, or North Korea which has recently taken important steps toward full nuclear weaponization and deployment capabilities; and on the other hand will be facing allies, such as Israel which already has a nuclear capability and is intent upon protecting its monopoly in the Middle East, or Saudi Arabia which may be tipped toward a decision on developing an indigenous nuclear capability to counter Iran. This variety of nuclear threshold challenges and diverse interlocutors will require creative, culturally aware and carefully tailored policy options, which our approach seeks to provide.

NOTES

1. Portions of this chapter previously appeared in Jeannie L. Johnson and Matthew T. Berrett, "Cultural Topography: A New Research Tool for Intelligence." *Studies in Intelligence*, Vol. 55, No. 2 (June 2011).
2. Johnston, "Thinking About Strategic Culture," 32–64; Glenn, "Realism versus Strategic Culture: Competition and Collaboration?"; Greathouse, "Examining the Role and Methodology of Strategic Culture."
3. Bloomfield, "Time to Move On: Reconceptualizing the Strategic Culture Debate"; Greathouse, "Examining the Role and Methodology of Strategic Culture."
4. Haglund, "What Good Is Strategic Culture?"
5. Snyder, *The Soviet Strategic Culture: Implications for Limited Nuclear Operations*, 8.
6. See Waltz, "The Anarchic Structure of World Politics," 29–49.
7. Ken Booth, "The Concept of Strategic Culture Affirmed," in Carl G. Jacobsen, ed., *Strategic Power: The United States of America and the USSR* (London: Macmillan Press, 1990): 125–126.
8. An exception is Meyer's work on the EU as a superstate structure: "The Purpose and Pitfalls of Constructivist Forecasting: Insights from Strategic Culture Research for the European Union's Evolution as Military Power," 669–690; "Convergence Towards a European Strategic Culture? A Constructivist Framework for Explaining Changing Norms," 523–549.
9. Twomey, "Lacunae in the Study of Culture in International Security," 338–357.
10. See Jeffrey Knopf's critique of the first generation of strategic culture scholarship, *Rationality, Culture and Deterrence*, PASCC Report Number 2013 009.

11. Johnson and Berrett, "Cultural Topography: A New Research Tool for Intelligence," 2.
12. See discussion in Maines, M., and Danks, J., et al., *Cultural Analytic Framework*, Appendix A, 41–42 (University of Maryland, 2011).
13. See Johnson, J., & Berrett, M. (2011), Cultural Topography: A New Research Tool for Intelligence Analysis. *Studies in Intelligence*, 55(2), 1–22.
14. Peter Wilson's article captures the research philosophy and data-extraction process pursued within the CTAF and offers a strong argument for attention to the interpretivist method, Grounded Theory, and the English School for future analysis in international relations: "The English School Meets the Chicago School: The Case for a Grounded Theory of International Institutions." *International Studies Review*, 14 (2012): 567—90. See also Glaser, Barney G., and Anselm L. Strauss. *The Discovery of Grounded Theory: Strategies for Qualitative Research*. Chicago: Aldine Publishing, 1967; and Chap. 1 "Know Thyself: Turning the Strategic Culture Tool Inward," in Jeannie L. Johnson, *The Marines, Counterinsurgency, and Strategic Culture: Lessons Learned and Lost in America's Wars* (Georgetown University Press, 2018).
15. Nye, J. *Soft Power: The Means to Success in World Politics*. Introduction, page x and 5–10. Public Affairs, Perseus Book Group, 2004.
16. Joseph S. Nye Jr., *The Future of Power* (New York: Public Affairs, 2011).
17. See Hillary Clinton's confirmation speech before the Senate Foreign Relations Committee, delivered on January 13, 2009.
18. Nye, J. *The Paradox of American Power* (Oxford University Press, 2002): 8–9.
19. Maines, M., & Danks, J., et al., *The Cultural Analytic Framework*, Appendix D, 46–50 (University of Maryland, 2011).
20. See Rublee, M.R. *Nonproliferation Norms: Why States Choose Nuclear Restraint* (Athens: The University of Georgia Press, 2009): 16–19, for a more detailed discussion in terms of social psychology on the difference between the terms "identification" and "persuasion" in regard to acceptance of nuclear norms.
21. Ibid. 16–19; see also Alastair Ian Johnston, "Treating International Institutions as Social Environments," *International Studies Quarterly*, 45 (2001): 487–515.

CHAPTER 3

Iran's Strategic Culture: Implications for Nuclear Policy

Nima Gerami

This chapter assesses the principal drivers of Iran's strategic culture and their broader implications for the country's nuclear decisionmaking and policies in light of the comprehensive nuclear agreement reached on July 14, 2015, between Iran and the P5+1 (the United States, United Kingdom, France, Germany, Russia, and China). The nuclear agreement, formally known as the Joint Comprehensive Plan of Action (JCPOA), is intended to verifiably prevent Iran from producing sufficient fissile material—either weapons-grade uranium or plutonium—for a single nuclear weapon for at least 10 to 15 years.

If fully implemented by all states parties, the physical constraints and verification provisions of the JCPOA, supplemented by national intelligence efforts, would effectively extend Iran's "breakout" capacity to one year and reduce the probability of an Iranian bomb until at least 2030.[1] Nevertheless,

The author is indebted to Rameez Abbas, Gawdat Bahgat, Michael Connell, Michael Eisenstadt, Thomas Lynch, and the book editors for their helpful comments on earlier drafts of this chapter. The views expressed herein are those of the author and do not reflect the official policy or position of the National Defense University, the Defense Department, or the US government.

N. Gerami (✉)
National Defense University, Washington, DC, USA

the JCPOA does not eliminate the risk that Tehran might seek to increase its enrichment levels and stocks of enriched uranium to achieve a "threshold" nuclear weapons capability—the ability to quickly develop nuclear weapons at a time of its choosing—after 15 years, when all of the physical constraints on Iran's enrichment capacity imposed by the JCPOA will be lifted. At that point, the central question will become whether Iranian leaders can be deterred from making the decision to cross the threshold and build nuclear weapons, in abrogation of the country's nonproliferation and safeguards commitments under the Nuclear Nonproliferation Treaty (NPT).

In the near term, there is considerable uncertainty about whether the JCPOA will remain intact, given heightened US-Iran tensions following the election of US President Donald J. Trump. On October 13, 2017, the Trump administration rolled out its strategy to push back against Iran's regional ambitions and "deny the regime all paths to a nuclear weapon."[2] In unveiling this strategy, President Trump announced he would not recertify the JCPOA as required every 90 days under the Iran Nuclear Agreement Review Act (INARA), leading to speculation about US intent to withdraw from the deal.[3] Other signatories to the JCPOA, including France, Germany, and the United Kingdom, have urged Washington to maintain its commitment to the nuclear deal, noting that the International Atomic Energy Agency (IAEA) has "repeatedly confirmed Iran's compliance with the JCPOA through its long-term verification and monitoring program."[4]

Iran, for its part, has dismissed efforts to renegotiate the JCPOA and signaled it will continue to implement the deal notwithstanding the US move toward decertification, provided that other signatories remain committed to the deal and do not cooperate with any US attempt to reimpose sanctions. In the event that the JCPOA ultimately falls apart, however, the United States and its international partners will need to consider possible implications and appropriate steps to prevent Iran from obtaining nuclear weapons. In this context, a more comprehensive understanding of Iranian decisionmaking will enable policymakers to better anticipate Iran's actions and interact with its leaders in a clear, compelling manner.

This chapter examines the nexus between Iran's strategic culture and its nuclear program. It also evaluates the policy implications of adopting more tailored approaches to deter Iran in an increasingly volatile Middle East. Proponents of using strategic culture as an analytic framework advocate a "know thy enemy" approach, in which a better understanding of adversarial states allows policymakers to develop tailored deterrence strategies designed to influence or alter state behavior. This logic currently underlies many US policy decisions on the Middle East, yet little scholarly research has tested the extent to which a state's strategic culture actually impacts foreign policy decisions, particularly decisions concerning the development and use of weapons of mass destruction (WMD). Despite significant growth in the field over the past few decades, strategic culture theory is often unwieldy, ill-defined, and difficult to operationalize and implement from a policy perspective.[5]

Previous work on Iran's strategic culture has refuted the notion that Iran is "irrational" and formulates policy solely on religious-ideological grounds. Instead, scholars have characterized Iran as an anti-status quo power with a defensive military doctrine that seeks to minimize risk, preserve plausible deniability, prevent conflict escalation, and enhance its deterrence capabilities. In his examination of Iran's "way of war," Michael Eisenstadt identifies key elements of Iran's strategic culture as indirection, ambiguity, incrementalism, and strategic patience.[6] Rather than being guided solely by religion, Iranian leaders base decisions upon the principle of *maslehat* (expediency) and national interest, according to Eisenstadt.[7] Indeed, one could argue that traditional realist theory explains much of Iran's behavior and preference for pragmatic policies that maximize its national interest. Strategic culture scholars have contended that their framework is not intended to supplant traditional theories of international relations but instead to supplement our understanding of state behavior on another level. Like Iran, Alastair Ian Johnston observes that China possesses a dual strategic culture, "one a symbolic or idealized set of assumptions and ranked preferences, and one an operational set that had a nontrivial effect on strategic choice."[8] Thus, a state may exhibit classic elements of realpolitik in its decisionmaking processes while remaining bound by the parameters of its unique strategic culture.

Nevertheless, religion, ideology, and culture do shape the parameters of Iranian decisionmaking. While Iran is a rational state actor, Matthew McInnis argues that religion and ideology provide a framework within which the country's leaders make national security decisions and justify their policies.[9] Iran's penchant for asymmetric warfare, for example, may be derived partly from Shia narratives of martyrdom, injustice, and the need to confront stronger, immoral powers, as well as from a cultural preference for ambiguity and indirectness. The concept of *taqiyya* in Shiism, whereby adherents lie about their faith to enemies if their lives are at stake, also provides a religious justification for dissembling.[10] Moreover, Islam has significantly influenced Iranian notions of grand strategy, deterrence, and victory, thereby providing the "national objectives for which the use of violence is permissible."[11] Iranian attitudes toward war are therefore "less goal-oriented than western concepts," and, as Gregory Giles asserts, "defeat is not necessarily equated with failure."[12] Victory is defined as outlasting the enemy in the long term, and religious narratives of sacrifice and *jihad*, or holy war, fuel Iran's ability to tolerate substantial losses for the sake of resisting external oppression.[13]

This chapter seeks to build on previous studies and apply a more systematic approach to analyzing Iran's strategic culture, drawing on the Cultural Analytic Topography Framework. The first section of this chapter outlines the history of Iran's nuclear program from the pre-revolutionary era to present. The next section identifies key individuals and institutions—or "keepers" of Iran's strategic culture—which influence nuclear decisionmaking. The third section highlights how elements of Iran's strategic culture—including its identity, values, norms, and perceptual lens—shape the way Iranian leaders perceive threats, respond to aggression, and formulate nuclear policies. The final section suggests possible traditional and nontraditional points of leverage to enhance US policy efforts to engage and deter Iran. Whatever the fate of the JCPOA, cultural considerations are likely to become increasingly important in discerning Iran's nuclear intent and, in the long term, determining whether its leaders believe their national interest is best served by pursuing nuclear weapons.

Origins and Evolution of Iran's Nuclear Program

During the rule of Shah Mohammad Reza Pahlavi, Iran first established its nuclear program in 1957 on the basis of a civil nuclear cooperation agreement with the United States, under the auspices of President Dwight D. Eisenhower's Atoms for Peace program. Iran was among the first countries to sign the NPT in 1968 and concluded a safeguards agreement with the IAEA in 1974.

Ironically, the same nationalist narrative that characterized the Shah's nuclear ambitions prefigured the Islamic Republic's present-day claims about its inherent right to pursue nuclear energy for peaceful purposes. The Shah's vision of transforming Iran into a modern, industrialized state—coupled with the oil shock of 1973–1974 and subsequent search for alternative power sources—accelerated Iran's pursuit of nuclear energy.[14] In 1974, the Shah established the Atomic Energy Organization of Iran (AEOI) to start a "full-fledged nuclear power industry" with a virtually unlimited budget.[15] As part of its peaceful nuclear cooperation agreement with the United States, Iran sent officials and AEOI scientists to American universities for training.[16] These officials—including current AEOI head Ali Akbar Salehi and Foreign Minister Mohammad Javad Zarif—play a leading role in Iran's nuclear decisionmaking and implementation of the JCPOA today.

Although the Shah publicly disavowed nuclear weapons, his insistence on mastering the complete nuclear fuel cycle and acquiring plutonium reprocessing capabilities aroused US suspicions about Iran's long-term nuclear ambitions.[17] The Shah eventually agreed to forgo plans to build a plutonium processing plant and ship spent nuclear fuel to the United States, but these negotiations were cut short by political turmoil that culminated in the 1979 Islamic Revolution.

After the overthrow of the Shah, Ayatollah Ruhollah Khomeini announced the formation of the Islamic Republic and instituted *velayat-e faqih* (guardianship of the jurist), the Shia doctrine granting absolute political and religious authority to the Supreme Leader. The new revolutionary government inherited a sizeable nuclear infrastructure that became a symbol of the excesses and irresponsibility of the ancien régime. After acceding to power, one of Khomeini's priorities was to reevaluate Iran's nuclear program and associated business contracts with the West. Against the backdrop of the seizure of the US Embassy in Tehran and the 444-day hostage crisis that ensued, American and other foreign companies ceased nuclear cooperation with Iran. The new head of the AEOI, Fereydoun Sahabi, recommended the Islamic Republic's abandonment of all nuclear power plants under construction for "political, economic, social, human, and technical reasons."[18] By 1980, the Islamic Republic announced the official suspension of large parts of the country's nuclear power program, stating that its construction had begun under the Shah "on the basis of colonialist and imposed treaties" and constituted a symbol of Iran's dependence on the West.[19]

Despite the Islamic Republic's initial opposition to the nuclear program and the exodus of nuclear scientists after the revolution, nuclear research continued unabated.[20] The devastating impact of the Iran-Iraq War and the international community's failure to condemn Iraq's use of chemical weapons likely contributed to Tehran's decision to begin chemical weapons research and restart its nuclear program as a potential deterrent against Baghdad.[21] Iran's efforts to achieve the full nuclear fuel cycle evolved in five discrete phases:

- *Phase I: Decision to Restart the Nuclear Program and Initiate Procurement (1984–1988).*

In a high-level meeting in 1984 at the Presidential Palace in Tehran, then President Ali Khamenei announced that Supreme Leader Khomeini had decided to secretly restart Iran's nuclear program in order to "secure the very essence of the Islamic Revolution from the schemes of its enemies, especially the United States and Israel."[22] In 1985, Iran began pursuing a gas centrifuge enrichment program and took steps leading to the acquisition of centrifuge enrichment technology. Henceforth, the Islamic Republic began procuring key components for a domestic enrichment program from the A. Q. Khan network in Pakistan and upgrading the Tehran Research Reactor (TRR) with fuel purchased from Argentina.

- *Phase II: Accelerated Procurement and Enrichment Activities (1988–2002).*

Despite Khomeini's death in 1989, Iran expanded its uranium mining and conversion capabilities, indigenous heavy water production plant, and enrichment program. In 1990, Iran signed a nuclear cooperation agreement with China and secretly imported uranium hexafluoride (UF6)—the feedstock for enrichment—one year later. Between 1994 and 1996, Iran purchased additional design drawings and components for P-1 centrifuges from the Khan network. In 1995, Iran secured a contract with Russia to complete the reactor unit at Bushehr.[23] Six years later, Iran initiated construction of a clandestine enrichment facility near Natanz.

- *Phase III: Public Disclosures and International Diplomacy (2003–2006).*

In 2002, an exiled Iranian opposition group, the National Council of Resistance of Iran, publicly disclosed the existence of sites at Natanz and Arak that had been constructed in contravention of Iran's NPT safeguards commitments. The EU-3—France, Germany, and the United Kingdom—initiated a series of negotiations ultimately resulting in Iran's agreement to enhance safeguards (the IAEA's Additional Protocol) and to temporarily suspend its nuclear fuel cycle-related activities. However, negotiations became deadlocked over the EU-3's insistence that Iran give up enrichment. By 2005, Supreme Leader Khamenei ordered the resumption of uranium conversion activities and the IAEA referred Iran's nuclear dossier to the United Nations (UN) Security Council.

- *Phase IV: Deepening Internal Divisions and International Tensions (2006–2012).*

In 2006, the United States, Russia, and China joined EU-3 diplomatic efforts with Iran, forming the P5+1. During the next two years, additional UN Security Council sanctions resolutions were imposed on Iran, including restrictions on arms imports and exports, financial services, and civil nuclear assistance. These sanctions may have played a role in slowing Iran's nuclear progress by limiting access to foreign materials and assistance. The alleged US-Israel Stuxnet cyberattacks in 2009 and 2010 also disrupted centrifuge operations at Natanz.

Upon taking office in 2009, US President Barack Obama signaled a willingness to engage with Iran as part of a dual-track policy of diplomacy and coercive sanctions. The United States supported an IAEA-brokered fuel swap agreement to refuel Iran's TRR, but this initiative broke down after the deal failed to garner support from Tehran's divided political factions. The turmoil following Iran's disputed presidential election in 2009 and increased technical progress in the nuclear realm, including the enrichment of up to 20% at Natanz, further complicated US outreach efforts toward the Iranian government.

In May 2010, Iranian President Mahmoud Ahmadinejad attempted a last-ditch effort to revive TRR negotiations through a Joint Declaration signed by Iran, Brazil, and Turkey, but the United States did not support the proposal because it did not satisfactorily address Iran's production of 20% enriched uranium and accumulation of low-enriched uranium (LEU). Increased US and European Union (EU) financial sanctions and the oil embargo in 2011–2012 further isolated Iran from the international banking system and embargoed roughly 40% of Iran's oil exports. Amidst mounting tensions, the United States held secret bilateral nuclear talks with Iran in Oman in 2011.

- *Phase V: From "Resistance" to "Heroic Flexibility" (2012–Present).*

The election of Iranian President Hassan Rouhani—who ran on a platform of economic reform and constructive engagement with the West—renewed momentum for nuclear negotiations. The US-Iran negotiating channel ran alongside formal Iran-P5+1 talks, which were renewed in 2012 in Istanbul, Turkey. The P5+1 pursued a confidence-building agreement to compel Iran to freeze its production of 20% enriched LEU, including activities at the Fordow enrichment facility, and to reduce its existing stockpile of LEU by either shipping the material abroad or converting it to fuel.

The dual-track negotiations led to the interim Joint Plan of Action in Geneva in November 2013, three months after Rouhani's inauguration. For the first time, Supreme Leader Khamenei publicly supported the negotiations and permitted direct talks with the United States under the banner of "heroic flexibility." After nearly two years of intensive negotiations, the final JCPOA was announced in Vienna on July 14, 2015. The detailed, 159-page nonproliferation agreement imposed physical constraints and verification provisions to prevent Iran from producing sufficient fissile material for nuclear weapons for 10 to 15 years in return for the comprehensive lifting of all nuclear-related sanctions.[24]

In short, the JCPOA constrains Iran's nuclear weapons option until 2030 through a combination of physical limits on fissile material production at declared facilities and robust inspection and verification provisions. The JCPOA, however, also allows Iran to retain a substantial nuclear infrastructure—including virtually all of the physical infrastructure associated with its uranium enrichment program—and the technical capacity to expand its enrichment program after the agreement's key restrictions expire. While the JCPOA increases the probability that the IAEA would detect any new covert nuclear facilities in Iran, the agreement is less likely to deter or detect small-scale illicit activities not involving nuclear material, such as research on nuclear weapons or the production of non-nuclear weapons components.[25]

Iran's decision to accept temporary constraints on its enrichment program and halt alleged weapons-related efforts raises fundamental questions about nuclear intent: does the JCPOA signal a strategic shift in Tehran to forgo nuclear weapons altogether or a tactical decision to hedge?[26] JCPOA proponents argue the nuclear agreement will ultimately undermine advocates of nuclear weapons inside Iran by reducing the threat of military conflict with the United States and increasing the benefits of economic integration. JCPOA opponents, on the other hand, claim the agreement will legitimize Iran's status as a nuclear threshold state and neither fundamentally alter Tehran's hostility toward the West nor address its destabilizing regional behavior.[27] In the long term, the nuclear issue will remain a key policy concern requiring a deeper understanding of Iran's unique strategic culture and the impact of cultural factors on Tehran's future nuclear calculus.

Iran's Nuclear Decisionmaking

Iran's national security and nuclear decisionmaking takes place within multiple, overlapping political institutions heavily influenced by informal power networks. The Supreme Leader, who is formally selected by the Assembly of Experts (*Majlis-e khobregan*), sets the overall direction and tone of policy guidance at the strategic level. The Supreme Leader appoints six clerics to the Guardian Council (*Shura-ye negahban-e qanun-e asasi*) as well as the head of the judiciary, who appoints the other six clerics on the Council. The Guardian Council is charged with ensuring all legislation accords with Islamic law and approving the qualifications of candidates for the presidency, parliament (*Majlis*), and Assembly of Experts. The Expediency Discernment Council (*Majma'-e tashkhis-e maslehat-e nezam*) is responsible for resolving disputes between the *Majlis* and the Guardian Council. The Supreme Leader is the head of the armed forces, namely the regular military (*Artesh*) and the Islamic Revolutionary Guard Corps (*Sepah-e pasdaran-e enqelab-e eslami* or IRGC). The IRGC reports directly to the Supreme Leader rather than the president, though the president and *Majlis* exercise a degree of control through oversight of the national budget.

The Supreme Leader retains ultimate say in all policy decisions, including those surrounding the nuclear program, but he rules through consensus. Despite Iran's deeply divisive domestic politics, substantive matters of national security and foreign policy such as the nuclear program tend to elicit relatively greater levels of elite and mass consensus coordinated through the Supreme National Security Council (*Shura-ye ali-ye amniyat-e melli* or SNSC) and its representatives, implemented by the president, and overseen by the *Majlis* (as reflected in Fig. 3.1). Constitutionally, the SNSC embodies the highest decisionmaking body in Iran. In practice, however, the IRGC

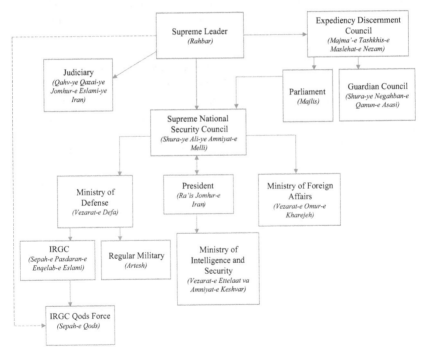

Fig. 3.1 A strategic overview of Iran's national security decisionmaking process. The dotted line represents a special, direct relationship of power and influence. Author's own work

represents the single most influential group of individuals in national security matters.[28]

The core group of traditional decisionmakers is relatively insulated from turnover resulting from elections or regional and international developments, providing some sense of regime stability and continuity. Nonetheless, the formal apparatus of power overlaps with, and at times is subordinated to, an informal and complex network of multiple individuals and factions (equivalent to interest or pressure groups), including charitable foundations (*bonyads*), think tanks, clerical seminaries, IRGC veteran groups, and miscellaneous individuals who amass power based on religious status and education, political affiliation, kinship, military service, or personal wealth.

Traditional Keepers of Iran's Strategic Culture

The SNSC formulates national security policy at the strategic level, coordinates the implementation of these policies among various institutions, and oversees other government entities. Its formal membership, with others invited on an ad-hoc basis, includes the head of the executive (SNSC chairman); heads of the legislative (*Majlis* speaker) and judicial branches; chief of the Supreme Command Council of the Armed Forces; Ministers of Foreign Affairs, Interior, and Intelligence and Security; Commanders of the IRGC and the *Artesh*; representative of the Planning and Budget Organization; and two representatives of the Supreme Leader, one of whom is the SNSC secretary and, in practice, serves as the national security advisor.

Of prevailing national security issues, none are as sensitive as Iran's nuclear program. Rouhani served as Khamenei's representative to the SNSC and its secretary for nearly two decades (1989–2005). After the public disclosures of Iran's clandestine nuclear efforts in 2002, a pyramidal structure for nuclear decisionmaking was put into place via the SNSC, with committees at the director, deputy, and ministerial levels. Representatives of the ministerial committee within the SNSC secretariat, known as the Supreme Nuclear Committee, were appointed by the Supreme Leader but are also Iran's highest level decisionmakers (i.e., the Council of Heads).

While there is careful deference to the Supreme Leader's wishes on all policy matters, Iranian officials often seek consensus in decisionmaking as a means of sharing the responsibilities and risks associated with sensitive national security policies. Before and since the conclusion of the JCPOA,

Rouhani and his nuclear negotiating team have insisted that Khamenei knew the details of secret bilateral talks with the United States—a shifting narrative since negotiations were well under way before Rouhani was elected president (and apparently without his knowledge).[29]

The Supreme Leader retains absolute authority on the nuclear issue, though he often maintains distance from specific policy decisions to preserve ambiguity and avoid blame for failure. While different presidential administrations may have varying tactics and ideological preferences, Iranian officials ultimately rely on the Supreme Leader to validate and legitimize the country's nuclear policies. In turn, the Supreme Leader relies on the IRGC as his power base to safeguard the regime against internal and external threats.

The IRGC is an unelected organization wielding considerable economic and political power in domestic and national security affairs, far surpassing that of other institutional actors. IRGC ideological fealty to the revolution has made it the chief custodian of sensitive weapons systems, as opposed to the *Artesh* (indeed, the Ministry of Defense is not even included in SNSC permanent membership). IRGC leaders typically do not take public sides in regime infighting, but their views, generally aligned with those of the Supreme Leader, carry significant weight in national security decisionmaking.

IRGC Qods Force Commander Qassem Soleimani—one of the most influential voices in Khamenei's inner circle—has gained public notoriety in recent years as the face of Iran's regional campaigns in Iraq, Syria, and Yemen. Once a shadowy figure, Soleimani has become a national hero whose photos on Twitter and Instagram show him evading Islamic State of Iraq and Syria (ISIS) attacks and near-death experiences in Iraq as well as brazenly traveling to Russia in defiance of international sanctions. His memoirs are replete with photos of Soleimani posing with Shiite brethren in solidarity against the West.[30] IRGC leaders tend to publicly support an unbridled nuclear program—without technical constraints imposed by the West—to promote an image of strength and deter Iran's regional adversaries.[31] While most IRGC officials initially contested nuclear negotiations, the Supreme Leader stifled criticism of the deal by calling on officials to demonstrate unified support for the JCPOA. Rouhani further promised the IRGC that sanctions would be "cancelled"—an attractive prospect for an organization facing resource constraints in Iraq, Syria, and elsewhere throughout the region. IRGC Commander Ali Jafari in July 2015 clarified the organization's position: "First, I have to state one more time there is not one official in the Islamic Republic that is opposed to a good deal in the negotiations. Therefore, the foreign media have tried to create untrue polarization on the issue of the nuclear negotiations in the country.... For me, as a military official, what is more important than anything else.... is the protection and promotion of Iran's defensive abilities."[32]

In contrast, the AEOI oversees the civil side of the nuclear program and is primarily concerned with Iran's scientific and technical prowess in order to justify its research and development budget. Current AEOI head Salehi played an important behind-the-scenes role in shepherding US-Iran negotiations, having served in three successive administrations (first as Ambassador to the IAEA, later Minister of Foreign Affairs, and now AEOI head). The nuclear dossier under the purview of AEOI was reassigned to the SNSC after the 2002 revelations.

Iran's Ministry of Foreign Affairs is primarily concerned with the international ramifications of Iran's nuclear program and reluctant to sacrifice economic and political opportunities for the country's nuclear capabilities. The Foreign Ministry, however, plays only an ancillary role in national security matters, mainly serving as the conduit for negotiations that led to the nuclear deal and ongoing discussions with the P5+1 and IAEA on JCPOA implementation issues. Under the Rouhani administration, Foreign Minister Zarif has been responsible for conducting nuclear negotiations in consultation with the SNSC, but he has little if any authority over technical aspects of Iran's nuclear program. During Rouhani's second term, the Foreign Ministry is poised to expand its influence over the nuclear file and a bill is being considered in the *Majlis* that would transfer responsibility for the JCPOA to the Ministry's political department.[33]

Politicization of the nuclear issue in recent years has exacerbated internal political divisions, making it a lightning rod in the broader debate among Iran's elite about the core tenets of the Islamic Republic and its place in the world. Personal rivalries, bureaucratic infighting, and the Supreme Leader's ambiguous guidance on the nuclear issue further compound this problem, creating a political environment that could potentially make implementation of the JCPOA difficult to sustain over the long term.

Nontraditional Keepers of Iran's Strategic Culture

Nontraditional actors also have a crucial role in shaping the nuclear debate in Iran. These actors are clerics, businessmen (*bazaaris*), political scientists, intelligentsia, and former government officials who remain connected to powerful Iranian leaders and therefore continue to exert influence on political decisionmaking from behind the scenes. Individual influence within this system depends on proximity to the Supreme Leader, revolutionary or clerical credentials, and the ability to build a strong coalition of supporters from diverse political backgrounds. Prominent examples of nontraditional keepers of Iran's strategic culture include Hossein Shariatmadari, editor-in-chief of the hardline daily *Kayhan* and unofficial mouthpiece of the Supreme Leader; Ayatollah Mahmoud Hashemi Shahroudi, widely considered the primary candidate to succeed Khamenei and his chosen replacement for the late Ali Akbar Hashemi Rafsajani as the chair of the Expediency Council; Javad Larijani, close advisor to Khamenei and brother of Ali Larijani (current *Majlis* speaker) and Sadegh Larijani (judiciary head); and Ali Akbar Velayati, the Supreme Leader's advisor on international affairs and head of the Center for Strategic Research, an influential think tank based in Tehran.

CHARACTERISTICS OF IRAN'S STRATEGIC CULTURE

The characteristics of Iran's strategic culture, outlined in Fig. 3.2, provide insight into how Iranian leaders process information, formulate and implement policy, and engage with the international community. Encompassing these traits, and as a provisional simplification, Iran's strategic culture can broadly be defined as a *revolutionary technocratic* type with a dualistic view of itself as an Islamic (revolutionary-clerical) country and a technocratic republic that shapes the discursive boundaries and manner in which the country's security policies and threat perceptions are framed. This tension is exemplified by recent power shifts in Tehran between technocrats, currently led by President Rouhani, and relative hardliners represented in Iran's conservative-dominated *Majlis* alongside elements of the judiciary, armed forces, and clerical establishment.

The following examination of Iran's strategic culture elucidates how Iran perceives threats and prioritizes competing policy objectives. The subsequent sections explore how these traits shape Iranian nuclear decisionmaking and offer policy implications for effectively engaging and deterring Iran. These sections benefit from previous research on Iran's strategic culture as well as analysis of Persian-language memoirs and speeches made by senior Iranian political and military figures, including Khamenei, Rouhani, Rafsanjani, Salehi, Jafari, and Soleimani.

Identity and Values:

- Dualism permeates Iranian identity
- Strategic patience is rewarded
- Historical "right" to hegemony
- Resistance is key to action and power
- World order is unjust, victimizes the weak

Norms and Perceptual Lens:

- Deterrence is the best defense
- Ambiguity complicates decisionmaking
- Islam and Shia martyrdom bolster regime legitimacy
- National interests supersede revolutionary ideals
- Proportionate responses preferable to escalation
- Combination of soft and hard power most effective for resisting enemies
- Rationalism and heroic flexibility key for survival

Fig. 3.2 Characteristics of Iran's *revolutionary technocratic* strategic culture. Author's own work

Dualism Permeates Iranian Identity

Dualism has permeated Iranian identity since pre-Islamic, Zoroastrian times (600 BCE–650 CE). Zoroastrianism was one of the first monotheistic religions to distinguish between opposing forces of good and evil. In modern Iran, the Islamic Republic derives legitimacy from nationalism and religion, particularly Twelver Shia Islam and the divine rule of the Supreme Leader. The inherent dichotomy between Iran's nationalist and Islamic identities has, at times, created tension within the political system.[34] Iranian leaders resolve this tension through adherence to the principle of *maslehat* (expediency), which allows them to forgo certain Islamic obligations in order to preserve the regime's political power.[35] According to this cultural norm, national security priorities may supersede religious ideology temporarily, though the two are often mutually reinforcing.

Iranian officials since the 1979 revolution have rejected Hobbesian notions of statecraft and embraced aspirations of becoming the spiritual leader of the Islamic world. Iran's perception of itself as the vanguard of

Shia and Sunni Islam translates into a desire to play a transformative role in regional and world affairs. Iranian nationalism and its revolutionary brand of Islam fuels military adventurism in the region, but Iran's effective use of soft power allows it to build long-term influence by translating military gains into strategic advantages.[36]

Strategic Patience Is Rewarded

Iranian culture values strategic patience, or long-term gains, in its decisionmaking process and formulation of national security policies. Iran's foreign policy and military doctrine advocate imposing costs on enemies through strategies of delay, attrition, and reliance on soft power to build long-term influence. Strategic patience is further reflected in the Islamic Republic's political structure insofar as senior officials—most notably the Supreme Leader—have held unelected positions continuously since the Iran-Iraq War.[37]

Iran's concept of strategic patience is based on ancient Persian notions of time as spiritual, infinite, and nonlinear.[38] The Zoroastrian view of *zaman* (time) is associated with the Persian deity *Zurvan*, the father of the god of eternally returning time. When the Arabs invaded the Persian Empire in the seventh century CE, they brought with them the idea of *dahr*—the infinite extension of time—which entered Persian folklore and Sufi references to all-pervading time and irreversible fate.[39] Historical examples of the benefits of strategic patience include the eventual selection of Imam Ali as the fourth caliph after he was passed over following the death of the prophet Mohammad; Iran's persistence in retaining the Persian script after the Arab conquest; and the eventual co-optation of Iran's Macedonian, Mongol, and Arab conquerors and the successful preservation of Iranian identity.[40]

Iran's long-term approach to decisionmaking translates into a preference to avoid conflict escalation and respond indirectly to perceived acts of aggression. This proclivity for indirect conflict is in line with Iran's reliance on asymmetric warfare to defeat more powerful adversaries. In practice, the result is a leadership culture seeking to avoid offensive military operations unless they are intended to punish the aggressor as a means of reestablishing deterrence.[41] For example, although Saddam Hussein initiated the war with Iran in 1980, Khomeini rejected the Iraqi offer of ceasefire in 1982 and decided to prolong the war, thus generating a war of attrition. During the US-led war against Iraq in 2003, Iran gradually wore down coalition forces through proxy attacks using Explosively Formed Projectiles (EFPs) and Improvised Rocket-Assisted Munitions (IRAMs), contributing to the eventual drawdown of the multinational force in Iraq in 2007 and the complete withdrawal in 2011. After Saudi Arabia invaded Bahrain in 2011 to suppress Shiite uprisings, Iran waited six months to retaliate before implementing the thwarted plot to assassinate the Saudi ambassador in Washington, DC.

More recently, Iran demonstrated strategic patience by avoiding the opening of a new front against Israel following the January 2015 air strikes in Syria that killed IRGC Brigadier General Mohammad Ali Allahdadi and the son of former Lebanese Hezbollah Commander Imad Mughniyeh.[42] After Saudi Arabia's execution of Shiite cleric Sheikh Nimr al-Nimr, which was widely perceived as Saudi escalation given the proxy war in Yemen, Iranian Foreign Minister Zarif claimed "Iran has no desire to escalate tension" and refused to break or downgrade diplomatic relations with Saudi Arabia.[43] Similarly, Iran chose not to escalate tensions with the United States on the eve of Implementation Day of the JCPOA in January 2016, when it captured and released 10 US naval officers who had strayed into Iranian territorial waters in the Persian Gulf.[44]

Furthermore, Iran has demonstrated strategic patience by not dashing to the bomb but instead pursuing a deliberately gradual approach vis-à-vis the nuclear issue, which was resolved after nearly a decade of negotiations with the EU-3, P5+1, and United States. Iranian officials have stated on numerous occasions that engagement with the P5+1 was intended to buy time to advance Iran's nuclear fuel cycle capabilities and to protect the program from military attack.[45] In memoirs of his time as Iran's chief nuclear negotiator, Rouhani recounts that he "strongly believed and still believes that success in the important nuclear issue will not be gained except through patience, careful scrutiny, pragmatism, and prudence. Undoubtedly, the use of these principles, both in policymaking and in practice, requires untiring efforts and abundant patience."[46]

Iran Has a Historical "Right" to Hegemony

Iran's strategic culture is defined by its longevity and resilience as a Persian nation and ancient civilization. Iran has a long history of not only surviving foreign conquests but also exerting influence over its invaders. The cultural and scientific achievements of Iran's Achaemenid

Empire survived its conquest by Alexander the Great, who adopted many Persian customs in order to rule more effectively. Iran resisted the Arab conquest of the Sassanids in the middle of the seventh century CE, as well as the subsequent conversion to Islam from Zoroastrianism, by largely keeping the Persian language intact. In modern history, Iran maintained its national identity during the Anglo-Soviet occupation following World War II, which deposed the Shah and installed a new ruler in Iran until the 1979 revolution.[47] Iran, moreover, continued efforts to nationalize critical oil and transportation infrastructure, despite the 1953 Anglo-American coup against the popularly elected Prime Minister Mohammad Mossadegh. To this day, Iranian law prohibits any foreign entity from owning a majority share of infrastructure projects. Iranian narratives of resistance against Western intervention are therefore deeply embedded in the popular consciousness and rooted in historical experience.[48]

The idea that Iran is culturally superior to its Arab neighbors and has an intrinsic right to regional hegemony is deeply ingrained in Iranian identity. Iranian officials argue the Islamic Republic should be the dominant power in the region by dint of history, religion, geography, demography, and natural resources.[49] This translates into Iran's desire to control the Gulf militarily and assert its vital interests against regional adversaries.[50] Most recently, this tendency has manifested itself in Iranian support to Shiite groups in Bahrain, Saudi Arabia, Yemen, and elsewhere throughout the region.

In this context, it is not surprising that Iranian officials frame the nuclear issue in nationalist terms and as an affirmation of Iran's rightful place in the world. In August 2015, Iranian Defense Minister Hossein Dehghan described the nuclear deal as a source of Iranian national pride: "Today, Iran has attained such status that the superpowers have surrendered to it because of its majesty, its steadfastness, its resistance, and its unity. Despite their great pride, the regime of arrogance [the West, led by the United States] sat humbly behind the negotiating table and obeyed the rights of the Iranian nation."[51] Likewise, Rouhani has acknowledged that the Iranian government deliberately tried to cultivate nationalist sentiment around the nuclear program: "propaganda should be concentrated on creating national pride, not just in the ability to acquire nuclear technology, but also in the ability to protect it from enemy threats while protecting national security."[52]

Resistance Is Key to Action and Power

The notion that Iran is destined to lead the so-called "axis of resistance" is deeply infused in its national identity and bolsters Iran's self-image as the vanguard of the Islamic world. This axis comprises Shiite proxy groups in Syria, Iraq, Lebanon, Palestine, Bahrain, and Yemen, as well as Sunni extremist groups such as Hamas and the Palestinian Islamic Jihad. By relying on this network to support its foreign policy objectives abroad, Iran is able to effectively leverage soft and hard power, while maintaining a veneer of plausible deniability. Iranian military officials boast frequently that Iran now controls four Arab capitals in Damascus, Baghdad, Beirut, and Sanaa. They refer to Syria as the "golden ring" in the axis of resistance, owing to its strategic importance as the key access route for weapons shipments to Hezbollah in Lebanon.[53] Iran will fight to preserve this axis, notwithstanding mounting casualties of IRGC officers in Syria, because it is a central tenet of Iran's defense against Israel and overall national security strategy.

Another mode of Iranian resistance is self-sufficiency and economic development. Since the revolution, Iranian leaders have emphasized the need for the Islamic Republic to distance itself from foreign powers and to become self-reliant through scientific advancements.[54] The slogan that came to characterize the revolution, "*na sharq, na gharb*" (neither East nor West), underscores Iran's perceived need for strength through self-reliance. For this reason, historic figures such as Ibn Sina, Biruni, and Razi have become sources of national pride for Iranians as great scientists, mathematicians, philosophers, and physicians.

Iran's relative military and economic insecurity fuels its search for regional strategic depth and preference for self-reliance. The Supreme Leader's decree in 2014 for Iran to establish a "resistance economy" emphasized subsidy reforms to optimize energy consumption, increase employment, and target the promotion of export goods. Khamenei also reiterated the importance of resistance in his open letter to Rouhani following the adoption of the JCPOA:

> In conclusion, as it has been notified in numerous meetings to you and other government officials and also to our dear people in public gatherings, although the lifting of sanctions is a necessary job in order to remove injustice [imposed on people] and regain the rights of the Iranian nation, economic overture and better livelihood and surmounting the current challenges will not be easy unless the economy of resistance is taken seri-

ously and followed up on entirely. It is hoped that this objective will be pursued with full seriousness and special attention would be paid to enhancing national production. You should also watch out so that unbridled imports would not follow the lifting of sanctions, and particularly importing any consumer materials from the United States must be seriously avoided.[55]

World Order Is Unjust, Victimizes the Weak

Iran's history of invasion by foreign powers reinforces its belief in the need to restore equality between powerful and weak countries, obtain *edellaat* (justice) for the *mustazafun* (victims) of aggression, and defeat the *mustakbirun* (arrogant) foreign interventionist powers. Khomeini's rejection of *gharbzadegi* (Westoxification) in the early years of the revolution helped justify the concept of *velayat-e faqih* and immediately influenced all aspects of governance, including the nuclear program which came to symbolize the embodiment of the Islamic Republic's anti-imperialist narrative. Indeed, some studies have shown that a small but politically significant portion of the Iranian population believes the nuclear program has become a sacred value, in the sense that it represents Iran's defiance of Western efforts to prevent it from acting autonomously.[56] More broadly, *gharbzadegi*—a cultural norm popularized ironically by secular Marxist writer Jalal Al-e Ahmad—has become a staple of post-revolutionary lexicon by remolding traditional Islamic tenets and heroes into religious dialectics about class struggle and universal moral values.

This narrative encompasses Shia notions of injustice and Iran's historical experience of invasion by foreign powers. Iranian leaders appeal to this sense of historical injustice to gain support for "resistance" against the West.[57] Similarly, Iranian officials are quick to allege Western double standards in international affairs and will insist on a fair playing field as a precondition to negotiations. Appealing to populist ideologies also allows Tehran to justify its policies domestically and abroad. Khamenei in a 2007 speech explains:

Why, you may ask, should we adopt an offensive stance? Are we at war with the world? No, that is not the meaning. Over the issue of the colonial policies of the colonial world, we are owed something. Over the issue of provoking internal conflicts in Iran and arming with various types of weapons, the world is answerable to us. Over the issue of proliferation of nuclear weapons, chemical weapons, and biological weapons, the world owes us something.[58]

Iranian leaders' perception of victimhood and an unjust world order manifests itself at times in a paranoid view of world politics.[59] Political polemics in Iran are replete with terms such as *tuteh* (plot), *jasouz* (spy), *khatar-e kharejeh* (foreign danger), and *nafouz-e biganeh* (alien influence). Khomeini and later Khamenei frequently warned that Western powers, particularly the United States and United Kingdom, were plotting to destroy Iran from within through subversive elements or *sotun-e panjom* (the fifth column).[60] This worldview and deep mistrust of foreign powers underlies all decisionmaking, prompting Iranian leaders to view international institutions, such as the IAEA, as Western mechanisms designed to subjugate developing nations by any means.

Impact of Strategic Culture on Iran's Nuclear Policy

Since there is no official document defining Iran's nuclear policies, nuclear decisionmaking often reflects competing visions for the Islamic Republic that stem from notions of identity, values, and cultural norms. Fundamentally, Iranian officials are divided over whether the country should focus on internal development or pursue external expansion.[61] These divisions are manifested in Iranian arguments that an overt nuclear weapons program would endanger regime security and that the country has paid high costs to build a civil nuclear power program alone.

In Rouhani's own account, internal political divisions over Iran's nuclear strategy first emerged following the Iran-Iraq War.[62] One camp claimed Iran should be *hefz-mahvari* (preservation-oriented)—focused on internal development and defending against existential threats—while the other argued Iran should be *bast-mahvari* (expansion-oriented)—focused on regional expansion and exporting revolutionary values.[63] The nuclear deal may indicate that Rouhani has persuaded the Supreme Leader to at least temporarily focus on improving Iran's deteriorating economy and expanding its power projection in the region while accepting some constraints on the nuclear program. The focus on improving Iran's economic development, however, does not appear to have significantly affected Iran's support for regional conflicts.

Iran's strategic culture reveals deep-seated concerns about its ability to manage multiple conflicts and growing regional isolation despite the growing perception among Gulf Arab states that the nuclear deal has emboldened Iran. Iranian leaders value regime survival and internal stability above all else. To that end, Iran's main strategic goals are to mitigate its relative isolation while deterring potential attacks from Israel and neighboring Gulf Arab rivals. A sense of relative insecurity can be seen in much of Tehran's behavior, including its search for greater strategic depth in the region and preference for asymmetric deterrence capabilities.

Deterrence Is the Best Defense

Iran's military doctrine is defensive, with long-standing norms of seeking to deter enemies through a combination of proxy and asymmetric warfare, ballistic missile capabilities, and threats couched in bombastic rhetoric. Given its conventional military inferiority relative to Israel and the West, Iran has focused on developing asymmetric warfare capabilities through proxy networks, terrorist attacks, naval exercises, cyber operations, and the expansion of its ballistic missile program. Iran relies on Hezbollah in Lebanon and Shiite proxy groups in Iraq, Syria, and Yemen to deter the West from intervening in regional conflicts. Similarly, Iran conducts regular naval exercises to show the West that it is capable of closing strategic waterways such as the Strait of Hormuz or Bab al-Mandab Strait. Iran is improving the range and accuracy of its ballistic missiles, which can strike any strategic target within the region, to deter Israel and Gulf Arab states from attacking major Iranian cities or nuclear sites.

While Iran lacks an official deterrence doctrine, it has adopted the idea of *baazdarandegi*, the closest approximation to the Western concept of deterrence. *Baazdarandegi* is a vague term in Iranian discourse that is often used interchangeably with *defa* (defense) or *talafi* (retaliation or revenge).[64] This Islamist notion of deterrence, while influenced by the Cold War, focuses on outlasting enemy attacks, inflicting high potential costs on adversaries, and maintaining the illusion of strength and power.[65] In this context, preserving Iran's reputation and *aberu* (saving face) is critical for its deterrence and defense posture. Iranian leaders may feel compelled to respond to threats—particularly if they are perceived as posturing—to avoid the reputational costs of failed deterrence. Building a strong deterrence against Iran therefore necessitates an understanding of Iran's strategic values and priorities, which might conflict with

Western cultural assumptions, in order to create a threat that Iranian leaders will perceive as credible and intolerable.

At the height of the Iran-Iraq War in 1984, then President Khamenei told political and security officials in Tehran that a nuclear arsenal would serve as a "deterrent in the hands of God's soldiers."[66] In a revealing interview in October 2015, Rafsanjani also confirmed that senior Iranian officials considered developing a nuclear deterrent capability during the Iran-Iraq War, but claimed the idea was never realized: "When we first began, we were at war and we sought to have that possibility for the day that the enemy might use a nuclear weapon. That was the thinking. But it never became real."[67] He added, "Our basic doctrine was always a peaceful nuclear application, but it never left our minds that if one day we should be threatened and it was imperative, we should be able to go down the other path."[68]

Iranian military leaders have emphasized the importance of *baazdarandegi fael* (active deterrence) in formulating the country's five-year defense plan and intimidating Iran's adversaries. This focus seems to track most closely with the Western concept of deterrence by denial—the notion that Iran has the ability to inflict considerable damage on its adversaries, not in counter-attack, but in defense of the homeland or its allies. IRGC Qods Force Commander Soleimani in his memoirs claims, "[to] attack is the best means of defense," a strategy that he appears to be implementing in Iraq, Syria, and Yemen.[69] Ali Fadavi, IRGC Naval Commander, praised Iranian deterrence following the conclusion of the JCPOA: "[the West] perceived the Iranian nation's resistance and steadfastness in the eight-year Holy Defense [Iran-Iraq War] and thus the power of the Islamic Republic's deterrence allows it to attack its enemies.... The will of our enemies to destroy the existence of the Islamic Republic grows stronger and more robust every day, but the power of our deterrence enables us to prevent enemy attacks."[70] Similarly, Yadollah Javani, a senior advisor to Khamenei in the IRGC, interpreted the nuclear deal as testament of the power of Iran's deterrence strategy:

> So far the Americans have not attacked, because of Iran's deterrence, which is steadily increasing. A decade ago, the Americans were stronger than they are today, and the Islamic Republic of Iran was weaker. In the past decade, the power of America and its allies in the region has eroded, while the power

of the Islamic Republic and its allies has only increased. Therefore, the regional upheavals during the past decade have worked in Iran's favor, and to the detriment of the US. Thanks to the nuclear agreement, this process will not take a turn for the worse for Iran, but could only add special might to it.[71]

In the wake of the JCPOA, Iran has sought to enhance its conventional deterrence posture by conducting a series of short- and long-range ballistic missile tests. In October 2015, a Special Commission of the *Majlis* set up to review the JCPOA recommended that Iran bolster its military capabilities to fight against "US-created terrorism" and reiterated Iran's right to self-defense against potential attacks on its nuclear program.[72] To that end, Iran publicized its long-range ballistic missile tests, despite continued UN sanctions and potential reprisals by the international community. In response to the threat of new US ballistic missile designations, Rouhani decried US actions and publicly ordered the Defense Ministry to expand Iran's ballistic missile program in December 2015.[73] Rouhani wrote in a letter to Defense Minister Dehghan published on the state news agency IRNA, "As the US government is clearly still pursuing its hostile policies and illegal meddling…. the armed forces need to quickly and significantly increase their missile capability."[74]

While affirming its commitment to the nuclear deal, the Rouhani administration has repeatedly threatened to walk away from the JCPOA if the United States continues to impose unilateral sanctions on Iran's missile program. Rouhani has warned Iran will forcefully respond to perceived threats and "return to our previous situation in a much stronger position," a subtle indication that Iran is willing to resume nuclear activities if the JCPOA falls apart.[75] In further defiance of US actions, the *Majlis* in August 2017 passed a bill allocating $303 million to Iran's ballistic missile program and another $303 million to the Qods Force to "combat the adventurous and terrorist actions of the United States in the region."[76] The bill was proposed after the Trump administration signed a law imposing new sanctions on Iran over its missile program the same month, underscoring Iran's propensity to react to perceived threats in a proportionate manner. Iran's strategic culture and official statements indicate it will continue to seek new ways to deter its adversaries, whether through nuclear or conventional military means.

Ambiguity Complicates Decisionmaking Process

Ambiguity is a cultural norm that defines Iranian political life and allows its leaders to balance religious ideology with geostrategic realties. Iranians refer to this ambiguity in the political system as *do-gohanehgi* (duality)—the idea that every policy decision has two faces or sides, one that is seen and the other that is hidden.

Iranian officials use ambiguity as a tool to increase uncertainty about the country's military capabilities and to create a psychological deterrent. The Supreme Leader has claimed on several occasions that Iran is not seeking nuclear weapons, while alluding to the fact that Iran has the technical prowess to pursue such a capability should it choose to do so. In a speech in April 2015, Khamenei declared, "We are not after nuclear weapons.... A nuclear weapon is a source of trouble for a country like ours—I do not want to expand upon this matter. So, nuclear achievements are very important and pursuing this industry and industrializing the country is a very important task."[77] More recently, AEOI head Salehi and President Rouhani argued that Iran remains committed to the JCPOA, while threatening to resume enrichment and other nuclear-related activities at "a more advanced level than at the beginning of negotiations" in response to US sanctions against Iran.[78] Iran has used such vague threats to maintain a position of nuclear opacity, while demonstrating a firm resolve to maintain advanced nuclear capabilities and expand its ballistic missile program, which could be used as a means to deliver nuclear weapons.

Tehran's policy of nuclear ambiguity potentially complicates efforts to establish a regional security architecture to deter and contain Iran's nuclear ambitions in a post-JCPOA environment. US allies in the Persian Gulf increasingly perceive that Washington has reconciled itself to Iran's eventual acquisition of nuclear weapons, both advancing Tehran's goal of gaining recognition as a latent nuclear weapons state and increasing the risk of miscalculation and instability in the region. The 2016 decision of several Gulf Arab states, led by Saudi Arabia, to sever diplomatic relations with Iran following protests against the Saudi Embassy in Tehran does not augur well for efforts to engineer a rapprochement between Iran and Gulf Cooperation Council (GCC) member states—Bahrain, Kuwait, Oman, Qatar, Saudi Arabia, and the United Arab Emirates—in the post-JCPOA environment.

Islam and Shia Martyrdom Bolster Regime Legitimacy

Iranian officials cultivate the image of Iran as a dangerous, radical state willing to absorb heavy costs in the name of martyrdom and revolutionary values. Iran's religious rhetoric increases the potential for miscalculation and inadvertent escalation of conflicts, particularly with Iran's Sunni Arab neighbors. It also complicates US deterrence efforts against Iran, since Israel and many Gulf Arab states perceive a nuclear-capable Iran as unpredictable and undeterrable.

This perception is strengthened by Iran's adherence to the Islamic doctrine of *taqiyya*—a Shiite practice of deliberately dissembling or disguising one's religious or political beliefs in order to protect the Shia sect from mainstream Sunni Islam and perceived adversaries. *Taqiyya* permits Iranian leaders to lie, potentially about the nuclear program, when faced with existential threats. The Supreme Leader's religious fatwa banning Iran's production or use of nuclear weapons could thus be recanted if deemed politically expedient.

Iranian leaders espouse a worldview attributing great importance to future gain, even at great risk, in keeping with the religious and ideological values of the regime. Iranian religious attitudes toward war are less goal-oriented than in the West and tend to praise struggle and adversity as a sign of commitment to the Shia faith. In the context of the nuclear program, Iran is willing to sacrifice blood and treasure to attain the technical capability it seeks, as evidenced by Iran's declaration that its assassinated nuclear scientists were "martyrs" who would attain great rewards in the afterlife.

Martyrdom is a value integral to Shia Islam—an honor accorded to those who give their life to defend faith, defeat not necessarily equated with failure. Iranian officials claim Iran is a *melat-e shahid parvar* (nation of martyrs) to energize the regime's support base, intimidate Iran's enemies, and strengthen the country's deterrent posture.[79] During the Iran-Iraq War, Iranian leaders used martyrdom, tales of Ashura, and the Battle of Karbala to increase recruitment and inspire young volunteers to launch human wave attacks on Iraqi positions. In 1985, Khomeini framed the decision to keep fighting Iraq in ideological terms: "It is our belief that Saddam wishes to return Islam to blasphemy and polytheism.... if America becomes victorious.... and grants victory to Saddam, Islam will receive such a blow that it will not be able to raise its head for a long time.... The issue is one of Islam versus blasphemy, and not of Iran versus Iraq."[80] The IRGC advanced under the slogans "War, War until Victory" and "The Road to Jerusalem Goes through Karbala," while paramilitary *Basij* volunteers signed admission forms that were called "Passports to Paradise" and wore keys around their necks to open the doors of heaven when they were "martyred".[81] Iran continues to use religious narratives and images of martyrdom today to encourage Iranian and foreign proxy forces to deploy to conflicts in Iraq and Syria.

National Interests Supersede Revolutionary Ideals

Iranian officials adhere to the religious principle of *maslehat*, which states that Iran can forgo certain Islamic obligations in order to preserve regime stability.[82] Khomeini articulated the principle of *maslehat* in a series of letters to then President Khamenei and the Guardian Council in December 1987 and January 1988, in which he asserted the Supreme Leader had the authority to suspend observance of Islamic precepts in order to preserve the Islamic Republic. The Supreme Leader established the Expediency Council in February 1988 to help discern when national security interests superseded religious ideology and to resolve disputes between the *Majlis* and Guardian Council. This was the first time the Islamic principle allowing Muslims to suspend the five pillars of faith was applied to Iran's political sphere.[83] In conjunction with *maslehat*, *velayat-e faqih* provides the Supreme Leader with the authority to determine which policies are compatible with Islamic values and to suspend some Islamic obligations if necessary.

A potential consequence of *maslehat* is that it could be used to justify the development or use of WMD. Despite Khamenei's fatwa—reportedly issued in October 2003—proscribing the development, stockpiling, and use of nuclear weapons, Iranian officials could choose to ignore or overrule this religious decree if they deemed it was in the national interest.[84] When Khomeini drank from the "poisoned chalice" and agreed to the ceasefire that ended the Iran-Iraq War in 1988, he revealed in a letter released by former President Rafsanjani in September 2006 that Iran considered developing "a substantial number of laser and atomic weapons" as a practical necessity to win the war.[85] Similarly, despite frequent claims that the development or use of chemical weapons is *haram* (forbidden), Iranian officials considered developing these weapons in response to Iraq's use of chemical warfare. As *Majlis* speaker and acting commander-in-chief of the armed forces, Rafsanjani stated in a 1988 speech to military officers, "Chemical and biological weapons are the poor man's atomic bombs and can easily be produced. We should at least consider them for our defense."[86] In spite of Khamenei's nuclear fatwa, Iran carried out a "coordinated effort" to design and conduct tests relevant to nuclear weapons until the end of 2003 and conducted "feasibility and scientific studies" until 2009, according to the IAEA.[87]

While national security exigencies may temporarily supersede religious ideology, the two are mutually reinforcing. Ideology determines the tenor of Iran's foreign policy priorities and goals, but pragmatism prevails in the implementation of these strategies at a tactical level. As political scientist Kamran Taremi puts it:

> Islam has set down the national objectives for which the use of violence is permissible. It has also dictated a defensive military strategy based on deterrence by denial using conventional forces. In addition, it has driven Iran to rely as far as possible on its own resources for its defense. Moreover, it has defined the meaning of victory on the battlefield and spelled out the factors which give the armed forces the strength to defeat the enemy. It is uneven because most of the impact of ideology can be seen at the level of national goals, military strategy, and to some extent at the level of operational strategy. But its effects on battlefield tactics have been minor. As one descends the ladder of strategy, the influence of ideology diminishes.[88]

The fundamental issue, then, becomes discerning when Iran's national interests trump ideological concerns, assuming there is little to no overlap between the two. Iran tends to forsake values and ideological preferences, such as the Supreme Leader's red line on negotiations with the United States, when Iran perceives it is facing an immediate or credible threat. Iran's Deputy Foreign Minister and senior nuclear negotiator Abbas Araghchi, in an off-the-record meeting with state radio and television officials following the JCPOA, revealed that Iran had engaged in backchannel negotiations with the United States since 2003 due to fears of an imminent military invasion:

> People may not know the details, but our friends in the military and Islamic Revolutionary Guard Corps (IRGC) know that.... we were worried every night that they might install the necessary equipment for attacking all over Iran the next morning.... In meetings with our military friends, they were showing military bases on the map and explaining which planes were on standby at which bases, and attacking Iran required nothing but Mr. Obama's political will."[89]

Moreover, Iran has frequently engaged in direct backchannel talks with the United States over the years, despite its enmity toward the West.

Zalmay Khalilzad, former US Ambassador to Iraq (2005–2007), revealed in his memoirs that he met with then Iranian Ambassador to the UN Javad Zarif to discuss the US decision to invade Iraq prior to March 2003. The United States, according to Khalilzad, tacitly signaled its intention to refrain from attacking Iran while seeking an Iranian commitment to "not fire on US aircraft if they accidentally flew over Iranian territory" and to help "encourage Iraqi Shia to participate constructively in establishing a new government in Iraq."[90] Zarif allegedly agreed to this condition and US and Iranian interlocutors continued to meet until May 2003 to discuss terrorism and a possible prisoner exchange for al-Qaeda members residing in Iran. In 2006, Iranian officials again planned to meet with a US delegation to discuss postwar Iraq, but the talks were cancelled at the last minute. Talks on Iran's nuclear program began in Oman in 2009 at the end of the Bush administration and gained traction under the Obama administration until the culmination of the JCPOA in 2015. This channel was also used to negotiate the release of American citizens taken hostage by the IRGC.[91]

Backchannel negotiations have been critical to US efforts to message Iran and deescalate tensions. Tehran backed away from its threats to close the Strait of Hormuz in response to new oil and gas sanctions in January 2012, after President Obama allegedly sent a secret message to Iran's Supreme Leader warning that closure of the strait would cross a "red line that would provoke an American [military] response."[92] More recently, Iran reversed a decision to send a convoy with military aid destined for Houthi rebels in Yemen, despite the Saudi naval blockade, after learning that a US carrier strike group was following the Iranian vessels.[93] These examples highlight Iran's prioritization of national security concerns over religious ideology when faced with credible military threats.

Proportionate Responses Preferable to Escalation

Iran tends to adopt a tit-for-tat mentality and prefers to respond in-kind if attacked.[94] This norm was evident during the Iran-Iraq War, when Tehran responded proportionately to Iraqi air strikes against Iranian cities by launching rockets and missiles at Iraq in what became known as the "War of the Cities."[95] In February 2012, Iran avenged the assassinations of its nuclear scientists through a series of planned terrorist attacks against Israeli diplomats in Turkey, Georgia, India, and Thailand. Starting in January 2012, Iran launched a wave of cyberattacks against the US financial sector, in response to sanctions and the alleged US-Israeli Stuxnet cyberattack against Iran's nuclear program. Iran also conducted a data-deletion attack against the computer network of Aramco—the Saudi state-owned oil company—in response to the strengthening of multilateral oil and gas sanctions against Iran. Iran's preference for proportionality favors symbolically similar modes of retaliation that send a warning to adversaries.[96] Thus, Iranian leaders may believe they are calibrating their response to send a message to the West, while Western leaders perceive these actions to be aggressive and escalatory.[97]

The need to respond in-kind to perceived aggression is balanced by Iran's concerns about regime stability and its limited military capabilities. Iranian leaders prefer to limit escalation by engaging in low-intensity, proxy, and asymmetric warfare in order to manage risk and avoid direct confrontation. For example, Tehran did not follow through on its threats to close the Strait of Hormuz in December 2011, fearing potential military retaliation by the United States. According to IRGC Commander Jafari, Iran enriched its stocks of uranium up to 20% as part of "a strategy to gain leverage" in nuclear negotiations with the West. It subsequently reduced its enrichment levels in exchange for technical concessions under the JCPOA.[98] Iran also delayed completion of the heavy water reactor at Arak and converted its stockpile of 20% enriched uranium to fuel plates for the TRR, presumably to avoid crossing Israeli red lines that could provoke an attack.

Iran values plausible deniability as part of its strategy for avoiding direct military confrontation. Iran has relied on Iraqi Shiite militants, Lebanese Hezbollah, Hamas, and other militant proxies to carry out attacks against its adversaries worldwide. In the cyber realm, Iranian officials use Virtual Private Networks (VPNs), fraudulent websites, and covert influence operations to deny responsibility for cyberattacks against the West and Saudi Arabia. Iran's most sophisticated cyberattack to date—the data-deletion attack in 2011 that destroyed billions of dollars' worth of equipment at Aramco—was carried out in the name of a fabricated group of Saudi hackers.

In the nuclear realm, Iran has sought to respond proportionately to perceived threats, even though its rhetoric on the issue often seems inflammatory. After the US Congress passed new sanctions against Iran in August 2017, for example, the latter threatened to abrogate the JCPOA but ultimately decided to respond with reciprocal sanctions against US entities. When Iran announced a package of "16 retaliatory measures" in response to US actions, members of Iran's JCPOA Oversight Committee explicitly stated that they sought to respond in a "proportional" manner.[99] In an interview on state television, Iranian Deputy Foreign Minister Araghchi also promised that Iran would deal with the US sanctions in a "prudent and calculated" way.[100]

Combination of Soft and Hard Power Most Effective for Resisting Enemies

Iranian officials rely on anti-imperialist rhetoric to gain credibility with discontented Arab peoples, enabling them to extend regional influence through militant proxy networks.[101] Iran's axis of resistance allows it to span Shia-Sunni sectarian divides in pursuit of broader foreign policy objectives.[102] According to Iranian presidential advisor and former Intelligence Minister Ali Younesi, Iran has established a sphere of influence spanning China to the Persian Gulf: "Currently, Iraq is not only part of our civilizational influence, but it is our identity, culture, center and capital.... Because Iran and Iraq's geography and culture are inseparable, either we fight one another or we become one."[103] In July 2015, the IRGC-affiliated *Javan* website also declared:

> It is not unreasonable that America believes that our military capabilities do not surpass its own, but it fears [Iran's] soft power, which is stronger than military bombardment.... This soft power has two main avenues: a covenant between the nation and the Imam [Ayatollah Ruhollah Khomeini].... and an alliance with the countries of the region [that is based on] emotion and faith. The Iraqi nation is an example of this alliance; there, America sacrificed 4,400 troops and ousted Saddam [Hussein], but the friends of the Islamic Revolution [of Iran] sat on Saddam's throne and did not in any way allow [the Americans] to seize power there. This soft power cannot carry out a military assault, which is why the Islamic Revolution's increasing might has caused America to transform itself, due to fear, from a stupid enemy into a relatively clever one.[104]

The axis of resistance is the most distinctive feature of Iran's foreign and military policies and reflects its dualist identity. As a cultural norm, Iran prefers to exercise soft power rather than hard power in these efforts but employs both with vigor. The network projects Iranian influence and ideas while providing Tehran with clandestine means to project power, deter perceived adversaries, and compete with rivals. While Iran's conventional military power is primarily defensive, Iran projects offensive power through asymmetric warfare and proxy networks.

Iran's emphasis on guarding against cultural infiltration and controlling the public narrative plays an instrumental role in shaping Iranian attitudes toward the nuclear program. The overwhelming majority of Iranians support the nuclear energy program, according to recent polls, probably in part because of the high degree of censorship surrounding the issue.[105] The SNSC continues to issue strict guidance to Iranian media to refrain from criticizing the country's nuclear policies and even threatened to fine *Kayhan*, a hardline daily with close ties to Khamenei.[106] This atmosphere of secrecy complicates analysis of Iran's nuclear intent because the issue is highly compartmentalized and Iranian officials have only recently begun discussing it in the public sphere.[107]

Rationalism and Heroic Flexibility Key for Survival

Iranian officials value *mantiq* (rationality) and "heroic flexibility" in foreign policy decisionmaking and international negotiations. Rationality in Iranian culture has a slightly different meaning from the Western equivalent, emphasizing spiritual and intellectual enlightenment over calculated, hard power considerations. In Rouhani's account of negotiations with the EU-3 during his tenure as chief nuclear negotiator (1989–2005), he alludes to the value of *mantiq*, stating: "the Europeans adopted a much more logical approach to the issue."[108] In the aftermath of the JCPOA, conservative and reformist Iranian editorials alike claimed the agreement was a signal that the United States had adopted a "more rational" approach to its policies toward Iran.

Iran's preference to appear rational and credible in international negotiations prompts it to periodically demonstrate flexibility on sensitive political issues, such as on the nuclear program. In a series of interviews with the Iranian foreign policy magazine *Diplomat*, AEOI head Salehi recounted that in 2011 he had persuaded the Supreme Leader to agree to backchannel negotiations with the United States on the nuclear issue by arguing, "If we do not go [to the talks with the Americans] the credibility of the Islamic Republic will be at risk."[109] Salehi further claimed he had told Khamenei, "If we reach a conclusion, then nothing, and if not, we will be in the same situation.... and we will know that the establishment has taken all measures to solve things peacefully, and people will also know that the establishment was ready for negotiations and that it was the Americans who refused."[110] In response, the Supreme Leader noted that the United States was not a trustworthy partner but eventually agreed to the backchannel under the following conditions: "First, that negotiations should be held at a level below that of foreign ministers, meaning the foreign ministers of the two countries should not meet. Also, that negotiations should not be held for the sake of negotiations.... and that negotiations should only be about the nuclear issue and not political relations and the like."[111]

In September 2013, Khamenei invoked heroic flexibility to justify the necessity of accepting a nuclear deal with the West to reduce sanctions levied against Iran: "I support the strategic effort that I called 'heroic flexibility' years ago. This tactic works well when you need to understand and grasp the intentions of your opponent.... [when] a wrestler allows himself to be compromised, [he] does not forget who his opponent is nor what his main goal is."[112] Iranian views on heroism are also often deeply intertwined with religious narratives about revered Quranic figures, such as Imam Hussein's peace treaty with the second caliph of the Ummayid clan.

The cultural norm of heroic flexibility is directly at odds with the radical image Iran's hardliners perpetuate to deter the country's regional adversaries. By appealing to the notion of *sarnavesht* (destiny), heroic flexibility allows Iranian officials to save face when conceding to adversarial demands in order to ensure regime survival. Importantly, the concept of heroic flexibility bridges factional divides in Iran, since moderates prefer a flexible, rational approach to interactions with the international community and hardliners gravitate toward heroic displays of strength.

POLICY IMPLICATIONS AND RECOMMENDATIONS

Iran's strategic culture has a profound impact on its foreign policy behavior and nuclear decisionmaking. While there are limits to the predictive value of strategic culture analysis, cultural factors are likely to grow increasingly important in discerning Iran's nuclear intent in the latter years of the JCPOA, when key restrictions on Iran's enrichment capacity begin to expire, or in the event that the deal collapses altogether. The question will then become whether Iran perceives that its status as a nuclear threshold state affords it an adequate level of deterrence to respond to real or imagined threats.

Iranian leaders perceive threats, deterrence, and power through a different cultural lens than their foreign counterparts. Absent serious acknowledgment of cultural differences, Iranian leaders are likely to perceive threats where there are none and miscalculate when it comes to US red lines. The risk of failed signaling and ineffective deterrence between Iran and the United States is particularly high at present, given mixed messages emerging from the Trump administration and increasing rhetorical bluster on both sides. The Trump administration's decertification of the JCPOA and continuing efforts to tighten sanctions against Iran's IRGC Qods Force and missile program have only further antagonized Iranian leaders while doing little to effectively constrain Iran's military power or regional aspirations.

The United States has already started to move away from a "carrot and stick" approach to Iran, which has not worked in the past and contravenes Iran's strategic culture and sense of national pride. A review of Rouhani's memoirs and of statements made by Zarif, Araghchi, and Salehi during the nuclear negotiations indicate Iran does not respond well to transactional approaches to foreign policy. For example, Iran long refused to halt its nuclear activities in exchange for sanctions relief and only agreed to do so after the international community tacitly recognized Iran's right to enrich uranium.[113] After adopting the JCPOA, Iran also waited to take irreversible steps to alter its nuclear program—such as removing the calandria, or reactor core, from the Arak heavy water reactor—until the IAEA publicly closed its 12-year investigation into the "possible military dimensions" (PMD) of Iran's nuclear program. Despite the fact that closure of the PMD file was not a necessary condition for Iran to reach JCPOA Implementation Day and obtain sanctions relief, the Supreme Leader declared the IAEA must immediately close the file to demonstrate there were no lingering questions about the weapons-related aspects of Iran's nuclear program. These examples demonstrate Iran's concerns about respect, mutual trust, and international recognition of Iran's rightful place in the world.

Lessons learned from the negotiations, as well as a better understanding of Iran's strategic culture, help inform a more comprehensive approach to influencing Iranian decisionmaking in a post-JCPOA environment and beyond. This approach relies on smart power—the combination of hard and soft power tactics—and applies both traditional (diplomatic, economic, and military) and nontraditional (cyber, strategic messaging, covert influence) levers of influence in concert. A key challenge for US policymakers going forward will be to redefine Iran's role in an international system that Iranian officials view as unjust and inherently opposed to Iran's national interests. Tailoring US transparency measures to ensure they take into account Iranian norms and values—by engaging Iran as an equal power broker, demonstrating flexibility, and respecting Iran's national dignity—is an important first step toward attaining this goal. To that end, the following policy recommendations are designed to counter Iranian influence while also preventing regional tensions from escalating further:

Conduct Strategic Messaging and Limit Transactional Engagement. In the soft power realm, appeals to Iran's sense of greatness and perception that it should play a larger role on the world stage resonate among keepers of its strategic culture. Regardless of their political affiliation, all Iranian officials believe Iran can and should play an influential role on the world stage. The Obama administration understood this aspect of Iran's strategic culture and sought to influence Iranian leaders by bringing Iran into multilateral talks on Syria and emphasizing the important role Iran could play in bringing peace and stability to the Middle East. Indeed, Iran is less likely to play the spoiler role in multilateral talks if it feels that it has a "seat at the table." Inclusion of Iran in multilateral fora, however, is likely to alienate Washington's traditional allies such as Israel and Saudi Arabia absent significant reassurances of continued US aid.

Parallel direct talks with Iran have also occasionally undermined progress made in these multilateral settings. Rather than focusing on direct bilateral engagement, which have often devolved into US officials seeking talks with Iran merely for the sake of continuing open lines of communication, it would be preferable to encourage increased Iranian participation in multilateral fora and to initiate new regional security dialogues in coordination with European allies, Russia, or the Gulf. When possible, the United States should rely on regional partners with close relations to Iran, such as Oman and Iraq, to help signal US intentions and broker agreements on sensitive issues.

Washington and its allies could take incremental steps to show that it is serious in partnering on these issues, such as by providing Tehran with credible information on terrorist plots inside Iran. Moreover, the United States should explore the possibility, in the aftermath of the nuclear deal, that Iran could transform into a "half religious, half civil society" state that is more responsive to the overwhelmingly moderate proclivities of its populace.[114] The United States, through multilateral fora, should engage with the Iranian people by encouraging the growth of civil society in Iran through greater press freedoms, the reduction of Internet controls, and open political dialogue. US leaders must take care, however, to avoid directly commenting on Iranian domestic politics, as Iranian leaders are likely to view any overt attempts at reform as part of a US "cultural invasion" aimed at regime subversion.[115] The Trump administration's vocal support for widespread Iranian protests on economic issues in January 2018, for example, have only bolstered the Supreme Leader's claim that the United States is responsible for domestic unrest in Iran.

In line with Iran's strategic culture, Washington should also avoid transactional engagement with Tehran that provides the regime with resources and a veneer of legitimacy without "prompting any improvement in Iranian polices on matters of core importance to the United States and its allies."[116] In the long term, engagement with Iran should not simply continue for the sake of engagement itself, but rather aim to gradually influence Iran's behavior by appealing to its national interests and allaying fears that fuel the security dilemma in the region.

Demonstrate Resolve, Credibility, and Strategic Patience. Iran will not be deterred through messaging alone; it must also observe consistent patterns in policymaking that indicate the United States will follow through on its threats every time. In order for deterrence to be effective, Tehran must believe that it risks a credible military response for defined acts of aggression. Zalmay Khalilzad, the former US Ambassador to Iraq, claims the United States failed to prevent Iran from gaining influence in Iraq because the US did not "combine diplomatic engagement with forcible actions [that] could have shaped Iran's meddling decisively."[117] The United States and its allies should also avoid responding reflexively to Iran, instead acting patiently and methodically to address Iranian challenges to American interests. In short, the United States must learn to play the long game with Iran.

Overt military threats are likely to backfire either because Iranian leaders do not believe they are credible or because they empower hardliners and bolster anti-American narratives. These threats must also be backed up with action, such as maneuvering of ships near Iranian waters, insofar as Iranian leaders tend to view verbal threats more as insults than as security dilemmas. Critically, military maneuvering with minimal, restrained rhetoric, would send a strong message to Iranian leaders without forcing them to respond for fear of losing face. At the same time, US military leaders must recognize tripwires that could provoke Iran to lash out and calibrate force accordingly. US strikes that killed senior IRGC officials in Syria or Yemen, for example, whether deliberate or inadvertent, would probably provoke Iran to retaliate against US military forces in the region. US strikes against Iranian-backed Houthi targets in Yemen or Shiite militia in Syria, in contrast, would not likely provoke the same response. In its dealings with adversaries, Iran accepts the use of force when it is circumspect, proportionate, and in response to a clearly defined provocation.

Hold Iran Accountable for Plausibly Deniable Actions. Iranian officials calibrate policy decisions to avoid provoking a direct military response, often by creating ambiguity and a veneer of plausible deniability through reliance on extensive proxy networks. This ambiguity allows Iran to avoid responsibility for its actions and blame Western plots instead, in line with its paranoid style of politics. Iranian leaders may be deterred from taking particularly aggressive actions, however, if they believe their actions will be publicly exposed and risk retaliation. To that end, the United States and its allies should make public, whenever possible, specific details and evidence of Iranian involvement in arming proxy groups, illicitly acquiring and proliferating weapons, conducting cyber or terrorist attacks, exacerbating sectarian tensions, and generally contributing to instability in the Middle East. Iran must be held accountable for its direct and indirect actions, including those of its proxies, in order to deter it from perpetuating asymmetric warfare against its neighbors.

Increase Support to Allies and Strengthen Existing Regional Security Structures to Counter Iranian Influence. The United States should strengthen regional security initiatives and expand provision of defensive military equipment to regional allies, particularly in the area of missile defense. In support of these efforts, Washington should consider extending a security umbrella to the region, expanding intelligence sharing and joint collection operations with Arab states, and encouraging nascent Arab-Israel cooperation to counter Iranian influence and proxy forces in the region. US allies in the region would also benefit from capabilities that will help them defend against Iranian asymmetric warfare in the proxy, terrorist, and cyber realms. Moreover, the United States must demonstrate its commitment to freedom of navigation in the Persian Gulf and Strait of Hormuz by increasing its forward operating naval presence in the Gulf and making it clear to Tehran that Washington will not countenance any Iranian or Iranian-backed proxy attacks on international shipping.

CONCLUSION

Iran's strategic culture provides the lens through which Iranian leaders perceive risk and formulate nuclear strategy. As a *revolutionary technocratic* state, Iran has a unique dualistic view of itself as an Islamic and secular power pursuing legitimate national security interests. Iran's strategic culture posits that it must resist hard and soft power threats, as it has done historically, by whatever means possible, even at the risk of violating religious principles. Therefore, Iran will employ vague language, deception, or fatwas when necessary to maintain a strong deterrent posture and prevent its adversaries from discerning its true strategic objectives.

At the same time, Iranian leaders may not be in a rush to determine the ultimate objective of the nuclear program or to develop nuclear strategies and postures. Given Iranian views of time as nonlinear and infinite, Iranian leaders probably prefer to play the long game when it comes to making important policy decisions that have a corresponding high amount of risk. Iran's penchant for ambiguity may also extend to its internal decisionmaking processes, with many Iranian officials themselves unsure of the nuclear program's ultimate objective. If this is the case, it will be extremely difficult for the United States or its allies to gain any definitive insight into Iran's over-the-horizon nuclear plans and intentions.

Regardless of intent, Iran's strategic culture also dictates that its leaders will approach any eventual decision to cross the nuclear threshold with great caution. Iran's history of tactical flexibility and preference for indirect confrontation suggests it will avoid crossing nuclear red lines, particularly if there is a high degree of certainty that it will be caught—and punished—for cheating. However, Iran's views of itself as a great civilization on par with global superpowers and its legitimate interest in scientific development will fuel its sense of entitlement to advanced nuclear fuel cycle technologies. Despite Tehran's accession to numerous nonproliferation treaties and enhanced IAEA monitoring under the JCPOA, Iranian leaders will likely seek ways to circumvent what they view as Westernprescribed rules and norms, due to their deep mistrust of the Westphalian international system.

If fully implemented by all states parties, the JCPOA will effectively prevent Iran from developing a nuclear weapon for the next 10 to 15 years. But the JCPOA also leaves substantial physical nuclear infrastructure intact, thereby affirming Iran's status as a nuclear threshold state. After key JCPOA restrictions begin to expire, Iran could in theory scale up its enrichment program to the point where it would have sufficient capacity to produce nuclear weapons in the span of a few weeks, should it choose to do so. Despite robust monitoring and verification measures in place to detect such a breakout, the question of Iran's nuclear intent will grow increasingly important over the next decade.

While cultural factors cannot definitively predict Iran's strategic behavior and are only one of several kinds of variables that impact its complex nuclear calculus, they are likely to become increasingly important indicators of Iran's nuclear intent in a post-JCPOA environment or in the event that either side decides to abrogate the deal. Iran is unlikely to forgo a nuclear weapons option, as long as it remains strategically isolated in the region and perceives a need to project power, influence, and self-reliance. Absent direct intelligence on Iran's nuclear intentions, cultural factors are likely to play a significant and complementary role alongside other indicators in determining Iran's propensity to cheat on the JCPOA and its ability to overcome long-standing ideological hostilities with the West.

Given the current political climate in the United States and Iran, as well as uncertainty surrounding the future of the nuclear deal itself, the prospects for a gradual US-Iran rapprochement post-JCPOA have diminished. Anti-American sentiment, meanwhile, remains deeply rooted in Iran's strategic culture, both as a symbol of resistance against oppression and as a byproduct of internal political machinations aimed at garnering hardliner support. The uptick in arrests of Iranians accused of working for a US "espionage network," as well as increased hostilities between Iranian- and American-backed elements in Syria, are further indicators of a negative trajectory in US-Iran relations.

For these reasons, it is critical to understand the cultural factors underlying Iran's strategic calculus. Iranian officials view the nuclear issue as a symbol of Iran's resistance against the West and a source of pride for the nation. The nuclear program represents not only Iran's technical achievements but also its ability to influence international affairs. The culmination of the JCPOA validated Iran's approach to the nuclear negotiations, in which it successfully employed tactics such as ambiguity, proportionality, and strategic patience. While the future of the deal remains uncertain, key questions concern how Iran's strategic culture will continue to evolve and whether the next generation of Iranian leaders will share the same values and attitudes shaping Iran's current nuclear strategy.

NOTES

1. Breakout is defined as the amount of time it would take to produce sufficient weapons-grade uranium or plutonium for one nuclear weapon. See, for example, Olli Heinonen, "Iran's Nuclear Breakout Time: A Fact Sheet," The Washington Institute, PolicyWatch No. 2394, March 28, 2015, http://www.washingtoninstitute.org/policy-analysis/view/irans-nuclear-breakout-time-a-fact-sheet

2. "Remarks by President Trump on Iran Strategy," White House Briefing Statement, October 13, 2017, https://www.whitehouse.gov/briefings-statements/remarks-president-trump-iran-strategy/

3. INARA requires the US president to certify every 90 days that: (1) Iran is transparently, verifiably, and fully implementing the JCPOA, including all related technical or additional agreements; (2) Iran has not committed a material breach with respect to the agreement or, if Iran has committed a material breach, Iran has cured the material breach; (3) Iran has not taken any action, including covert activities, that could significantly advance its nuclear weapons program; and (4) suspension of sanctions related to Iran pursuant to the agreement is: (i) appropriate and proportionate to the specific and verifiable measures taken by Iran with respect to terminating its illicit nuclear program; and (ii) vital to the national security interests of the United States. Full details available at: https://www.congress.gov/bill/114th-congress/house-bill/1191

4. "Declaration by the Heads of State and Government of France, Germany, and the United Kingdom," October 13, 2017, https://www.gov.uk/government/news/declaration-by-the-heads-of-state-and-government-of-france-germany-and-the-united-kingdom

5. Few studies, for example, explore how material and ideational factors interact and shape policy outcomes within a state's unique strategic culture. For a review of strategic culture theory, see Jeannie L. Johnson, "Conclusion: Toward a Standard Methodological Approach," and Colin Gray, "Out of the Wilderness: Prime Time for Strategic Culture," in *Strategic Culture and Weapons of Mass Destruction: Culturally Based Insights into Comparative National Security Policymaking*, Jeannie L. Johnson, Kerry M. Kartchner and Jeffrey A. Larsen, eds. (New York: Palgrave Macmillan, 2009).

6. Michael Eisenstadt, "The Strategic Culture of the Islamic Republic of Iran: Religion, Expediency, and Soft Power in an Era of Disruptive Change," The Washington Institute, MES Monograph No. 7, November 2015, 15.

7. Ibid., 5.

8. Alastair Ian Johnston, *Cultural Realism: Strategic Culture and Grand Strategy in Chinese History* (Princeton: Princeton University Press, 1995), page x; and Jeffrey Lantis, "Strategic Culture: From Clausewitz to Constructivism," Defense Threat Reduction Agency, October 2006.

9. J. Matthew McInnis, "The Future of Iran's Security Policy: Inside Tehran's Strategic Thinking," *American Enterprise Institute*, May 2017, 95–101.

10. Gregory F. Giles, "The Crucible of Radical Islam: Iran's Leaders and Strategic Culture," in *Know Thy Enemy: Profiles of Adversary Leaders and Their Strategic Cultures*, Barry R. Schneider and Jerrold M. Post, eds. (Maxwell AFB, USAF Counterproliferation Center, 2003), 145–147.

11. For a comprehensive assessment of the impact of Islam on Iran's strategic culture, see Kamran Taremi, "Iranian Strategic Culture: The Impact of Ayatollah Khomeini's Interpretation of Shiite Islam," *Contemporary Security Policy*, 35(1), March 2014, 3–25.

12. Giles, "The Crucible of Radical Islam," 147.

13. "Strategic Culture of Iran" in *Strategic Culture*, Russell D. Howard, ed. (MacDill AFB: Joint Special Operations University), December 2013, 42.

14. For a detailed account of Iran's nuclear ambitions during the Shah's era, see Bijan Mossavar-Rahmani, "Iran's Nuclear Power Programme Revisited," *Energy Policy*, 8(3), 1980; Leonard S. Spector, *Nuclear Ambitions: The Spread of Nuclear Weapons: 1989–1990* (Boulder: Westview Press, 1990), 207–209; and David Patrikarakos, *Nuclear Iran: The Birth of an Atomic State* (New York: I.B. Tauris, 2012).

15. The AEOI annual budget increased from $30.8 million in 1975 to over $3 billion in 1977, second only to the National Iranian Oil Company. See Ali Vaez and Karim Sadjadpour, "Iran's Nuclear Odyssey: Costs and Risks," Carnegie Endowment for International Peace, 2013, 5.

16. "Rouhani's "U.S. Educated Cabinet," US Institute of Peace, *Iran Primer*, November 13, 2014, http://iranprimer.usip.org/blog/2014/nov/13/rouhani%E2%80%99s-us-educated-cabinet

17. Excellent historical treatments of US-Iran nuclear negotiations from 1974–1976 include William Burr, "A Brief History of U.S.-Iranian Nuclear Negotiations," *Bulletin of the Atomic Scientists*, 65(1), January 2009; and Roham Alvandi, *Nixon, Kissinger, and the Shah: The United States and Iran in the Cold War* (Oxford: Oxford University Press, 2014).

18. Norman Gall, "The Twilight of Nuclear Exports," *The Ecologist*, 9(7), October–November 1979, 234.

19. Patrikarakos, *Nuclear Iran*, 98–99.

20. In 1981, the AEOI began to conduct laboratory-scale experiments related to uranium conversion at the Isfahan Nuclear Technology Center. In 1983, the AEOI also approached the IAEA for help with a research program in production of UO2 and UF6 but was rebuffed after the United States directly intervened.

21. Eisenstadt, "What Iran's Chemical Past Tells Us about Its Nuclear Future," The Washington Institute, Research Note No. 17, April 2014, 7.

22. As quoted in David Albright, *Peddling Peril: How the Secret Nuclear Trade Arms America's Enemies* (New York: Free Press, 2010), 71. In a letter dated May 9, 2008, the IAEA reportedly asked Iran to provide information regarding the 1984 meeting (see IAEA, "Implementation of the NPT Safeguards Agreement and Relevant Provisions of Security Council Resolutions 1737 (2006), 1747 (2007), and 1803 (2008) in the Islamic Republic of Iran," GOV/2008/15, May 26, 2008, Annex, 3). Iran's follow up on the matter does not appear in subsequent IAEA reports.

23. The original contract also included a Russian centrifuge enrichment plant that was eventually dropped from the agreement due to US pressure. See Michael Eisenstadt, "Iran's Military Power: Capabilities and Intentions," The Washington Institute, Policy Paper No. 42, 1996, 106–107.

24. Full text of the JCPOA is available at: https://www.state.gov/e/eb/tfs/spi/iran/jcpoa/

25. See, for example, Robert Einhorn, "Debating the Nuclear Deal: A Former American Negotiator Outlines the Battleground Issues," Brookings Institution, August 12, 2015, https://www.brookings.edu/research/debating-the-iran-nuclear-deal-a-former-american-negotiator-outlines-the-battleground-issues/

26. Nuclear hedging is defined as "maintaining, or at least appearing to maintain, a viable option for the relatively rapid acquisition of nuclear weapons, based on an indigenous technical capacity to produce them within a relatively short timeframe from several weeks to a few years." See Ariel E. Levite, "Never Say Never Again: Nuclear Reversal Revisited," *International Security*, 27(3), Winter 2002, 69. For further discussion on Iran's strategy of nuclear hedging in a post-JCPOA context, see Wyn Bowen and Matthew Moran, "Living with Nuclear Hedging: The Implications of Iran's Nuclear Strategy," *International Affairs*, 91(4), 2015.

27. For a useful overview of the JCPOA and the major arguments for and against the agreement, see Gary Samore, ed., *The Iran Nuclear Deal: A*

Definitive Guide (Cambridge Belfer Center for Science and International Affairs, 2015).

28. Hassan Rouhani, *Amniyat-e Melli va Diplomasi-e Hasta'i* (Tehran: Markaz-e Tahqiqat-e Istiratizhik, 2011).

29. Rouhani, *Amniyat-e Melli,* 62. See also Mehdi Khalaji, "Iran's Shifting Nuclear Narratives," The Washington Institute, PolicyWatch No. 2469, August 12, 2015, http://www.washingtoninstitute.org/policy-analysis/view/irans-shifting-nuclear-narratives

30. Ali Akbar Mozdabadi, *Hajj Qassem: Jostari dar Khatarat-e Hajj Qassem Soleimani* (Tehran: Ya Zahra, 2015).

31. See author's "Leadership Divided? The Domestic Politics of Iran's Nuclear Debate," The Washington Institute, Policy Focus No. 134, February 2014, 20–21.

32. "Har mousabeh-ye shura-ye amniyat barayeh tahdid-e tavaanamandi taslihaati iran 'bi 'itabaar' ast," *Tasnim News,* July 20, 2015, https://www.tasnimnews.com/fa/news/1394/04/29/804960

33. "Taghyeeraat dar saakhtaar-e vezarat-e kharejeh/cheh ma'avanathai hezf mishvanad?" *Tasnim News,* August 8, 2017, https://www.tasnimnews.com/fa/news/1396/05/17/1482665

34. For more information on the tension between Iranian nationalism and Islam, see Alam Saleh, *Ethnic Identity and the State in Iran* (New York: Palgrave Macmillan, 2013), 45–58.

35. Asghar Schirazi, *The Constitution of Iran: Politics and the State in the Islamic Republic* (New York: I.B. Taurus, 1997), 233–246.

36. For more on the impact of religion on Iran's foreign policy, see Rouhani, *Andishe-ye Siasi-ye Eslam: Sisasat-e Kharaji* (Tehran: Markaz-e Tahqiqat-e Istiratizhik, 2009), 71–96.

37. Eisenstadt, "The Strategic Culture of the Islamic Republic of Iran," 18.

38. For more background on the Islamic concept of time, see Gerhard Bowering, "The Concept of Time in Islam," *Proceedings of the American Philosophical Society,* 141(1), 1997.

39. Ibid., 77–89.

40. Eisenstadt, "The Strategic Culture of the Islamic Republic of Iran," 19.

41. Iran has historically sought to avoid direct military conflict with its neighbors and confined itself to limited strikes designed to send a warning. During the Iran-Iraq War, for example, Iran attacked Arab vessels transiting the Persian Gulf to dissuade them from aiding Iraq and resupplying it with weapons. See Nadia El-Sayed, *The Gulf Tanker War: Iran and Iraq's Maritime Swordplay* (New York: St. Martin's Press, 1989); and Martin S. Navias and E. R. Hooton, *Tanker Wars: The Assault on Merchant Shipping during the Iran-Iraq Conflict, 1980–1988* (London: I.B. Tauris, 1996).

42. The Israeli attack inflicted a blow to Iranian military operations in Syria. Despite IRGC Commander Jafari's threat to unleash "devastating thunderbolts" in retaliation, Iran at present remains focused on operations in Syria.

43. Mohammad Javad Zarif, "Saudi Arabia's Reckless Extremism," *New York Times*, January 10, 2016, http://www.nytimes.com/2016/01/11/opinion/mohammad-javad-zarif-saudi-arabias-reckless-extremism.html?_r=0

44. David E. Sanger, Eric Schmitt, Helene Cooper, "Iran's Swift Release of U.S. Sailors Hailed as a Sign of Warmer Relations," *New York Times*, January 13, 2016, https://www.nytimes.com/2016/01/14/world/middleeast/iran-navy-crew-release.html

45. For example, Basij commander Mohammad Reza Naqdi claimed that the purpose of negotiations with the West was "to buy time for Iran to build a nuclear bomb." See "Mowzu-ye hasta'i-ye jomhuri-ye eslami az zaban-e namayande-ye vali faqiyeh dar sepah," *Kayhan*, September 11, 2013. See also Rouhani, *Amniyat-e Melli*, 335, 414; and "Chief Iranian Nuclear Affairs Negotiator Hossein Mousavian: The Negotiations with Europe Bought Us Time to Complete the Esfahan UCF Project and the Work on the Centrifuges in Natanz," MEMRI Special Dispatch No. 957, August 12, 2005.

46. Rouhani, *Amniyat-e Melli*, 489. Rouhani goes on to compare the nuclear negotiations to an Iranian proverb that "a stone turns into a ruby through patience, but becomes a ruby only after hard work."

47. The famous Iranian novel, *My Uncle Napoleon* (1973) humorously depicts this time period and Iranians' tendency to blame the British for all ills that have beset the country.

48. McInnis, "The Future of Iran's Security Policy," 2015.

49. Rouhani, *Andishe-ye Siasi-ye Eslam*, 57.

50. Ibid., 99–146.

51. "Iranian Defense Minister: The Superpowers Surrendered to Iran and 'Obeyed Iranian Rights,'" *Tasnim News*, August 30, 2015.

52. Rouhani, *Amniyat-e Melli*, 341.

53. "Velayati: Syria is Golden Ring in Line of Resistance," *Islamic Republic News Agency*, May 18, 2016, http://www.irna.ir/en/News/82080242.

54. Rouhani, *Andishe-ye Siasi-ye Eslam*.

55. "In a Letter to President Hassan Rouhani: Ayatollah Khamenei: Sanctions Snapback Means JCPOA Violation," Office of the Supreme Leader, October 21, 2015, http://www.leader.ir/langs/en/index.php?p=contentShow&id=13791

56. Morteza Dehghani et al., "Sacred Values and Conflict over Iran's Nuclear Program," *Journal of Judgment and Decision Making*, 5(7), December 2010, 540–546.

57. Eisenstadt, "The Strategic Culture of the Islamic Republic of Iran," 19–20.

58. Cited in Michael Axworthy, *Iran: Empire of the Mind – A History from the Zoroaster to the Present Day* (London: Penguin Books, 2008), 289.

59. For a fuller treatment of this issue, see Ervand Abrahamian, "The Paranoid Style in Iranian Politics," PBS Frontline Tehran Bureau, August 27, 2009, http://www.pbs.org/wgbh/pages/frontline/tehranbureau/2009/08/the-paranoid-style-in-iranian-politics.html

60. Ibid.

61. Rouhani, *Andishe-ye Siasi-ye Eslam*.

62. Ibid., 41–43.

63. Ibid.

64. "Pishraft-e istratejhi-ye baazdarandegi-ye iran hamzamaan ba tamhidaat-e jadid-e amrika va israel," *IR Diplomacy*, September 25, 2009, http://www.irdiplomacy.ir/fa/page/11333; and "Hasht baazdarandegi-ye jomhuri eslami-ye iran va tasaavir, *Akfar News*, October 11, 2014.

65. Yoel Guzansky and Avner Golov, "The Rational Limitations of a Nonconventional Deterrence Regime: The Iranian Case," *Comparative Strategy*, 34(2), 2015, 169–184.

66. "Internal IAEA Information Links the Supreme Leader to 1984 Decision to Seek a Nuclear Arsenal," Institute for Science and International Security, April 20, 2012, http://isis-online.org/uploads/isis-reports/documents/Khamenei_1984_statement_20April2012.pdf

67. "Rafsanjani: Iran Considered Nuclear Deterrent in 1980s," *Radio Free Europe/Radio Liberty*, October 29, 2015, http://www.rferl.org/content/iran-rafsanjani-nuclear-deterrent/27333079.html

68. Ibid.

69. Mozdabadi, *Hajj Qassem*, 165.

70. "Farmaande-ye nirou-ye daryai-e sepah-e pasdaran: tavaan-e baazdarandegi-ye iran ejazeh-ye hamleh ra az doshmanan migirad," *Jamejam Online*, September 23, 2017, http://jamejamonline.ir/online/1873324414754019974

71. "Pasokh qata' beh gostakhi amrikaiha," *Sobh-e Sadeq*, July 27, 2015.

72. "Matn-e kamel gozaresh-e comision-e vijheh barresi barjam dar majlis," *Fars News*, October 4, 2015, http://www.farsnews.com/newstext.php?nn=13940712000110

73. "Rouhani Expands Iran's Missile Program despite U.S. Sanctions Threat," *Reuters*, December 31, 2015, http://www.reuters.com/article/us-iran-nuclear-usa-sanctions-idUSKBN0UE0QT20151231

74. "Baaztaab-e baynalmalalli nameh-ye rohani beh vazer-e defa," *Fararu News*, January 1, 2016, http://fararu.com/fa/news/257450

75. "Iran Says It Could Quit Nuclear Deal if US Keeps Adding Sanctions," *Guardian*, August 16, 2017, https://www.theguardian.com/world/2017/aug/16/iran-says-it-could-quit-nuclear-deal-if-us-keeps-adding-sanctions

76. "Tasvib-e komak-e miliaardi barayeh taqviat-e tavaan-e defaa'i dar majlis," *Mashregh News*, August 13, 2017, http://www.mashreghnews.ir/news/761622; and "Dolat maklif beh ikhtsaas dar hezaar miliaard riyal

bodjeh beh niyrou-ye qods-e sepah-e pasdaran shod," *Iranian Students News Agency*, August 13, 2017, http://www.isna/ir/news/96052213312

77. "Reason is Telling Us Not to Pursue Nuclear Weapons," Office of the Supreme Leader, April 9, 2015, www.khamenei.ir/Opinions/tnuclear

78. IRIB State TV, August 2017.

79. After the 1979 revolution, the Islamic Republic of Iran replaced street names with names of the *shahid* (martyrs). Many more street names were changed after the Iran-Iraq War, since every soldier who died was considered a martyr, and portraits of deceased soldiers were painted on murals lining the streets. Themes of martyrdom were also evident in children's textbooks, with as much as 10% of the texts depicting themes of death and martyrdom. For more information, see Samih K. Farsoun and Mehrdad Mashayekhi, *Political Culture in the Islamic Republic* (London: Routledge, 1992), 172; and Zahra Kamalkhani, *Women's Islam* (New York: Columbia University Press, 1998), 81.

80. As quoted in Daniel Brumberg, *Reinventing Khomeini: The Struggle for Reform in Iran* (Chicago: University of Chicago Press, 2001), 132–134.

81. Efraim Karsh, *The Iran-Iraq War 1980–1988* (London: Osprey, 2002), 38; and Ervand Abrahamian, *History of Modern Iran* (London: Cambridge University Press, 2008), 171, 175.

82. Rouhani, *Enqelab-e Eslami: Risha va Chalesha* (Tehran: Markaz-e Tahqiqat-e Istiratizhik, 1997).

83. Schirazi, *The Constitution of Iran*, 233–246.

84. See, for example, Michael Eisenstadt and Mehdi Khalaji, "Nuclear Fatwa: Religion and Politics in Iran's Proliferation Strategy," The Washington Institute, Policy Focus No. 115, September 2011.

85. After the letter appeared on Rafsanjani's website, the word "nuclear" was removed from the letter's text at the request of the Supreme National Security Council.

86. *Islamic Republic News Agency*, October 19, 1988. More recently, before his death Rafsanjani reportedly condemned the use of chemical weapons by the Assad regime in Syria.

87. The IAEA's 2015 report echoes the US government's 2007 National Intelligence Estimate (NIE), which stated Iran suspended nuclear weapons research in 2003, though the NIE judged with "moderate confidence [that] Tehran had not restarted its nuclear weapons programs as of mid-2007." See IAEA, "Final Assessment on Past and Present Outstanding Issues regarding Iran's Nuclear Programme," December 2, 2015, https://www.iaea.org/sites/default/files/gov-2015-68.pdf

88. Taremi, "Iranian Strategic Culture," 6.

89. Araghchi is known for being the closest person to Khamenei among the negotiators and was tasked with briefing the Supreme Leader on the details of the talks and passing his advice to his team, under both Saeed Jalili and Javad Zarif. Less than 24 hours after the IRIB published details

of Araghchi's meeting online, the website took down the post due to "technical errors." See "Araghchi dar sadosima: fareidoun mataalb ra sorkheh-ye ba tehran dar miyaan migozasht/dar jang paaii keh qata' shod aazaar dehandeh bod ama chareh-ye nabod," *Bourse News*, August 1, 2015, http://www.boursenews.ir/fa/news/152331

90. Zalmay Khalilzad, *The Envoy: From Kabul to the White House, My Journey Through a Turbulent World* (New York: St. Martin's Press, 2016), 160–165.

91. Mark Landler, *Alter Egos: Hillary Clinton, Barack Obama, and the Twilight Struggle over American Power* (New York: Random House Publishing, 2016), 236–248.

92. Elisabeth Bumiller, Eric Schmitt and Thom Shanker, "U.S. Sends Top Iranian Leader a Warning on Strait Threat," *New York Times*, January 12, 2012, http://www.nytimes.com/2012/01/13/world/middleeast/us-warns-top-iran-leader-not-to-shut-strait-of-hormuz.html?_r=0

93. Kay Armin Serjoie, "Iran Challenges U.S. and Saudi Arabia by Sending Aid Ship to Rebels in Yemen," *Time*, May 18, 2015, http://time.com/3882293/iran-saudi-aid-ship/

94. In Persian, Iran refers to the concept of proportionality as responding "threat with threat." For more background, see Eisenstadt, "Not by Sanctions Alone: Using Military and Other Means to Bolster Nuclear Diplomacy with Iran," The Washington Institute, Strategic Report No. 13, July 2013, 24, http://www.washingtoninstitute.org/uploads/Documents/pubs/StrategicReport13_Eisenstadt2.pdf

95. Eisenstadt, "What Iran's Chemical Past Tells Us About Its Nuclear Future," 2.

96. For a fuller treatment of the influence of Islam on Iranian notions of pro-portionality, see Asghar Eftekhari and Fatallah Kalantari, "Evaluating and Defining the 'Threat in Response to Threat' Strategy in Iran's Defense Policy," *Journal of Defense Policy*, 22(88), Fall 2014.

97. For example, Iran's decision to mine international shipping lanes in the Persian Gulf during the Iran-Iraq War was viewed by US policymakers at the time as a provocative and disproportionate response to US pledges to protect freedom of navigation throughout the region. Iranian leaders, however, including then Supreme Leader Khomeini and President Rafsanjani, instructed the Iranian military to "retaliate without provoking the Americans" and viewed mining as a proportionate, non-escalatory response to US actions. See Rafsanjani, *The End of Defense, The Beginning of Reconstruction: The Memories and Records of Hashemi Rafsanjani of the Year 1367* (Tehran: Daftar-e Nashre Moarefe Enqelab), 119.

98. In addition, AEOI head Salehi warned Iran would enrich uranium up to 20% if the United States sought to renegotiate or abrogate the JCPOA.

"Iran Says Only 5 Days Needed to Ramp Up Uranium Enrichment," August 22, 2017, *US News & World Report*, https://www.usnews.com/news/world/articles/2017-08-22/iran-says-only-5-days-needed-to-ramp-up-uranium-enrichment

99. Members of the JCPOA Oversight Committee are appointed by Khamenei and include: President Hassan Rouhani, Majlis Speaker Ali Larijani, Foreign Minister Mohammad Javad Zarif, Defense Minister Hossein Dehghan, SNSC Secretary Ali Shamkhani, AEOI head Ali Akbar Salehi, former nuclear negotiator Saeed Jalili, senior foreign policy advisor to Khamenei Ali Akbar Velayati, and Deputy Foreign Minister Abbas Araghchi. See "Qassemi: Iran haq-e pasokh beh aqdaamat-e zed-e irani-ye amrika ra barayeh khod mahfoz midarad," *ISNA*, August 3, 2017, http://www.isna.ir/news/96051207550; and "Musahbeh-ye akhir-e amrika aqdaami doshmananeh va khosmaneh," *Fars News*, July 29, 2017, http://www.farsnews.com/newstext.php?nn=13960507001995

100. "Musahbeh-ye akhir amrika aqdaami doshmananeh va khosmaneh," *Fars News*, July 29, 2017, http://www.farsnews.com/newstext.php?nn=13960507001995

101. Rafsanjani, *Souye Sarnevesht* (Tehran: Daftar-e Nashre Moarefe Enqelab, 2008), 54.

102. For more on Iran's use of soft power to further its regional objectives, see Hassan Rouhani, *Andishe-ye Siasi-ye Eslam*, 64–65.

103. Hamdi Malik and Maysam Behravesh, "Is Iran Creating Its Own State Within Iraq?" *Guardian*, May 18, 2015, http://www.theguardian.com/world/2015/may/18/irans-state-within-state-in-iraq-shia

104. *Javan Online*, July 15, 2015.

105. "Iranian Public Opinion on the Nuclear Negotiations," University of Maryland Center for International and Security Studies, June 2015, http://www.cissm.umd.edu/publications/iranian-public-opinion-nuclear-negotiations

106. "Iran Bans Newspaper of Nuclear Deal Critic, Warns Others," *Hurriyet Daily News*, August 3, 2015, http://www.hurriyetdailynews.com/iran-bans-newspaper-of-nuclear-deal-critic-warns-others.aspx?pageID=238&nID=86379&NewsCatID=352

107. For more on Iran's censorship of the nuclear issue see Chapter 2 of author's "Leadership Divided? The Domestic Politics of Iran's Nuclear Debate," 3–8.

108. Rouhani, *Amniyat-e Melli*, 251.

109. "Muzakereh-ye diplomat ba ali akbar salehi," *Diplomat*, http://thediplomat.ir/417

110. Ibid.

111. "Salehi Reveals New Details of Secret US, Iran Back Channel," *Al-Monitor*, December 23, 2015, http://www.al-monitor.com/pulse/originals/2015/12/salehi-interview-conveys-new-details-of-secret-backchannel.html#ixzz3vYLaS48a

112. "Rahbar-e enqelab-e eslami bar istefadeh az taaktik-e 'narmesh qhrmaa-naaneh' takid kardand," *ISNA*, September 17, 2013, http://www.isna.ir/news/92062616573

113. White House correspondent Mark Landler suggests Iran agreed to the nuclear negotiations only after its baseline demand was met and that it be allowed to continue to enrich uranium. Landler claims then Senator John Kerry told Iranian officials during backchannel talks that Iran might be allowed to enrich uranium under a future nuclear agreement. See Landler, *Alter Egos*, 236–248.

114. See Sadegh Zibakalam's analysis of the critical turning points in Iran's political history, "Noqteh ataf taarikhi: roznameh-ye sharq," July 15, 2015, http://www.zibakalam.com/news/2075

115. *BBC Persian*, August 26, 2015, http://www.bbc.com/persian/iran/2015/08/150826

116. Michael Singh, "Deterring Tehran: An Iran Policy for the New Administration," The Washington Institute, Policy Note No. 36, March 2017, 1–3.

117. Khalilzad, 276.

CHAPTER 4

Prospects for Proliferation in Saudi Arabia

J. E. Peterson

Speculation regarding the acquisition of nuclear weapons by the Kingdom of Saudi Arabia (KSA) has been percolating for at least several decades. To date, there is no reliable evidence that any attempt has been made to either purchase such weapons or to begin a process to produce them. In addition, most of the speculation has been made by observers who either have little understanding of the KSA beyond the headlines or have an ideological ax to grind—or both.

While there remains a possibility of Saudi Arabian proliferation—no matter how remote as viewed at present—the decision to take that path is made difficult by both the complicated structure of Saudi society and politics (which runs contrary to popular wisdom) and the complex matrix of variables that the Saudi leadership must consider. While some of these are purely political, a rich variety of cultural determinants also factor in the mix.

Regarding KSA intent, a number of fundamental points need to be kept in mind. First, although the kingdom is an authoritarian monarchy with ultimate power resting with the king, various actors within KSA possess a variety of contributory roles and carry variable importance and weight in any debate over Saudi domestic and foreign policies, including nuclearization. Decisionmaking in KSA is tightly controlled within a small central

J. E. Peterson (✉)
University of Arizona, Tucson, AZ, USA

© The Author(s) 2018
J. L. Johnson et al. (eds.), *Crossing Nuclear Thresholds*,
Initiatives in Strategic Studies: Issues and Policies,
https://doi.org/10.1007/978-3-319-72670-0_4

elite and public input is limited to diffused perception of public opinion, generally through traditional filtered means. There is no single view or homogeneity of opinion on many issues. Furthermore, leadership, elite, and public opinion may evidence opposing viewpoints. The multiplicity of issues bearing on nuclear attitudes is likely to make KSA decisionmaking unclear. With regard to the impact on the United States, it should be noted that for some years, KSA-US relations have been strong and troubled at the same time. This underlying factor introduces ambiguity into relations as well as lessens the range of options available regarding a single issue.

BACKGROUND ON SAUDI NUCLEAR INTEREST

Contentions that the KSA has been developing nuclear capability, including delivery systems, geared particularly toward weapons capability can be dated back more than 30 years. A key assumption in these allegations relates to the kingdom's purchase a quarter of a century ago of Chinese missiles. KSA acquired some 50–60 CSS-2 "East Wind" ballistic missiles from China about 1987. These were theoretically nuclear-capable but they had been modified to carry non-nuclear warheads. Their purchase and installation were kept completely secret, especially from the United States. A strongly worded American official complaint provoked Saudi reaction, ending with the US ambassador to Riyadh Hume Horan being declared *persona non grata*.

One of the earliest of the contentions that KSA was seeking nuclear capability occurred in 1994 when KSA diplomat Muhammad al-Khilawi sought asylum in the United States with allegations that KSA had been seeking to share Iraqi nuclear technology for 20 years and that in the 1970s KSA had bankrolled the Pakistani bomb project. Additional documents asserted by Khilawi claimed that KSA had tried to buy nuclear reactors from China. He subsequently claimed that KSA had two undeclared research reactors but offered no proof. Khilawi's allegations were never backed up by hard evidence.[1]

Then in 1999, according to journalist Simon Henderson, the KSA's minister of defense Prince Sultan bin 'Abd al-'Aziz allegedly visited Pakistan's Kahuta uranium enrichment and missile assembly factory. This was said to prompt a formal diplomatic complaint from the United States.[2] A few years later (2003), Britain's *Guardian* newspaper reported that KSA was carrying out a strategic review, including the acquisition of nuclear weapons, in response to allegations of an Iranian nuclear program. Options being considered were said (1) to acquire a nuclear capability as a deterrent, (2) to maintain or enter into an alliance with an existing nuclear power that would offer protection, and (3) to try to reach a regional agreement on having a nuclear-free Middle East.[3]

Around the same time, journalist Arnaud de Borchgrave reported that KSA and Pakistan had concluded a secret agreement providing KSA with nuclear weapons technology in exchange for cheap oil. This was said to be arranged by Crown Prince 'Abdullah during his 2003 trip to Islamabad and President George H.W. Bush was said to have confronted Pakistan's prime minister, Pervez Musharraf, over the Saudi nuclear issue at Camp David in the same year. The allegation was denied by both the US and Saudi Arabian governments.[4] It should be noted that many of these allegations were made or promoted by individuals and organizations that were hostile to KSA, and thus their veracity is of considerable doubt.

In 2005, reports surfaced that the KSA was about to sign a "small-quantity protocol" with the International Atomic Energy Agency (IAEA) that would restrict IAEA inspections of the kingdom's nuclear status. Although the protocol had been arranged for many developing countries, the United States sought to persuade the KSA to withdraw their protocol request and to submit to independent verification of its nuclear status on a voluntary basis. Riyadh declined and its request was approved. This attention emerged despite the fact that there still was no evidence that Riyadh was indeed pursuing a nuclear weapons strategy of any sort.[5]

These reports circulated at a time when it became known that KSA was in fact interested in pursuing a nuclear energy program, as was the case with a number of other Arab states. Indeed, the kingdom had established an Atomic Energy Research Institute as early as 1988.[6] The KSA joined the IAEA's board of governors on 20 September 2007 and the KSA and the United States signed a memorandum of understanding on civil nuclear energy cooperation on 16 May 2008.[7]

Hints that the kingdom was continuing its interest in civil nuclear energy continued through the following years. The KSA minister of water and electricity declared in 2009 that the kingdom was thinking about building a pilot plant, apparently with French assistance. Nevertheless, the realization of any plans remained a long time off.[8] To this end, nuclear cooperation agreements were signed with the United States (2008), South Korea (2011), China (2012), and Jordan (2014) and discussions were underway with another six to eight countries.

In the midst of this more general concern about nuclear energy and possible weaponization, fears that Iran was seeking to produce nuclear weapons acquired prominent attention. Saudi Arabia has been one of the most vocal opponents of Iran's acquisition of such weapons and this factor has in turn raised concern about Saudi intentions. These were stoked by the comments in 2011 of Prince Turki al-Faysal, a former Saudi head of intelligence and ambassador and the brother of the then-foreign minister:

> We are committed to a Middle East Zone Free of Weapons of Mass Destruction, but if our efforts and the efforts of the world community fail to bring about the dismantling of the Israeli arsenals of nuclear, chemical and biological weapons and the prevention of Iran acquiring the same by failing to construct such a Zone, then why shouldn't we at least, and as a duty toward our nations and our peoples, study, seriously, all of the available options, including acquiring WMDs so that future generations will not blame us for neglecting any course of action that will keep looming dangers away from us?[9]

This led *The Times* of London shortly afterward to declare that the KSA planned, in case of an Iranian nuclear test, to immediately launch a twin-track nuclear weapons program by purchasing weapons and converting its civil nuclear program, with hints of upgrading the kingdom's aging Chinese missiles.[10] Two years later, the BBC reported on the possibilities that the KSA had arranged with Pakistan to hold nuclear weapons for release to the KSA on demand, together with rumors that Pakistan had delivered Shaheen mobile ballistic missiles to KSA but without warheads. The BBC followed up its story by declaring that the KSA embassy in London had refused to deny the story while lamenting the failure of the UN to make the Middle East a nuclear-free area [read Iran] and warning that the "lack of international action has put the region under the threat of a time bomb that cannot be refused by manoeuvring around it."[11] Saudi concerns were echoed by the words of Prince Turki al-Faysal in South Korea in 2015: "Whatever the Iranians have, we will have, too." This was said to be same message given to President Obama at Camp David.[12] Jamal Khashoggi, a well-known and connected Saudi journalist, added that "I think Saudi Arabia would seriously try to get the bomb if Iran did. It's just like India and Pakistan. The Pakistanis said for years they didn't want one, but when India got it, so did they."[13]

The effect of the Iran nuclear threat was to spur the KSA into more focused action regarding nuclear energy. Multinational discussions with Iran renewed KSA frustration with the "stalled" 123 nuclear agreement with United States, which had been foundering on US insistence on forbidding the KSA to enrich uranium or reprocess plutonium. As an apparent consequence, the King Abdullah City for Atomic and Renewable Energy (KA-CARE) announced a deal with Russia for help in building the 16 nuclear reactors.[14] In another seeming signal of Riyadh's intention to develop alternative nuclear arrangements, a letter of intent was signed with France just a few days later on 24 June for the construction of two nuclear reactors, as part of a larger arms deal.[15]

All of this material fed into Saudi—and Gulf—reactions to the signing of the JCPOA. A report out of Russia claimed that the KSA might be the first foreign purchaser of a Russian missile system capable of carrying nuclear warheads.[16] According to the *New York Times*, before the May 2015 Camp David summit with Gulf Cooperation Council (GCC) leaders, the KSA indicated that it wanted a formal "defense treaty with the US pledging to defend them if they came under external attack."[17] Jamal Khashoggi contended that oil exports would immunize the KSA from any international pressure over nuclear plans.[18] Abdullah Al Shayji of Kuwait University wrote that the Iran deal "will not calm our fears. On the contrary it could be even more a destabilizing factor in our region. GCC states need to forcefully make the argument and insist that their fears and skepticism should be addressed both strategically and militarily."[19] In large part, the Gulf fears of Iranian nuclear intentions formed just one aspect of a larger threat perception. As a Saudi columnist wrote, "Probably the most important question is whether our problem with Iran is limited to the nuclear deal. Many feel that the problem has its roots in Iran's political policies in the region. Tehran seems to insist on intervening in internal Arab affairs and inciting sectarianism in Iraq, Syria, Lebanon, Bahrain, and Yemen."[20] The Gulf worried in particular about the absence from the JCPOA of any mention of missile systems. This was expressed at the US-GCC foreign ministers summit in August 2015, when the six states endorsed the JCPOA deal.[21] This was thought to be in return for additional military equipment, especially missile defense systems. There has been some fear that KSA aggressiveness in its campaign in Yemen (assisted by four of the five other GCC members) is a direct result of its perception of Iranian interference in Yemen and its encirclement of the GCC.

Saudi and Gulf reactions in turn fueled American concerns over possible Saudi intentions. For many, Saudi comments constituted a blustering intended to force America's hand vis-à-vis Iran. For example, former US Secretary of Defense Robert Gates said in an August 2015 speech that the Iran deal "will provoke other countries in the region to pursue equivalent nuclear capabilities, almost certainly Saudi Arabia."[22] The discussion reached a nadir, however, with a silly column by Fareed Zakaria in the *Washington Post* that snorted "Oh, please! Saudi Arabia cannot build a nuclear weapon. Saudi Arabia has not even built a car … Saudi Arabia can dig holes in the ground and pump out oil but little else."[23]

The JCPOA was certainly a major spur driving King Salman to Washington in September for talks with President Obama, only a few months after he had declined an invitation to join his fellow GCC rulers at Camp David. During the meeting, the JCPOA and Iranian activities in the Middle East were prominent topics of discussion, along with the situation in Yemen and Syria, terrorism, Lebanon, global climate change, and bilateral relations—but seemingly remained a low-key topic. Obama's only spoken reference to the JCPOA came in his opening remarks: "We'll discuss the importance of effectively implementing the deal to ensure that Iran does not have a nuclear weapon while counteracting its destabilizing activities in the region." King Salman did not mention Iran in response. The joint statement was similarly low-key: "The two parties affirmed the need to continue efforts to maintain security, prosperity and stability in the region and in particular to counter Iran's destabilizing activities. In this regard, King Salman expressed his support for the Joint Comprehensive Plan of Action (JCPOA) between Iran and the P5 + 1 countries, which once fully implemented will prevent Iran from obtaining a nuclear weapon and thereby enhance security in the region."[24] The downplaying of the issue may have been due to such factors as Obama's difficulty in getting Congressional approval for the deal, the KSA's acquiescence already (as signaled in the earlier GCC approval), the US sweetening the sting by offering new arms deals and assistance to the KSA in Yemen, and US silence on domestic reforms in the KSA.

An interesting development was the seeming emergence of a tacit alliance between the KSA and Israel regarding the Iranian threat. Israeli Prime Minister Benjamin Netanyahu emphasized Arab opposition as an argument against Congressional approval of the Iran deal, suggesting a new front of common interests between Israel, the KSA, Egypt, and

Jordan. However, any movement beyond common rhetoric seems unlikely as long as Israeli-Palestinian relations remain unsettled.[25]

SAUDI PERCEPTIONS OF THREAT AND OF THE UNITED STATES AS PARTNER

Threats Through the Saudi Perceptual Lens

While there would be multiple rationales behind any Saudi impetus to acquire nuclear capability, undoubtedly the principal driver would be the panoply of external threats that the kingdom perceives surrounding it in what has been referred to as an encirclement syndrome. Some perceived threats are regarded as more serious than others. Security perceptions are inevitably colored by the defensive nature of the Saudi regime's attitude. KSA leaders and elites display an easily provoked prickliness about a wide range of issues. Reasons for this may include the fact that the KSA was never colonized and so retains a strong sense of unfettered independence. At the same time, its religious origins—in particular the puritanical Wahhabi or *salafi* interpretation of Islam—combine with its guardianship of Islam's Holy Places to provide the KSA—in self-perception—with an unchallengeable voice of legitimacy. This may lead to actions that on the surface may appear high-risk or even counter-productive. Examples include the secret purchase of Chinese missiles in the 1980s, economic threats to Britain whenever a dispute arises over treatment of British citizens in the KSA, or the KSA's lobbying for a seat on the UN Security Council and then abruptly rejecting it when offered.

Yemen has long been seen as a source of insecurity and the KSA has taken the lead in the fighting there. But the nature of the threat is more one of spreading instability and the influx of Yemenis seeking work as well as radicals and terrorists; it is not an existential threat. Nor is that true of the Horn of Africa, another source of worry; particularly Somalia's fragmentation and Eritrea's weakness.

To the northeast, Israel has been a source of worry for more than a half-century due to the continued antagonism resulting from the never-ending Arab-Israeli conflict. The KSA opposes Israel's occupation of the West Bank and decries its treatment of Palestinians. Mutual antagonisms persist because of (from the Saudi point of view) the gradual shift in Israeli politics to the right, personified in the leadership of Ariel Sharon and now

Benjamin Netanyahu, with its rejection of a Palestinian state, unwillingness to share Jerusalem, and continued strife with Palestinians in occupied
territories. Beyond this, however, there is also a fear, no matter how subli-
mated, of the Israeli nuclear threat.

Still, the most serious threat perception by Riyadh (and its fellow GCC
members), by far, is that posed by Iran. Officially expressed KSA concerns
about Iran date back at least to the 1979 Iranian revolution but have
intensified in the last four years. There are a number of layers to this concern, which is voiced particularly by Saudi elite but is also shared to a large
extent by the country's citizenry. The most fundamental factor in the two
countries' shared antipathy is probably the long cultural/political antagonism between Persians and Arabs, stretching beyond the Islamic era. There
is a history of Persian expeditions to and occupation of territory on the
Arab side of the Gulf that reverberates in the Arab popular imagination
today and gives added emphasis to imagined Iranian designs on Bahrain
and indignation at the extension of Iranian control over the disputed
islands of Abu Musa and the two Tunbs near the entrance to the Gulf. The
islands, along with final demarcation of the Iranian-Iraqi border, were the
last boundary disputes between the two littorals, thus removing what had
been a contentious subject.

Beyond that, the new Islamic Republic of Iran's revolutionary Islamist
rhetoric and its actively threatening the status quo in the Gulf and the
Middle East complicated Arab perceptions in the aftermath of the Iranian
Revolution. Sectarian divisions between Sunnis and Shi'ah had always
existed but were of relatively minimal significance in the pre-1979 atmosphere. But the Iran-Iraq War deepened sectarian as well as political divisions and created Sunni popular suspicions of a Shi'ah expansion of
influence and of indigenous Shi'ah elements of the population as a potential or real fifth-column. This was particularly true in the KSA, where the
prevailing creed of Wahhabism reflected a deep antipathy to the heterodox
Shi'i strain of Islam. Spontaneous outbursts of dissidence in the Shi'ah
areas of the KSA's Eastern Province, inspired in 1979–1980 by the Iranian
revolution, were put down with ferocity. The kingdom's long and deep
hostility toward Shi'ism combines with a suspicion of Iranian imperialism
in its antagonistic relations with its trans-Gulf neighbor.

In recent years, the hostility of the Iranian revolutionary regime toward
Sunni Arab regimes—real and perceived—and support for dissident movements has pushed a quickening war of rhetoric. Apart from the hostilities
in Syria, this rivalry was amplified in the Saudi-Iranian proxy war in

Yemen.[26] Saudi enmity reached a crescendo with its warnings about Iranian nuclear ambitions and Riyadh fought hard with Washington against the JCPOA agreement. But, failing to achieve their goal of disruption, the Saudis gamely acquiesced in its implementation, albeit while continuing to press for increased US defense arrangements.

A final driver revolves around an emerging intensification of the old encirclement fears, particularly as the immediate region seems to descend into chaos. Diffuse threats emanate from numerous sources, including both hostile states and even more hostile movements. The Huthis of Yemen and their allies are in the forefront of KSA foes at present but they are hardly capable of striking seriously at the kingdom—nor do they seem to have any desire to expand hostilities beyond defense of their home area. A far more potent threat is posed by Da'ish (also known as ISIS or ISIL) in Syria and Iraq. While a Da'ish assault on KSA territory does not seem likely, there is a real threat that has been partially realized already of Da'ish teams carrying out terrorist actions within the kingdom.

Contrary to much Western opinion, the KSA regards both al-Qa'idah and Da'ish as serious threats.[27] It follows that the greater the danger of extremism is to attracting Saudi youth—as well as the blowback to terrorist activities within the KSA—the more Saudi leadership will be inclined to act against extremist groups with whatever means at its disposal. Recent Saudi activism in the Yemen campaign might just possibly signal a greater resolve to act unilaterally against Da'ish centers in Syria and Iraq.

Following on from the perception of encirclement, the KSA can also be quite protective of the smaller Gulf States, an attitude engendered partly because it is vulnerable to a soft underbelly along the Gulf and even more because in Saudi eyes, these states should have been incorporated into the Third Saudi State but were prevented from doing so because of the British presence. This has led to KSA peremptory attitudes and pressure vis-à-vis its fellow GCC members (as well as taking such controversial stances as sending troops to Bahrain in the aftermath of the 2011 demonstrations). As a consequence of this overbearing attitude, the other five GCC members have generally been reticent to strengthen GCC political functions for fear that it would increase Saudi domination.

The above movements of course do not constitute a threat against which nuclear weapons capability would be of any use. But they do contribute to a broader and more diffuse uneasiness that more specific state-derived threats help to provoke. In this sense, Saudi perceptions of the general situation may parallel the Pakistani example: Islamabad's push to create nuclear weapon capability seemed to be prompted generally by its perceived location in an uncertain neighborhood and specifically by Indian proliferation.

As remarked above, the KSA does have an ancillary desire and legitimate aspiration because of its expanding requirements for electricity and fuel for utilities to acquire nuclear energy facilities and has taken opening steps toward such an end. It is certainly not outside the realm of possibility that the kingdom might expand that goal to include nuclear weapons capability either overtly or covertly as a consequence of its perception of the direct and diffuse threats outlined above.

Perceptions of the United States

Real enemies or serious external threats from nearly all compass points are present and are perceived by the KSA as becoming increasingly serious. This fuels the citizenry's suspicion of outsiders and leads to widespread stereotypes. Northern Arabs are suspect because they believe themselves to be culturally superior, they are in the KSA only to earn money and leave, and they promote dangerous ideologies (secular radicalism in the past; Islamist extremism at present). Westerners are suspect because of lax morals and imperialist designs. Asian expatriates are perceived as being little more than menial laborers and threaten cultural contamination.

Attitudes to the United States are mixed. On the positive side, the two countries enjoy a long-standing economic partnership based on a number of key factors. The foundation factor was the exploitation of oil for decades by an American company that also played a pivotal role in early development; the company, although Saudiized, still exists as Saudi ARAMCO (Arabian-American Oil Company). The oil company connection was then strengthened by the development role of the US government from World War II on, first in providing loans when sorely needed and then through a wide range of development assistance. The two countries continued to share common interests in preserving the international oil structure and, as the KSA began to build a surplus from its oil revenues, it heavily invested it in US Treasury bonds. The KSA and the United States remain major trading partners.

More positive attitudes revolve around political and security cooperation. The United States and the KSA have tended to share worldviews: anti-Communism, anti-Islamist extremism, a laissez-faire global economy. For decades, the KSA has relied upon huge purchases of American weapons and other military purchases of US goods and services. This is often seen as a quid pro quo for the extension of a US security umbrella over the kingdom and its GCC neighbors. It also includes the exchange of security and political information on common issues. But it is debatable whether these common outlooks would be strong enough to provide the KSA with sufficient assurance of security and to dissuade it from acquiring the bomb if it looks as though Iran did.

In some respects, a cultural affinity has developed as well. A voracious appetite exists for American media, fashion, fast food, and so on in Saudi Arabia. A pro-American attitude is commonly retained by many Saudis who have studied in the United States.

However, there are a multitude of negative reactions to the United States. These can be grouped into several clusters. One revolves around religious and moral objections. There is a deep belief among many or most Saudis that Western culture is immoral and does not respect the family (Saudi students en route to the United States receive lectures from religious figures on this subject, thus reinforcing the antipathy of some). Religiously conservative elements may display a disdain for non-Muslims. Anecdotal observation indicates that perceptions are widespread and growing that Americans are anti-Arab and anti-Muslim. These perceptions grow with the reaction of some Americans to every terrorist attack worldwide by expressing increased hostility toward Muslims in the United States, which is widely reported in the United States and the Middle East. Beyond that, there is a deep belief that the US acts as an imperialist power, imposing its will on others and carrying out policies that serve its interests while indiscriminately harming others.

Some of these attitudes relate more directly to security concerns and the belief that the United States is not a reliable partner in security matters. This can be expressed in the observation that when the going gets tough, the United States gets going—and the examples of American involvement in and then quick retreat from Lebanon, Somalia, Iraq, and Afghanistan are brought up. Many Saudis remain strongly perturbed by the American-led invasion of Iraq, an act that devastated the country and put radical Shi'ah in power. More recently, the United States has failed to take effective action in Syria and seems to be content to allow Bashshar al-As'ad to remain in power. Finally, there is chafing over the impression that the United States regards the KSA as a very much junior partner and is not sufficiently attentive to the kingdom's needs and priorities.

More directly, there is frustration throughout most of Saudi society over core Middle East concerns. The United States is seen as not objective on Arab-Israeli matters. Second, the United States seems too willing to deal with Islamist (not extremist) movements, such as the Muslim Brotherhood in Egypt. Thirdly, the nuclear agreement with Iran threatens Saudi security directly and the United States' role in seeking it and accomplishing it demonstrates its indifference to Saudi concerns.

KEY PLAYERS AND DECISIONMAKING NORMS

Decisionmakers

Clearly, the king is the actual decisionmaker, including in the nuclear arena. He has the final say in establishing all policies and his decisions cannot be challenged by anyone. But it is a mistake to call him, as is often done in the West, an absolute monarch. The Saudi monarchy is built on its tribal ethos, which in its pure form demands access, consultation, and feedback. Even though the KSA has evolved into an authoritarian monarchy, these principles still play a significant role in the modern state. The long-term legitimacy of the regime depends heavily on building and maintaining consensus on major issues. Of course, the value of such consensus varies on the importance of the constituent group with whom the king and his advisers interact.

Not surprisingly, the top-most and most important elite in consensus-building consists of the senior members of the royal family. Despite internal differences and rivalries, they form a corporate group that maintains the survival of the royal family and the regime. Their overriding credo may be said to be, in paraphrasing Benjamin Franklin's words, to hang together instead of hanging separately. Some individuals—such as those of the same mother (e.g., the so-called Sudayri Seven who produced Kings Fahd, 'Abdullah, and Salman) or sons (most notably recently, Muhammad b. Salman, son of present King Salman who has named him minister of defense and heir apparent)—may carry considerable weight with the king. Alternatively, internal rivalries within the family may isolate individuals, especially when combined with their personality. Pertinent examples include Talal b. 'Abd al-'Aziz (a son of the modern kingdom's founder but outspoken in the past and present) or Bandar b. Sultan (son of a late crown prince who served as the KSA's ambassador to the United States for more than a decade but has been banished to the political wilderness).[28]

Some mention also should be made of the role of the other members of the extensive royal family. Most do not hold government positions and many are engaged in commerce. They may not be actively involved in decisionmaking except for issues that involve the royal family as a whole. But they certainly may unite to oppose a decision that seemingly threatens the position of the family or the "Saudi" in Saudi Arabia.

Perhaps next in importance to the senior royal family is the senior bureaucratic elite. This sector can be considered more or less non-ascriptive since its members increasingly receive their positions because of competence and education. This can even hold true for those members who are also from the royal family, such as the late Saʻud al-Faysal, the country's foreign minister for decades. Although the members of the elite do not make major decisions themselves, they play an influential role in shaping policy (particularly in the economy and some aspects of foreign affairs) by framing policy alternatives and consequences for the actual decisionmakers.

The religious establishment constitutes another ring in the circles surrounding the supreme decisionmaker, the king. This group, the *ulama*, is not composed of direct decisionmakers because the role of the religious establishment in the centuries-old partnership with the Al Saʻud has been to safeguard the morals of the people rather than oversee policy (as is the case in Iran). Although they are not the decisionmakers themselves, they do play a major role in the decisionmaking process because the state depends on them to rubber stamp policies via *fatwas* (religious opinions) and to vouchsafe the religious legitimacy of the regime. As a consequence, few major decisions are taken without considering the collective opinion of the clerics. Any government decision that contravenes clerical wishes (expressed before decisions are made and nearly always in private) is almost inevitably accompanied by another decision that meets with clerical approval.[29] The backing of the religious establishment has remained of key importance because of such factors as the need for the *ulama* to sanction the presence of Christian troops in the country before and during the 1991 Kuwait War, the emergence of a "loyal opposition" of independent *ulama* in the 1990s, and the emergence of first al-Qaʻidah and then Daʻish that both deny the Saudi monarchy's religious legitimacy and actively attempt to undermine the government through terror campaigns within the KSA.

In many countries, the military establishment plays a strong and constraining role vis-à-vis the government, even where it does not control it.

This is not the case in Saudi Arabia. All senior military officers are selected by the inner circle of the regime and the organization, placement, and use of the armed forces is directly controlled by the king and his advisers. While most of the senior positions are held by commoners, the Al Sa'ud has been careful to sprinkle members of the royal family and its cadet branches throughout the services as a check on other officers and to keep the family informed.

Decision Influencers

It can be argued that the previous groups could equally be called decision influencers. The difference, for the sake of argument here, is that the first groups generally play some more or less direct role in shaping or steering policy while the following groups provide feedback that the ruling elite interprets and considers.

The commercial elite has enjoyed something of a symbiotic relationship with regime. Although, generally speaking, of lower social standing than decisionmakers (since prominent merchant families rarely possess impeccable tribal genealogies), it forms an important part of the increasingly complex contemporary social milieu. Collectively, the merchants hold enormous economic weight. Individually, they are close to various senior figures in the regime.[30] It should be noted as well that members of merchant families also constitute a considerable cross-section of educated cadres and the bureaucratic elite. In earlier years of the oil age, merchant families had an edge in education over other members of society and a broader worldview because of travel and family "internships" abroad (such as India). When the kingdom began to fashion a modern government, members of merchant families were ideally placed to hold senior positions first. They remain well-represented in government circles.

The middle class continues to grow in size and importance. Increasingly, it forms the backbone of the new Saudi society and proportionally the most non-ascriptive sector. Prominent subsectors include mid-level government officials, intellectuals (including university faculty), small merchants, professionals, and military officers. The support of the middle class in regard to public opinion is an essential building block of KSA's rulers. While the class enjoys virtually no formal participation (apart from appointments to the Majlis al-Shura and elections to local councils), it does exercise considerable influence or restraint as a key source of public opinion. It is no over-statement to say that middle-class support is essential for the regime in both the short- and long-run.

Another key sector in the formation and leading of public opinion is that of the dissident clerics (particularly the Sahwah movement). It is important to note that they have been dissident but not disloyal. The state can and has co-opted prominent figures (most notably Salman al-'Awdah), as well as placating some by modifications of policy and also punishing recalcitrants. In contrast to state-supported clerics, dissidents keep the state grounded in perceived moral values and force the regime to defend and modify certain policies.

Intellectuals are capable of drawing international attention to controversial issues but they are essentially powerless to exact meaningful change (except perhaps over the very long-term given receptive monarchs). Public attitude to their stances and actions, particularly those often misleadingly characterized as "liberals," seems largely neutral or indifferent.

The most-feared segment of the future is that of the burgeoning legions of youth. The KSA has a huge and growing problem with restless youth, many of whom are unemployed and chafing against societal restrictions. Not surprisingly, it is the segment of the population that is most susceptible to extremist recruitment. Altogether, these groups have the potential to help shape national attitudes on nuclear issues or, at the very least, to coalesce public opinion in opposition to nuclear decisions.

Regime Opponents

Some mention should be made of regime opponents. In decades past, these would have been secular leftists, whether Arab nationalist or Marxist. In the past decade or two, however, opponents are essentially restricted to members of or sympathizers with Islamist extremist groups. The Saudi role in the formation and operation of al-Qa'idah is well-known—and equally well overstated. It is no secret that many of the rank and file of Da'ish are also Saudi. Equally overstated and simplified is the contention that the Saudi dominant creed of Wahhabism created Islamist extremism, whether the Taliban, al-Qa'idah, or Da'ish. Al-Qa'idah and Da'ish are sworn enemies of the Al Sa'ud regime: the former carried out a pervasive campaign of terrorism within the KSA during 2003–2007 and Da'ish has begun in the last few years to commit its own acts of terrorism. The goal of both groups is to create instability in the country that will cause the Al Sa'ud to fall. There is a direct security impact to their actions but as they are not states but groups, straightforward military action is not an option. Their role as decision influencers is justified by their ability to influence the opinion of conservative and disaffected sectors of citizenry, to recruit among disaffected youth, and to collect funds from sympathetic citizens.

Decisionmaking Norms

Whether decisionmakers or decision influencers, actors within Saudi society tend toward a common set of norms in state decisionmaking. A principal approach to politics is consensus-building. For this reason, it often seems to take very long to reach any decision. Generally, criticism or outspokenness is not accepted within the family, and therefore it is not accepted within society. Consequently, it is vastly preferable to achieve consensus within whichever circle is involved rather than risk confrontation.

Consensus and respect for authority form the foundation at the heart of the KSA's legitimacy. Most policies are enacted by the king after a consensus has been established among sociopolitical elites. The initial approach to disobedience and dissidence is to seek to "reform" the individual and bring him or her back into the fold and re-integrate them into harmonious society, as has been done with both clerical and liberal dissidents. But refusal to cooperate can provoke severe responses. The attitude to the Shi'ah is (mostly) benign neglect, owing to Sunni (and particularly Wahhabi) negative perceptions of Shi'ah. As a consequence, most Saudis are politically quiet. Few demonstrations occur, partly because participants face quick prosecution and partly because it contravenes the principles above.

Tradition and conformity are overwhelmingly desired attributes. Whatever an individual does or says is observed and known throughout his/her social circle. Negative talk or behavior brings shame on the family as well as the individual. As a consequence, personal relations are the glue that holds society together. Inability or unwillingness to cooperate risks exclusion and personal hardship. While this social reality certainly has its negative aspects, it also serves to bind society together and create a near uniformity of support for the state.[31] Consequently, open opposition to a state nuclear policy is very unlikely apart from dissidents abroad.

One of the fundamental tenets of Saudi politics and society is the legitimating requirement for access, consultation, and feedback. This follows on from the shared tribal ethos of the society, as perpetuated by the state.

Nearly all senior members of the royal family, many senior government officials, and most major merchants hold a regular *majlis* or gathering, often weekly, at which anyone generally can appear and take part in the discussion of the evening. While many of these *majlises* have no political focus, they provide a forum where diverse subjects of interest and issues of the day can be discussed. Information or feedback is thus permitted to flow up to the country's leadership.

While it is very unlikely that the question of whether the KSA should pursue nuclear weapons acquisition would be broached in a *majlis*, it is far more possible that discussion of Iran's nuclear program would be the subject of discussion. In this way, national leadership would have an opportunity to ascertain popular views pertaining to nuclear weapons, their utility, and desirability. While such views may have a political aspect, they are even more likely to display sentiments, whether culturally or religiously based, regarding the moral, as well as practical, implications of ownership and use of nuclear weapons. Either in or outside of a *majlis*, there may be some opportunity for educated Saudis and senior bureaucrats to articulate their positions on weapon of mass destruction (WMD) as part of an informal consultation process, in supplement to their formal roles.

Social status in the KSA at present is both ascribed and mobile. At the top, the ruling family (and ancillary families) forms a virtual caste, which is enforced through marriage restrictions. In the last few decades, social status has been increasingly infiltrated by wealth (through commerce) and education (through government service). The traditional elite of the Al al-Shaykh and religious notables is increasingly seen by growing numbers of citizenry (and probably most of the ruling family) as a still-necessary nuisance. Intellectuals are not well respected: they tend to be seen as either essentially irrelevant or as suspect dissidents. Another traditional elite comprising tribal leadership has lost position as tribes matter less in active political and many social affairs, despite the continuing fact that tribes retain social importance and identity.

The social hierarchy, although buffeted, still prevails. There is still tremendous respect for authority, which remains stirred but fundamentally intact. It is not acceptable to publicly question one's elders but one must defer to their judgment. This may be one result of a learning-by-rote education: traditional norms are instilled and questioning is frowned upon. In this regard, much or most of the population undoubtedly would passively accept a decision by the government to acquire nuclear weapons.

The influence of the royal family is enhanced further by its quasi-monopoly of the media (television and radio are state-owned while the private sector in media, both local and international, is owned by the elite and supports the government). Pro-government attitudes are constantly reinforced, both in media (TV, radio, and newspapers) but also in education (political, cultural, and religious indoctrination). The state is the source of all authority and therefore "truth." The majority of citizens accept the state's stated rationales, at least in foreign affairs. The "correct word" of the state is reinforced repeatedly in all media. Furthermore, a prominent historical myth promoted by the regime invokes the glory of the Arabs and the manifest destiny of the KSA led by the Al Sa'ud. Nearly all deviation from the accepted view is kept private. Disagreement with government policies and attitudes in public is generally viewed by citizenry with indifference or ostracization. Religious figures may receive more public attention and approval, therefore, government responses to vocal opposition tend to be more careful at first. In the event of a decision by the leadership to acquire WMD, very little public opposition might be expected, even if disquiet should exist.

VALUES AND THE PARADOXES IN SAUDI SOCIETY

All the strategic arguments for or against nuclear acquisition must be tempered with cultural considerations in a society such as Saudi Arabia. One primary concern of the royal family from the very beginning has been adhering to the precept of ruling in a just and Islamic way. The precept may have been nibbled around the edges and even flouted in certain cases, but the ethos remains intact. As a consequence, cultural factors must be regarded as a significant determinant in Saudi intentions.

It remains very much true in the KSA and the other Gulf monarchies that corporate identity is still valued far above individual identity. Central to this is the concept of honor and its opposite, shame. Saudi society is extremely transparent and every action by an individual is noted and reflects positively or negatively on one's corporate group.

Society is still often posited as a family writ large and the country continues to reference a bedouin ethos. The head of the tribe was regarded as the father of his tribe. It was his responsibility to protect the collective interests of the tribe (such as defense of territory, conducting warfare against tribal threats, presenting the tribe's needs to the ruler), to adjudicate in tribal disputes, and to look out for the needs of individual members of the tribe and families. The same concept is at the heart of the Saudi national identity: the king is regarded as the father of the national family and his role carries the same obligations and responsibilities. Of course the parallel is not completely true. The Saudi nation is far larger than a tribe, the personal ties (always so important in Saudi society) do not exist to anywhere near the same degree, and certainly not all Saudis trace their origins back to noble tribes. But in the recesses of the mind, the concept still retains relevance for a majority of the population.

In part, the idea of a supreme father figure rests on the belief that age and status are highly valued. Deference to the head of family is virtually unchallenged. Consequently, deference to authority is also very deeply ingrained.

Social mobility has been a visible hallmark of the oil era. The emergence of the middle class has incorporated disparate elements from nearly all sectors of pre-oil society. Some of the wealthiest individuals come from mean backgrounds (or even were originally not Saudi). Against this, it should be kept in mind that an under-current of social classification remains vibrant. It remains very rare for women from noble tribes to marry outside the tribe or tribes of equal status. At the top, of course, the Al Sa'ud forms an impenetrable caste.

The regime seems to play upon the value placed on a harmonious society. In the first place, it is a generally accepted precept in Sunni Islam that it is better to obey existing authority, even if that may be a tyrant, than to oppose and thereby create more harm and chaos. The oil era has brought prosperity to most Saudis and citizens of the Gulf States, highly welcomed in contrast to the extreme poverty of the area before the 1940s to 1960s. This has created what seems to be an overly materialistic society. The regime constantly but subtly reminds its people that life is good in the KSA, even without political participation, compared to what transpired during the revolution in Iran or has happened to Iraq and Syria. The lesson of the trade-off is not lost on most people.[32]

Not surprisingly, the KSA displays a number of aspects of a rentier state. A dependence on the state to provide nearly everything has been created in the last few decades. In addition, there is an expectation that the state will organize the domestic economy and politics and it will handle foreign relations as it sees fit. Consumerism has become a major feature of society, and along with it the desire to maintain the good, comfortable, life is a major reason for acceptance of the state as it is. There is a real fear of the unpalatable alternative posed by chaos in neighboring states, a fear that the regime has continued to emphasize. It may also be said that the Iranian system is perceived by most of the population as a threat to Saudi values and way of life, in addition to comprising a security threat.

Saudi Arabia in many ways presents a paradox. It is, officially and superficially, a very traditional society. This is certainly how the regime, and beyond it the religious establishment, likes to declare it—and it is true that millions of Saudis have never traveled abroad, speak few or no foreign languages, are religiously devout, and place considerable trust in their government. At the same time, however, there is a sizable sector of society that is more cosmopolitan and demands more of its political system. American and Western movies and television programs are widely watched through satellite television, video games are ubiquitous, and the kingdom—with 22 million users—ranks among the top 50 or so countries in Internet penetration. This creates a dialectic between the desire to remain unchanged and the drive for change, even radical change. The government in many ways is caught in the center.

The KSA, as a one-commodity producer, is particularly vulnerable to oil price fluctuations. The years of plenty with prices around $100/barrel have turned to prices of only $40 a barrel, and have fallen at times to less than that. The government is facing budgetary pressure to decrease current expenditures but will resist as long as possible, probably by borrowing and drawing down assets in its equivalent of a sovereign wealth fund. Typically, the government will seek to pacify an unruly population by continuing lavish spending on social services, salaries, and even direct payouts. For reasons of national pride and employment, it is unlikely the economic constraints will force a reduction in military purchases or size of force. It is more likely that efforts to achieve such capability will be postponed for financial reasons.

The economy, in large part because most income comes from oil revenues, remains stubbornly dirigiste despite government attempts to encourage the private sector. This factor gives the government a significant edge in leading its people to accept the purpose and rightness of their policies, including a possible nuclear weapons acquisition program.

This combination of factors presents the KSA with a burgeoning problem from its youth. The youth of the country must contend with persistent high levels of unemployment. But their employment, when jobs become available, is often resisted by employers who question the quality of their education and their work commitment. It can be contended that the youth of the KSA possess a broader worldview than their parents.

Among educated youth from elite families, Western pop culture is avidly followed while many are educated in English and are less competent in formal Arabic. Among non-privileged youth—the greatest part of the demographic range—there is growing anomie and resentment of the system, which is felt to have forgotten them. They are less likely to accept the situation as it is, and they are more likely to be recruited by Islamist extremists, in which case they may be more likely to favor WMDs.

FACTORS IN NUCLEAR DECISIONMAKING

Drivers

Cultural factors cannot be separated from strategic factors. Influences on the decisionmaking process regarding whether to pursue nuclearization are myriad. In the first instance, it must be recognized that the national leadership will be doing the actual decisionmaking; therefore, the personalities and conviction of those leaders are major determinants. Is a leader thoughtful and contemplative, or is he impetuous and hotheaded, driven by emotion more than logic? More globally, it can be assumed that the status of the relationship between the KSA and the United States would be a major driver: a deterioration in ties and confidence would undoubtedly spur greater Saudi resolve to pursue an independent security course. This may be influenced by existing or near-term KSA capabilities to pursue a nuclear program: if at least preliminary work had been done in achieving such capability, it is more likely that leadership would consider it a viable alternative and public opinion would be more receptive. The latter of course would particularly hold the more the citizenry feared existentialist external threats.

The role of prestige may also play a significant role. Nuclear capability would enhance the KSA's leadership status among Arab and Islamic nations and raise its standing on the global stage. This would be particularly effective among elites and other educated sectors of the population (including within the royal family) who share a more globalized outlook, although the majority of citizens may also regard it as a patriotic plus. More to the point, a nuclear policy may be regarded as an assertion of the KSA's national right, and the kingdom has always been very assertive of its perceived rights. At the same time, both leadership and citizenry may express an inability to comprehend why the nonproliferation regime should apply to the KSA.

Factors holding influence against proliferation may be economic, particularly relevant in the period of 2015–2017 when oil prices plummeted and the KSA's budget went into serious deficit. But religious and cultural norms against the possession and use of nuclear weapons undoubtedly would play a part in the decisionmaking process as well.

In part, this is due to the inordinately important role that the religious establishment plays in directing or at least constraining domestic policies. At the same time, this establishment has been given great latitude in carrying out a foreign policy that parallels—and sometimes conflicts with—the official foreign policy. For the question of nuclear acquisition, it is certain that the approval or at least acquiescence of the Islamic authorities in the KSA would be required. Such acquiescence would seem to depend on Islamic authorities' views on such points as waging war in defense, waging war against other Muslims, the moral right to possess nuclear weapons, and whether threats to the state would permit such a course of action.

Quranic injunctions that any combat engagement must distinguish between the innocent and the guilty while applying the minimum amount of force to achieve the objective and sparing the lives of noncombatants would seem to limit the acquisition and use of WMD.[33] At the same time, an argument has also been advanced for possessing nuclear capability as a deterrent.[34] At least one prominent conservative Saudi Arabian cleric has argued that WMD should not be used if victory can be achieved by using less powerful weapons but its use is permissible otherwise, particularly if it is suspected that the enemy might do so.[35] Another has used the analogy of early Islamic armies' use (including by the Prophet Muhammad) of catapults against enemy cities to justify WMD in extremis.[36]

Any clear-cut distinction within the religious establishment between religious justification of acquisition and religious abhorrence is likely to be distorted by the establishment's relationship with the country's secular authorities. The KSA's special perception of its role as protector of the Holy Places and thus serving as the guardian of Islam (as reflected in the king's other title, "Custodian of the Holy Places") gives its clerical establishment a certain power to establish the norm as regards Islamic injunctions concerning nuclear weapons.

Triggers

Triggers for acquisition are likely to be prompted by such causes as a concern over regional disintegration, Israeli provocation, KSA perceptions of regional and wider power status to be gained, and, especially, continued Iranian belligerence and involvement in regional crises. Proliferation may then be triggered by the deterioration of the JCPOA or evidence of direct Iranian provocation or interference in domestic affairs, such as has been claimed by Kuwait and Bahrain. Perhaps an even more compelling trigger would be the opening of a major breach in KSA-US relations. Still, it would seem that the actual use of nuclear weapons would remain restricted to perception of an existentialist threat to the KSA.

It is entirely possible—and unpredictably so—that one or more wildcards may play a significant role in distorting the picture outlined above. The emergence of a new king with a significantly different mindset and personality would of course be key. This may, for example, occur by way of generational change (as of 2015, all kings of Saudi Arabia since the death of 'Abd al-'Aziz have been sons of that king). The heir apparent, Muhammad b. Salman, is from the following generation of grandsons. Much has been made of the inflated role of Muhammad b. Salman in KSA decisionmaking in light of the seeming non-involvement of his father, King Salman. Muhammad, about 30 years old and with little experience in government or military affairs, has been regarded as the architect of the KSA's campaign in Yemen to restore a weak president to his capital by aggressively attacking the opposition forces, alleged in Riyadh to be actively supported by Iran. The war has been a quagmire; tens of millions of Yemeni civilians have been displaced and far more than 10,000 have lost their lives. He is also one of the main architects of the decision to besiege Qatar. If it were the decision of Muhammad to make, would he be less aggressive when it came to nuclear aspirations?

Another wildcard may well be a conservative backlash in public opinion against the possession or use of nuclear weapons. Public opinion does matter in the KSA, but for it to have an impact in this instance it would have to be uniformly and strongly presented in opposition to be taken seriously. On the other hand, it is within the realm of possibility that the opinion and influence of the non-royal-family elites and the middle class might coalesce as a voice for moderation.

US POLICY OPTIONS

A full panoply of policy options is open to the United States to inhibit or prevent the KSA from acquisition and proliferation of nuclear weapons. Deterrents are probably the measures that come to mind first, but the KSA is not an enemy or a hostile state. Assurance may in fact be more effective since the KSA is not an adversary. This section will detail each of the dissuasion or assurance policy options in turn and assess their effectiveness.

Dissuasion

The least threatening move in an effort to dissuade the kingdom from nuclear acquisition may be presidential or (less provocatively) administration hints at US displeasure. But this tactic has featured in KSA-US relations for many years, dating back to the oil crisis of the 1970s and continuing in Arab-Israeli matters without much significant success. Such action is unlikely to have positive effect and it is more likely to stiffen KSA resolve.

Similarly, the United States could take diplomatic action, such as not naming an ambassador to Riyadh. But this would probably result in a tit-for-tat, thus resulting in some damage to relations without achieving a positive result.

The United States could threaten to withdraw military support or announce its refusal to sell arms to the kingdom. In such a scenario, the KSA undoubtedly would turn to other suppliers: for example, France for reactors, Russia (and the European Union) for arms, and China for missiles. Riyadh has pursued a policy of diversification in economic and military goods and services for quite some time and this development would simply accelerate an existing trend. As a consequence, the United States would run the risk of losing political and moral influence in Riyadh and thus its ability to monitor KSA activities would be degraded.

The United States could threaten to enact sanctions or take other similar action against the KSA. But such an attempt would likely be disregarded by other states who are dependent on Saudi oil and desiring to maintain good relations with Riyadh, and could provoke KSA rhetoric and considerably impair direct relations.

This would of course be even more true if the United States actually attempted to apply sanctions. The question arises of what sanctions the United States could organize that would have serious impact on the

KSA. Would the United States be able to pressure Europe to join a sanctions regime? The KSA's reaction might well be to provoke it to an oil boycott of the United States. Even if the level of exports to the United States did not constitute a serious liability, the reduction in KSA crude production (a major part of global production) would affect the world as a whole and the global economy would undoubtedly suffer as it did in the 1970s.

The United States could make either public or covert attempts to interdict KSA-bound nuclear fuel and equipment. This may have some short-term success in impairing KSA nuclear abilities but it would also likely cause friction with the KSA's suppliers.

Assurance

Measures of assurance may well be more effective as long as US-KSA relations remain productive and friendly. The first cluster of options involves US official action vis-à-vis the KSA government. These may run from the provision of positive rhetoric supporting the security of the KSA to active support for and involvement in an effective nuclear-free zone in the Gulf. Another measure would be to rely on active assistance to the KSA in the acquisition of nuclear energy capability coupled with firm persuasion directed at the KSA government to abide by stringent international and American restrictions on nuclear activities. This might be accompanied by promises to provide more military support in both the short- and long-term. Independently or simultaneously, the validity of US assurance may well include an increase in the US military presence in the Gulf region. Stronger measures, applied as necessary, would involve a formal defense treaty or inclusion in a US-led alliance and, ultimately, basing nuclear weapons or fuel on KSA soil with limited KSA access but with a share in policy decisions, such as their storage or movement as well as protocols on use.

But measures need not be restricted to the official bilateral arena. The United States could appeal directly to Saudi opinion. In the first instance, this might mean reasoning with sympathetic members of the inner circle. This would include royal family members who can influence consensus-building, the bureaucratic elite who can present rational policy alternatives, military leaders who would be responsive to advising caution, and other elites who can present their views informally to senior members of the royal family. Beyond that, appeals could be made to public opinion, either through a nuanced media campaign or by outreach to Saudi students in the United States and after their return home. While the utility of enlisting military leaders, given their subservience to political authorities, may be limited, it is not inconsequential. Bonds and common outlooks between American military personnel and their Saudi counterparts, many of whom have been trained in the United States and/or by Americans, are strong.

Finally, a more complex and fruitful approach might consist of the reassessment and a redirection of the overall US-KSA relationship. Particularly effective here would be a skillful, patient, and constructive mix of addressing pertinent issues, including KSA democratization, toning down or stopping its aggressive export of conservative Islamic ideology, and supporting growing KSA involvement on the global stage, balanced by more meaningful manifestations of strong US support for the kingdom in security and political matters.

CONCLUSIONS

There is no evidence at present of Saudi intention to acquire nuclear weaponry. But heightened Saudi suspicions of Iran and fears raised by an increasingly chaotic region may have prompted Saudi interest in procuring that capability. Such a path can follow either the acquisition of technology and scientific knowledge that will allow the kingdom to move beyond nuclear energy toward weapons, or it can seek to acquire off-the-shelf weapons from another country—almost by default that would have to be Pakistan. The conventional wisdom that Pakistan would in fact not be willing to provide a bomb or assistance to the kingdom may be overstated. Given the American tilt to India, it is conceivable that Islamabad may value nuclear cooperation with Riyadh because such a policy would seem to provide leverage with the United States.

The principal factors in an internal Saudi assessment of the possibility are likely to be strategically based in the first instance, resting on the ruling elite's view of the geopolitical scene.[37] But a wide panoply of cultural factors may also play an influencing if not deciding role in the process. Among these, a shared sense of being threatened exhibited by nearly all sectors of Saudi society might encourage leadership to act. Equally, a strong sense of national cohesion and desire for consensus might both condition the population to passively accept whatever path upon which the leadership embarks and, more actively, to share the leadership's resolve and give its backing.

American policy options can involve either dissuasion or assurance but probably not both to any degree. The levers for dissuasion are limited in effectiveness, particularly since Saudi Arabia is not an adversary and the two countries have many strategic, economic, and political goals in common. While measures of assurance inevitably will appeal to strategic rationales, there is considerable scope for invoking cultural appeals.

Scott Sagan suggests that the "security" model explanation of "why states decide to build or refrain from developing nuclear weapons" may have been overstated and he makes an argument for advancement of "domestic politics" and "norms" models.[38] Many of the points advanced in the Background and US Policy Options sections of this paper elucidate rationales conforming to the security model. His emphasis within the domestic politics model on the role of bureaucratic politics and promotion by the scientific and military establishments does not apply in a significant way to the KSA where the authority of the king and his circle is overwhelming. Bureaucratic rivalries may indeed shape policy decisions but both the scientific and military establishments are clearly subordinate to tightly held policymaking at the top. Even his example of South Africa's decision to eliminate its nuclear arsenal does not seem to have a parallel in the KSA, where fears of an overthrow of the regime appear remote at present.

There is more scope for consideration of his norms model, "under which nuclear weapons decisions are made because weapons acquisition, or restraint in weapons development, provides an important normative symbol of a state's modernity and identity."[39] This is more likely to have an effect on the KSA's behavior. As noted above, the KSA places great pride in never having been colonized and in its custodianship of the holiest symbols of Islam. The expansion and creation of the kingdom in the twentieth century was accompanied by a belief in a Saudi divine mission that was limited only on most frontiers by the presence of British-protected states. Gradually through the following decades, the KSA developed its self-image as not only the most important state in the Arabian Peninsula but also a major power in the Middle East and Islamic world. Its ambitions and insistence on treatment as a world power have, if anything, accelerated to the present. It is not impossible to conceive that the KSA might in the near future, or already has, considered contingencies regarding nuclear weapons acquisition, particularly in consideration of an identity or national pride driver. If so, it clearly does not yet believe that pursuing such a path outweighs the political costs in terms of international and American opposition and in raising the risks of a regional arms war, not to mention altering its self-perceived image as a defensive actor in its neighborhood and securing the full support of its population.

Jacques Hymans takes Sagan's arguments further by suggesting that "top state leaders are unlikely to push for the bomb unless they hold an 'oppositional nationalist' conception of national identity—in other words, a combination of profound antagonism toward an external enemy with an equally profound sense of national self-esteem."[40] This comes closest to describing the KSA, with Iran of course as the prime enemy. But the willingness of the Saudi leadership to act on this basis would probably require a combination of two prerequisites: Iran's acquisition of nuclear weapon technology and the emergence of a "wildcard" figure as king, perhaps such as Prince Muhammad b. Salman. As heir apparent in March 2018, Muhammad denied that Saudi Arabia wanted nuclear weapons but simultaneously emphasized that if Iran developed a nuclear bomb, the KSA would quickly follow suit. The actions of a "wildcard" king may well be conditioned by his perceptual lens of Iran as posing a fundamental and even existential threat, perhaps even without evidence of Iran's possession of nuclear weapons. But even in the case of such a "wildcard," it cannot be assumed that any king can act independently of cultural considerations, social constraints, and the lack of consensus within the royal family and other elites.

US policy options to discourage Saudi Arabia from undertaking steps toward nuclear weaponry are limited from a strategic security point of view. Cultural appeals will probably have at least somewhat greater success but they are unlikely to work in isolation. The best course of action would seem to be fashioning a revised strategy of engagement that would incorporate multiple strategies of cultural interaction with a view to influencing Saudi policymakers and public alike. It may not require a great deal of persuasion to prevent Saudi Arabia from actively seeking nuclear weapons since no burning desire to do so seems to exist. Nevertheless, it is undoubtedly wiser to make the effort now than to risk a surprise later.

NOTES

1. *Sunday Times*, 24 and 31 July, 7 Aug. 1994; *International Herald Tribune*, 8 Aug. 1994.
2. *New York Times*, 10 July 1999.

3. *Guardian*, 18 Sept. 2003. The report was categorically denied by KSA's London embassy and dismissed by the IAEA. Reuters, 18 Sept. 2003.
4. Arnaud de Borchgrave, in the *Washington Times*, 22 Oct. 2003; VOA News, 22 Oct. 2003. A few months later in early 2004, KSA refuted another report that it was interested in Chinese missiles and bankrolling Pakistan's nuclear program. Reuters, 16 Feb. 2004.
5. Reuters, 1 and 16 June 2005; AP, 1 June 2015. The German magazine Cicero alleged in March 2006 that Pakistani scientists were employed in Saudi Arabia to help develop a secret nuclear program. AFP, 29 March 2006.
6. Reuters, 4 Nov. 2006; http://www.kacst.edu.sa/en/about/institutes/Pages/ae.aspx
7. AFP, 21 Sept. 2007; White House, Office of the Spokesman, "Media Note," 16 May 2008.
8. *The Peninsula* (Doha), 21 Aug. 2009. A further hint of Saudi intentions came in 2011 when a consultant for the King Abdullah City for Atomic and Renewable Energy (established 2010) said that the KSA intended to build 16 nuclear reactors by 2030. *Gulf News*, 30 Sept. 2011.
9. "Gulf and the Globe" Conference, Riyadh, Saudi Arabia, hosted by the Institute of Diplomatic Studies and the Gulf Research Center, 5 Dec. 2011.
10. *The Times*, 10 Feb. 2012.
11. BBC News, 6–7 Nov. 2013.
12. *Independent* (London), 14 May 2015.
13. Reuters, 22 July 2015.
14. Reuters, 19 June 2015.
15. AFP and AP, 25 June 2015. The deal followed a series of nuclear-related accords between the two countries between 2011 and 2014. *World Nuclear News*, 26 June 2015.
16. *Times of Israel* blog, 25 Aug. 2015.
17. Cited in a Tristan Volpe blog for *The Hill*, "Calling Out the Saudi Nuclear Bluff," 25 Aug. 2015, available at http://carnegieendowment.org/publications/?fa=61095
18. Reuters, 22 July 2015.
19. *Gulf News* (Dubai), 7 Sept. 2015.
20. Mohammed Fahad al-Harthi in *Arab News* (Jiddah), 2 Sept. 2015.
21. US Department of State, Office of the Spokesperson, Media Note, "Joint Statement of the US-GCC Foreign Ministers Meeting," 3 Aug. 2015.
22. Quoted in Volpe, "Calling Out the Saudi Nuclear Bluff," 25 Aug. 2015.
23. *Washington Post*, 11 June 2015. Zakaria's arguments were thoroughly and comprehensively skewered by Jeffrey Lewis on ForeignPolicy.com Voice, "Sorry, Fareed: Saudi Arabia Can Build a Bomb Any Damn Time It Wants To," 12 June 2015, available at http://foreignpolicy.com/2015/06/12/sorry-fareed-saudi-arabia-can-build-a-bomb-any-damn-time-it-wants-to/

24. White House, Office of the Press Secretary, "Joint Statement," 4 Sept. 2015. For analysis of the meeting, see the *Financial Times*, 4 Sept. 2015, and the *New York Times*, 4 and 5 Sept. 2015, as well as the reaction of the Gulf analyst Abdullah Al Shayji, *Gulf News*, 7 Sept. 2015.

25. The development is discussed by former Israeli ambassador Uri Savir on *Al-Monitor*, "Why it's time for Saudi Arabia to take the lead on Israeli-Palestinian peace process," 6 Sept. 2015, available at: http://www.al-monitor.com/pulse/en/originals/2015/09/palestinian-statehood-iran-agreement-regional-alliance.html

26. It should be noted that the proxy war was largely a construct of Saudi perceptions as material Iranian assistance to the Huthi rebels and their allies was minimal.

27. No systematic scientific opinion polling has ever been carried out in Saudi Arabia and the kingdom's media closely follows government positions. Consequently, many of the observations made in the following pages rely heavily upon material gathered during the author's numerous trips to Saudi Arabia and the Gulf over more than 40 years, diverse conversations with Saudis in the kingdom and outside, and close monitoring of Saudi media and government policy pronouncements, as well as the body of relevant scholarly literature.

28. The writing of this chapter was completed before the extensive arrests and detentions of members of the royal family, ministers, and prominent merchants in November 2017.

29. The classic example is the government's decision in the 1960s to enact compulsory education for girls. The trade-off involved the creation of a General Presidency for Girls' Education that was placed under the supervision of the *ulama*.

30. A pertinent example dates from 1986 when a royal decree imposed an income tax on expatriates working in the kingdom. There was a general outcry among merchants who complained in the *majlis*es of provincial governors, government ministers, and royal family members, contending that either expatriates would leave in droves or their employers would end up paying the tax through higher salaries. Less than 24 hours later, another royal decree suspended the first and no personal income taxes have ever been imposed in the KSA.

31. In recent years, the kingdom has sent around 100,000 Saudi students to the United States each year. The fact that all return home after the education may in part reflect economic opportunities in the KSA but it also validates the closeness of Saudi society.

32. Of course not all Saudi citizens have benefitted equally. Discrimination against the Shi'ah creates resentment but it does not seem to have mobilized a majority of the population into seeking an uprising. Similarly, the

segregation of women has disenfranchised them from many aspects of public life, yet it is not clear that most Saudi women are willing to take to the streets to demand equal rights.

33. Rolf Mowatt-Larssen, *Islam and the Bomb: Religious Justification For and Against Nuclear Weapons* (Cambridge, MA: Harvard Kennedy School, Belfer Center for Science and International Affairs, 2010), pp. 23–24. Mowatt-Larssen adds that Islamist extremists attempt to justify nuclear action as legitimate when used in retaliation. Ibid., pp. 25–26.

34. Ibid.; Faiqa Mahmood, "Islam and the Bomb," Arms Control Wonk website, http://www.armscontrolwonk.com/archive/1200516/islamand the bomb/, 25 Nov. 2015.

35. Norman Cigar, *Saudi Arabia and Nuclear Weapons* (London: Routledge, 2016); UCLA Center for Middle East Development Series, pp. 87–88. Cigar also notes that "Quite apart from the justification for acquiring nuclear weapons based on security concerns, the Saudis also routinely have raised the issues of justice and effectiveness in thinking on proliferation." Ibid., p. 220.

36. https://archive.org/stream/NasirAlFahd/NasirAl-fahd-TheRulingOnUs ingWeaponsOfMassDestructionAgainstTheInfidels_djvu.txt. It should be noted that neither of these two clerics, A'id al-Qarni and Nasir al-Fahd, is representative of the country's religious establishment and that the latter apparently remains under detention and may have indicated his support for the so-called Islamic State.

37. A comprehensive analysis of the strategic factors in Saudi Arabia's nuclear thinking, including discussion of Saudi reaction to the JCPOA, appeared after this chapter was written. See Op. cit. Cigar, *Saudi Arabia and Nuclear Weapons.*

38. Scott D. Sagan, "Why Do States Build Nuclear Weapons? Three Models in Search of a Bomb," *International Security*, Vol. 21, No. 3 (Winter 1996/97), pp. 54–86, quotations from p. 55.

39. Sagan, "Why Do States Build," p. 55.

40. Jacques E.C. Hymans, "No Cause for Panic: Key Lessons from the Political Science Literature on Nuclear Proliferation," *International Journal*, Vol. 69, No. 1 (2014), pp. 85–93; quotation from p. 87.

CHAPTER 5

Israeli Strategic Culture and the Iran "Preemption Scare" of 2009–2013

Gregory F. Giles

A Snapshot of Israel's Historical Engagement with Nuclear Issues

For decades, Israel has been widely perceived as a nuclear weapons state, so the focus of this chapter is not how the concept of strategic culture can be leveraged to discourage Israeli development of nuclear weapons but rather how strategic culture influences Israeli behavior with respect to maintaining its presumed nuclear weapons monopoly in the Middle East.

Preserving Israel's Nuclear Monopoly: The Begin Doctrine

Israel's national security rests, in part, on the three pillars of its nuclear policy. Namely, the indelible legacy of the Holocaust dictates that the Jewish people living in their ancestral homeland must possess the ultimate guarantor of national survival—nuclear weapons—to ensure against conventional military defeat and international isolation. Second, Israel needs to balance the benefits of nuclear possession against the risk of sparking a nuclear arms race that would leave it worse off or running afoul of the nonproliferation policy of its main supporter, the United States. Israel

G. F. Giles (✉)
Science Applications International Corporation (SAIC), Reston, Virginia, USA

© The Author(s) 2018
J. L. Johnson et al. (eds.), *Crossing Nuclear Thresholds,*
Initiatives in Strategic Studies: Issues and Policies,
https://doi.org/10.1007/978-3-319-72670-0_5

achieves this balance through "nuclear opacity," neither confirming nor denying to friend and foe alike its possession of nuclear weapons. The success of this posture stems from the willingness of the Israeli populace to forego public discussion of nuclear matters, reinforced by strict censorship laws to further discourage it. Third, Israel's enemies are presumed to be irrational, that is, not bound by the logic of mutual assured destruction, and therefore cannot be entrusted with nuclear weapons of their own. Therefore, the Jewish State must take active measures to preserve its presumed nuclear weapons monopoly.

This third pillar finds expression in Israel's proclivity to attack preemptively its adversaries' nuclear programs, using covert, overt, or unacknowledged means, as witnessed in the assassination of Egyptian scientists in the 1960s, the air strike against Iraq's Osirak reactor in 1981, and the unacknowledged destruction of Syria's al-Kibar reactor in 2007. This proclivity toward preemption is typically referred to as the "Begin Doctrine," named for Prime Minister Menachem Begin who undertook the daring 1981 raid. Begin defended the strike as "an act of supreme moral, legitimate self-defense" to save the Jewish State from another Holocaust at the hands of a "meshugana" (crazy person), Saddam Hussein.[1] To be sure, there are a variety of active measures available to derail an adversary's nuclear program, including warnings, sabotage, and, as noted, assassinations. For the purposes of analysis, however, this chapter invokes the Begin Doctrine in its most common understanding—the use of military forces to physically destroy enemy nuclear facilities.

From 2009 through 2013, Israel was seemingly gearing up to preemptively attack Iran's nuclear facilities, in part because covert and other means had failed to impede Tehran's nuclear progress. After prolonged and uncharacteristically public debate, Israel did not carry out a military strike against Iran. That outcome, like those of 1981 and 2007, was the result of the complex interaction of Israeli identity, norms, values, and perceptual lenses. Taken together, these factors can be said to constitute the country's "strategic culture," the shared interpretation of what behavior is or is not acceptable at any given time in the name of national security.

This chapter aims to address the following key questions:

- How does strategic culture explain Israel's consideration of, but failure to execute, a preemptive strike against Iran's nuclear facilities over 2009–2013?

- What influence did the United States have over this Israeli decisionmaking?
- How did Iran perceive and influence the situation?
- What does the episode and Israeli strategic culture tell us about the Jewish State's future willingness to use force against Iran's nuclear program?

The Begin Doctrine in Action: The September 2007 Destruction of Syria's Al-Kibar Reactor

As a point of departure, it is instructive to examine Israel's most recent application of the Begin Doctrine, the destruction of Syria's al-Kibar reactor.[2] Israeli intelligence managed to penetrate the Syrian Atomic Energy Commission, leading to credible evidence that the Assad regime had contracted North Korea to secretly build a plutonium production reactor at al-Kibar, in remote northeastern Syria. The reactor could only have one purpose, provide the fissile material for nuclear weapons. By March 2007, the reactor was at an advanced stage of construction.

After consulting with key Israeli officials, Prime Minister Ehud Olmert presented the matter to President George W. Bush, making it clear that the reactor was unacceptable to Israel. Olmert hoped the United States would destroy the reactor but warned if it did not, Israel was prepared to act unilaterally. Upon conferring with his advisors, President Bush informed Olmert that the United States had rejected a military option in favor of diplomacy, intending to bring Russia, China, France, and Britain into an ultimatum to Syrian President Bashar al-Assad to dismantle the reactor. Olmert expressed his disappointment at the American position, making clear that a Syrian capacity to unleash a nuclear holocaust "hits at the very serious nerves of this country."[3]

Having to go it alone, the Israeli Defense Forces (IDF) drew up its plans, and Olmert worked the constitutional approval process. Both were in place on the evening of September 5, when the air strike was launched. The raid completely destroyed the reactor without any Israeli losses. Israel kept mum and encouraged its neighbors to do the same to help encourage Assad not to retaliate and risk a wider war in the region. As Israeli intelligence had anticipated, Syria denied an Israeli attack had taken place. Damascus later sought to thwart an International Atomic Energy Agency (IAEA) investigation by sanitizing the site, although the IAEA reached the conclusion that there probably was a reactor being built at al-Kibar.

The decision to invoke the Begin Doctrine against Syria in 2007 was shaped by Israel's sense of identity, values, and norms, as well as the perceptual lens through which the leadership viewed the situation.

Identity. At center stage was the collective sense of the Israeli leadership that it bore a heavy responsibility to prevent another Holocaust from befalling the Jewish people, in this case by keeping nuclear weapons out of Syria's hands. The state imperative to protect its citizenry is by no means unique to Israel but the defining historical experience of the Nazi Holocaust accentuates it and instills in Israeli leaders a strong preference for action over passivity. But the notion that the Israeli state is sovereign in matters of national security is complicated by the nature of relations with Washington. The United States is seen by Israeli leaders as a critical, perhaps indispensable, ally of the Jewish State. Indeed, as exemplified by Prime Minister Olmert in the al-Kibar affair, the United States was expected not only to share Israel's security concerns but to agree on and carry out Israel's preferred solution, preemptive military attack. When President Bush acted otherwise, Olmert was surprised and disappointed. To balance Israeli sovereignty with the reality of US influence, Olmert carefully avoided asking for US "permission" to take out the reactor himself. While he did not seek, nor apparently receive, a "green light" from President Bush, neither did he receive a "red light" which enabled the Israeli strike to proceed without fear of US repercussions. Notably, IDF planning for a unilateral military strike appears not to have begun until it became clear that the United States would not do the job itself.

Values. The al-Kibar episode was a reinforcement of the tremendous importance the Jewish State places on keeping nuclear weapons out of the hands of its enemies but even this Israeli value had to compete with others. As noted above, maintaining good relations with Washington was a concern. Protecting the Israeli populace from enemy retaliation was another. Here, Israeli leaders hoped that the risk of retaliation could be mitigated by the particular circumstances of the situation, namely, that in contrast to Saddam Hussein in 1981, Bashar al-Assad was building his nuclear reactor in secret and therefore had real incentives not to strike back and blow his cover.

Norms. The attack on Syria in 2007 also illuminated Israeli norms. Chief among these was the need to act in accordance with Israeli constitutional law. While Prime Minister Olmert was convinced of the need to destroy the al-Kibar reactor, he could not order the strike on his own. He had to win the approval of the Ministerial Committee on Defense

(MCOD), which included political rivals. In a half-dozen meetings over five weeks, Olmert was able to persuade the MCOD to opt for a military strike. Defense Minister Ehud Barak initially advocated delaying the attack for what Olmert reportedly suspected were personal political motivations.[4] But on September 5, the Security Cabinet voted to strike—and granted Olmert, Barak, and Foreign Minister Livni sole power to approve the military approach and timing of the attack. The three voted unanimously to proceed with one of the IDF attack options that night.

The al-Kibar strike also reinforced Israeli decisionmaking patterns, namely, keeping the circle of advisors and decisionmakers quite small by virtue of their official capacities. In addition to Prime Minister Olmert, the key Israeli actors were the:

- Defense Minister (Amir Peretz until June 2007, then Ehud Barak);
- Foreign Minister (Tzipi Livni);
- Chief of Staff of the IDF (Gabi Ashkenazi);
- Director of Military Intelligence, AMAN (Amos Yadlin);
- Director of Foreign Intelligence, Mossad (Meir Dagan); and
- Director of Domestic Security, Shin Bet (Yuval Diskin).

Notably, Prime Minister Olmert also conferred individually with his predecessors: Shimon Peres and political rivals Ehud Barak and Benjamin Netanyahu. The willingness to do so underscored Olmert's sense of heightened threat, determination to act, and desire to build a political consensus. While leaking sensitive information is the norm in Israeli politics, Olmert took extraordinary measures to keep the al-Kibar deliberations secret, going so far as to meet with key figures individually at his home. Even to this day, Israeli officials will not speak of the al-Kibar incident publicly.

Perceptual Lenses. Israeli leaders approached the al-Kibar reactor as a *military* problem to be solved *militarily*. Their lack of faith in diplomacy was stark, tainted no doubt by the international stalemate over Iran's nuclear program which was in its fifth year by then with no end in sight. The military mindset among the top political leadership was reinforced by the pervasive influence of the IDF, the result of decades of conscription and the IDF's unrivaled planning expertise within the Israeli bureaucracy. The pervasive influence of the IDF over Israeli policymaking has been studied at length by Israeli scholars.[5]

Not only was al-Kibar a problem in need of a military solution, it was becoming an *urgent* problem, with the reactor soon to go critical. Often, Israeli decisionmaking is ad hoc, and tough problems get "kicked down the road" until they become dire.[6] This tends to reinforce other characteristics of Israeli identity and values. In particular, Israeli society is more accepting of military action when there is no other choice. This inclination itself is a reflection of the importance placed within Judaism on Just War.[7] The realization that the Syrian reactor would soon go "hot" and the window for decisive action would close helped to coalesce the MCOD behind the notion that they had no other choice but to attack, particularly once the United States demurred.

It would be naïve to imagine that domestic politics did not influence the Israeli decision to attack. As noted, Olmert was so concerned that the issue would be politicized that he went to extraordinary measures to shroud the leadership's deliberations in secrecy. But because he could not take credit publicly for the attack and avert Syrian retaliation, the Prime Minister was unable to accrue any political benefits himself. Indeed, Olmert's political fortunes continued to decline due to perceived mishandling of the 2006 Hezbollah conflict and allegations of personal corruption. Olmert announced in July 2008 that he would not seek re-election as leader of the Kadima Party, setting the stage for Netanyahu to take over as Prime Minister in early 2009.

These aspects of Israeli identity, values, norms, and perceptual lenses provide an important baseline for comparison with Prime Minister Netanyahu's handling of the Iranian nuclear program over 2009–2013. What was different about that period and how does strategic culture help explain the dissimilar outcome in Israeli decisionmaking?

ANALYSIS AND KEY INSIGHTS PROVIDED BY THE CULTURAL TOPOGRAPHY ANALYTICAL FRAMEWORK

Netanyahu at the Helm: "To Attack or Not to Attack"

After his first stint as Prime Minister 1996–1999, Benjamin "Bibi" Netanyahu returned to the office in February 2009. Bibi is the son of Benzion Netanyahu, a prominent Zionist with hawkish views. In 2009, Benzion said in an interview that a "vast majority of Israeli Arabs would choose to exterminate us if they had the option to do so. Because of our power they can't say this."[8] Benzion was a scholar of Judaic history and a professor at various American colleges. Bibi thus lived for a number of years in the United States; after graduating from high school in Philadelphia, he returned to Israel to serve in the IDF and was selected for the elite IDF commando unit, Sayeret Matkal. Under the command of Ehud Barak, Bibi participated in a 1972 mission to free a hijacked airliner in Tel Aviv. Netanyahu was wounded in the assault, which saved all but one of the passengers and killed or captured the hijackers. Four years later, Bibi's older brother Yonatan, serving as the commander of the Sayeret Matkal, was killed during an operation to free Israeli hostages in Entebbe, Uganda. In the early 1980s, Bibi made his first foray into politics, and returned to the United States where he served as Israel's ambassador, 1982–1984. He became Israel's youngest Prime Minister at age 47, no stranger to military daring and sacrifice, and with a deeper understanding of the United States than any of his predecessors. He routinely turned to Benzion for behind-the-scenes advice.[9]

For Bibi, the Islamic Republic of Iran was an existential menace to Israel, calling for the Jewish State's destruction and seeking the nuclear weapons that could enable it. Netanyahu invoked historical analogies, claiming that Iran was Nazi Germany and it was 1938 all over again. In his September 2009 speech to the United Nations General Assembly, he replied to Iranian President Ahmadinejad's denial of the Holocaust by waving the blueprints for Auschwitz and invoking the memory of his own family members killed by the Nazis.[10] In Netanyahu's perceptual lens, Iran was in the grip of an apocalyptic cult which would certainly use nuclear weapons if it could get its hands on them. He spoke of Ayatollah Rafsanjani, who proclaimed in 2001 that only a single nuclear weapon could destroy Israel, whereas the Muslim world could absorb multiple nuclear strikes and still prevail.[11]

Israeli public opinion showed some support for Netanyahu's views. In a survey conducted in 2009 by the Israeli Institute for National Security Studies, 21% of Israeli respondents believed that Iran would attack the Jewish State with nuclear weapons if it acquired them. The majority (35%), however, believed that Iran would threaten Israel with nuclear weapons but would refrain from actually using them for fear of Israel's presumed nuclear retaliation.[12]

With the Holocaust as his historical frame of reference, Netanyahu sought moral equivalence in order to steel Israel and the international community to preemptive action against Iran in order to avert a greater catastrophe later. He also knew how to exploit symbols of Israeli strategic culture. In a speech before the Knesset, he referenced the 2003 flyover of the Auschwitz death camp by Israeli F-15s, captured in an iconic photo that hangs in many government offices in Israel:

> This image says it all. This image epitomizes the great change in our people's history: from a people helpless before its enemies to a people that defends itself. Ultimately, when it comes to a threat to our very existence, we must not abandon our future to others. When it comes to our fate, we must rely only on ourselves.[13]

Netanyahu supplied imagery of his own, staging a photo of him sitting in the cockpit of an Israeli F-15 in August 2009 to convey a warning to Iran, just two years after the Begin Doctrine had been invoked against Syria.

Netanyahu's perceptual lens also extended to the United States and the Obama administration in particular. Like Olmert vis-à-vis Syria in 2007, Netanyahu's preference was for Washington to destroy Iran's nuclear program. The difference is Bibi said so publicly.[14] After an initially positive interaction with then-Senator Obama in 2007, Netanyahu soon came to distrust the President, first over the Palestinian issue and then over Iran. This distrust reflected the public mood by late-2009, with no more than 10% of the Israeli populace supportive of the new American president.[15] Their Oval Office encounters were charged and awkward, with Netanyahu lecturing Obama before the cameras, as if to educate the new president on the realities of the Middle East. Before long, the mistrust was mutual. Netanyahu doubted that Obama would use force to stop Iran's nuclear progress. Like Olmert, Bibi sought the President's approval or at least acquiescence for a unilateral Israeli strike.[16] US stakes were higher this time and neither would be forthcoming.

But did Netanyahu truly intend to attack Iran during the period 2009–2013? The foregoing composite sketch of identity, values, norms, and perceptual lenses would suggest "yes." Who in Israel would have known? Ehud Barak, the Defense Minister during this period, claims that he and the Prime Minister had decided to put the Israeli Air Force into action against Iran as early as 2009. However, Barak's claims are likely politically motivated. His perceptual lens is one of unseating Netanyahu, as he had done in 1999, but as Israel's savior during a period of upheaval; Charles De Gaulle is said to be his role model.[17] In the August 2015 leaked recordings of Barak's interview with his biographers, Barak wants to be seen as someone pushing hardest for the strike, in contrast to

Netanyahu who he characterized as "weak...someone who doesn't want to take difficult steps unless he's forced to...in the balance between fear and hope [Netanyahu] generally prefers to be more fearful."[18]

Not surprisingly, Israeli political culture hardly induces close confidants. Proportional representation sets the bar for entry to the Israeli Parliament very low. As a result, numerous parties are drawn into coalitions in order to achieve a governing majority. The Prime Minister, as chief broker, is constantly consumed by the need to hold his coalition together. With the different factions vying to increase their influence, policymaking deliberations are typically leaked for political advantage. For these particular reasons, as well as the importance attached to freedom of maneuver more broadly, the Prime Minister plays his or her cards very close to the vest, taking very few, if any into confidence.[19] All of this suggests that Barak's claims notwithstanding, it is likely that only Netanyahu himself knew if he really intended to strike Iran or had other objectives in mind.[20]

So Why Didn't Netanyahu Pull the Trigger?

Of the accounts that have emerged from Israel thus far, it seems that familiar leitmotifs of Israeli identity, values, and norms were present 2009–2013 but their relevance and robustness varied, and some new notes were also struck in what decisionmakers concluded was acceptable Israeli behavior towards Iran's nuclear program, namely, that overt intervention in US domestic politics was "fair game." In terms of cultural resonance, Prime Minister Netanyahu's March 2012 speech to the American Israeli Public Affairs Committee (AIPAC) in Washington, DC, could have been given by his predecessor Ehud Olmert in 2007 or Menachem Begin in 1981:

> The Jewish state will not allow those who seek our destruction to possess the means to achieve that goal. A nuclear armed Iran must be stopped ...
>
> Yet incredibly, some are prepared to accept ... a world in which the Ayatollahs have atomic bombs. Sure, they say, Iran is cruel, but it's not crazy. It's detestable but it's deterrable. My friends, responsible leaders should not bet the security of their countries on the belief that the world's most dangerous regimes won't use the world's most dangerous weapons. And I promise you that as Prime Minister, I will never gamble with the security of the State of Israel ...
>
> Of course, the best outcome would be if Iran decided to abandon its nuclear weapons program peacefully. No one would be happier than me and the people of Israel if Iran dismantled its program. But so far, that hasn't

happened. For fifteen years, I've been warning that a nuclear-armed Iran is a grave danger to my country and to the peace and security of the entire world.

For the last decade, the international community has tried diplomacy. It hasn't worked. For six years, the international community has applied sanctions. That hasn't worked either. I appreciate President Obama's recent efforts to impose even tougher sanctions against Iran. These sanctions are hurting Iran's economy, but unfortunately, Iran's nuclear program continues to march forward.

Israel has waited patiently for the international community to resolve this issue. We've waited for diplomacy to work. We've waited for sanctions to work. None of us can afford to wait much longer. As Prime Minister of Israel, I will never let my people live in the shadow of annihilation...

Today we have a state of our own. And the purpose of the Jewish state is to defend Jewish lives and to secure the Jewish future. Never again will we not be masters of the fate of our very survival. Never again. That is why Israel must always have the ability to defend itself, by itself, against any threat.

We deeply appreciate the great alliance between our two countries. But when it comes to Israel's survival, we must always remain the masters of our fate.

Ladies and Gentlemen, Israel's fate is to continue to be the forward position of freedom in the Middle East. The only place in the Middle East where minorities enjoy full civil rights; the only place in the Middle East where Arabs enjoy full civil rights; the only place in the Middle East where Christians are free to practice their faith; the only place in the Middle East where real judges protect the rule of law.[21]

All the familiar themes are there, from holocaust prevention as the raison d'être of the Jewish State, to the presumed irrationality of Israel's enemies, to the desire for American military intervention, and even Israel's democratic mores. But a single speech before a friendly foreign audience does not tell the whole tale.

Israeli values and norms are not fully deterministic; rather, they set a range of expected behaviors. They complement but can also compete with one another for prominence, particularly as they interact with other kinds of variables, such as individual ego and tangible military capacity. Indeed, Prime Minister Netanyahu may have sought to exploit Israeli strategic culture for political ends only to find it to tying his hands, as suggested by the following Israeli accounts as to why the Jewish State did not dispatch its air force against Iranian nuclear facilities during 2009–2013.

2009

While precise dates are lacking, it appears that Netanyahu had not been back in the Prime Minister's office long before he and Defense Minister Barak decided to ready the Israeli Air Force against Iran's nuclear installations. To be sure, a range of Israeli activities already had been underway to derail Iran's nuclear program, ranging from intelligence sharing with other countries to building diplomatic support for sanctions. Israel was also suspected of sabotaging Iran's nuclear program, and in time assassinating its nuclear scientists.[22] All of these actions were consistent with the Begin Doctrine and the Jewish tradition of only using force as a last resort, when there is no other choice. But a wrinkle in the planning to ultimately use force was the discovery that Iran was constructing a new enrichment facility deep beneath a mountain in Fordow where it could not be destroyed by existing Israeli "bunker buster" munitions. According to Barak, Netanyahu ordered the IDF to develop the requisite military capacity.[23]

2010

The following year, Netanyahu and Barak sought to put that military capacity into action. Bibi convened a meeting with his top six ministers, collectively referred to as the "Septet." This Inner Cabinet lacked constitutional standing but a majority there typically serves a springboard for the Prime Minister to sway the two bodies that do have constitutional authority on security affairs, the MCOD or the full Cabinet. At the session, the Prime Minister called upon IDF Chief of Staff Gabi Ashkenazi to put Israel's military forces into "P-Plus" mode, imminent readiness for a military strike on Iran.

The risks of such an alert were apparent to Ashkenazi who feared the Iranians would detect it and both sides would spiral into a war. Mossad chief Dagan also opposed the move on the grounds that the Septet did not have the authority to order it. He warned Netanyahu and Barak against "stealing a war" by issuing an illegal order. Pressed for an answer, Ashkenazi said that the IDF still lacked the operational capacity to execute a strike on Iran's nuclear sites, and in the face of Dagan's legal challenge, Netanyahu took "P-Plus" off the table. According to Barak, Ashkenazi's response stymied the Septet's ability to seek constitutional approval: "You can't go the cabinet when the [IDF] Chief of Staff says, 'excuse me, I told you no.'"[24]

2011

Some re-shuffling of the top Israeli leadership set the stage for Netanyahu and Barak's next attempt to green light a preemptive strike on Iran. In February 2011, Ashkenazi was replaced by Benny Gantz as IDF Chief of Staff. Finance Minister Yuval Steinitz, a Netanyahu loyalist, was brought into the Inner Cabinet, transforming it into the "Octet." Steinitz was a wounded veteran of the 1982 Lebanon War. That conflict had become a touch stone in Israeli strategic culture because it was not deemed to have been a "no choice" war but rather a costly and avoidable "war by choice."[25] Once again, Netanyahu brought the military and intelligence chiefs in to ascertain whether the IDF was ready to attack Iran and if he had enough support in the Octet to bring the motion forward for Cabinet authorization.

The new IDF Chief of Staff declared the capability ready but he also spelled out the very real risks involved, including a significant loss of Israeli lives. To deal with Fordow, the plan reportedly involved the landing of Israeli commandos to destroy the enrichment halls from the inside.[26] Mossad chief Dagan remained adamantly opposed to a strike and was joined by the Shin Bet director, Yuval Diskin, who made an impassioned case not to proceed.[27] Ministers Dan Meridor and Benny Begin, both of whom had served in the IDF armored corps, also were opposed.[28] Netanyahu, Barak, and Foreign Minister Lieberman (who also served in the IDF) supported a strike. It came down to Steinitz and Strategic Affairs Minister Moshe "Bogie" Ya'alon, a former IDF Chief of Staff. According to Barak, Netanyahu was confident both would support a strike but "with all the difficulties and the risks, including the possibility of losses" laid out by the IDF Chief of Staff, "You see before your very eyes how both Bogie and Steinitz melt."[29] Netanyahu could not establish a majority of the Octet in favor of attacking.

The showdown proved to be a career-ender for Dagan. After nearly a decade as Mossad chief, he took his views public. Dagan described an Israeli attack on Iran's nuclear program as the "stupidest idea [I'd] ever heard." "An attack on Iran now before exploring all other approaches is not the right way how to do it." He described Tehran as a "very rational regime...not exactly rational based on what I would call 'Western Thinking,' but no doubt they are considering all the implications of their [nuclear] actions."[30] In contrast, Dagan seemed more concerned about *Israeli* decisionmaking: "I decided to speak out because when I was in office, Diskin, Ashkenazi and I could block any dangerous adventure... Now I am afraid that there is no one to stop Bibi and Barak."[31]

Diskin, who left government service on good terms, was just as critical of Netanyahu and Barak. He accused them of "misleading the public" about the likely effectiveness of an Israeli attack on Iran's nuclear sites. Again, for all the talk of Iran's apocalyptic cult, it was *Israel's* leadership that worried Diskin: "I don't believe in a leadership that makes decisions based on messianic feelings...I have observed [Netanyahu and Barak] from up close...I fear very much that these are not the people I'd want at the wheel."[32]

2012

According to Barak, Israel most seriously considered striking Iran in early 2012. Opposition from Mossad, Shin Bet, and the IDF Chief of Staff was no longer a factor, given the turnover in those top positions. Netanyahu also appeared to have changed tactics, secretly polling key ministers individually rather than risk another "meltdown" in a group setting.[33] The attack was being readied for January but US entanglements threatened to get in the way. Just weeks before, Secretary of Defense Panetta very publicly warned that an Israeli attack on Iran would be blamed on America, leaving US interests in the region open to retaliation.[34] Austere Challenge 12, the long-planned and largest ever joint Israeli and American military exercise, would have brought US troops to Israel just as it was attacking Iran.

Barak, who was the point man on the Iran issue with Washington, sought to create enough freedom of maneuver for Israel to still launch its attack. "We intended to carry [the Iran strike] out, so I went to Panetta and asked him if we could change the date of the exercise...So they delayed it as much as they could...to a few days before the [November US Presidential] election."[35]

Instead of Israeli strike aircraft taking to the skies in early 2012, however, it was Netanyahu who took flight, to Washington for an Oval Office meeting on March 5. In the photo op prior to their meeting, President Obama implicitly reiterated Panetta's warning to Israel about not dragging the United States into a war with Iran: "I know that both the Prime Minister and I prefer to resolve this diplomatically. *We understand the costs of any military action*."[36] Netanyahu, for his part, used the President's speech to AIPAC the day before to underscore key tenets of Israeli identity, values, and norms:

[There are] two principles, longstanding principles of American policy that you reiterated yesterday in your speech—that Israel must have the ability always to defend itself by itself against any threat; and that when it comes to Israel's security, Israel has the right, the sovereign right to make its own decisions. I believe that's why you appreciate, Mr. President, that Israel must reserve the right to defend itself.

And after all, that's the very purpose of the Jewish state—to restore to the Jewish people control over our destiny. And that's why my supreme responsibility as Prime Minister of Israel is to ensure that Israel remains the master of its fate.[37]

If Netanyahu had hoped to persuade President Obama to lead the attack on Iran or at least acquiesce to an Israeli strike, he was surely disappointed. Media reports speculated that during the visit Israel sought to acquire from the United States airborne tankers and advanced "bunker buster" munitions that would have aided an Israeli strike, neither of which materialized.[38] If Obama was insisting on advance notice of an Israeli attack, he, too, may have come away disappointed.[39]

Ironically, by now, the majority of his Inner Cabinet reportedly favored a strike on Iran, but Netanyahu seemed to be in no hurry to convene it or the MCOD upon his return from Washington.[40] Barak remains vague on this point: "Things did not work out in the first part of 2012 and [the Iran strike] was pushed back toward the end [of the year]."[41]

Later in the year proved no better for Israel, however. Netanyahu and Barak appeared to have fallen into disagreement over Iran policy.[42] In April, Netanyahu's father Benzion passed away at age 102. The following month, Netanyahu had to re-shuffle the government to remain in power, bringing in the center-right Kadima party under the leadership of Shaul Mofaz. Mofaz, a former IDF Chief of Staff and Defense Minister who had served under Bibi's brother in the Entebbe raid, was known to oppose a unilateral Israeli attack on Iran's nuclear sites, believing such action should only be taken in conjunction with the United States.[43] By July, Mofaz pulled out of Netanyahu's government and, as opposition leader, announced that Kadima would not support any military "adventures" by Israel.[44] A survey of Israeli Jews conducted that month found that the senior security echelon's opposition to an Israeli attack on Iran was trusted far more than Bibi and Barak's inclination to strike.[45] In August, Secretary of Defense Panetta visited Israel, further disrupting Bibi and Barak's attack timing, followed by the aforementioned Austere Challenge exercise. In his September speech before the UN General Assembly, Netanyahu literally drew a red line across Iran's enrichment of uranium, warning that the time for decisive action against Iran would come by the following spring or summer. The year closed out with the re-election of Barak Obama in spite of Netanyahu's backing of Mitt Romney, Ehud Barak's decision to retire from politics, and no Israeli attack on Iran.

2013

With Ehud Barak out of Israeli politics in early 2013, he has had nothing to say about the state of Israeli preparations to attack Iran that year. Israeli media continued to stoke the embers of a unilateral Israeli strike on Iran's nuclear facilities, however. Much of Netanyahu's efforts were spent trying to get President Obama to commit to a red line for decisive US action against Iran's nuclear program. In March, Obama came close, telling Netanyahu that he would not allow the "P5+1" (i.e., United States, United Kingdom, France, Russia, China, and Germany) talks with Iran to run beyond the year without a major show of Iran's willingness to compromise. What the President did not tell the Prime Minister was that the United States had already opened up a secret backchannel to deal directly with the Iranians, for fear that Bibi would try to sabotage it.[46] That back channel was embraced by Hassan Rouhani who became Iran's president in August. It was not until their September meeting at the White House that Obama told Netanyahu about the secret talks.[47] Within a couple of months, the P5+1 and Iran announced their breakthrough agreement in Lausanne, Switzerland, to peacefully resolve concerns about Iran's nuclear program. For all intents and purposes, a unilateral Israeli strike on Iranian nuclear facilities had become moot by late 2013; in a poll conducted after the Lausanne breakthrough, less than half of Israeli Jews said they would now support an Israeli strike on Iran's nuclear program.[48]

ALTERNATE EXPLANATIONS OF ISRAEL'S FAILURE TO STRIKE IRAN

Within Israel, close observers of the political-military scene have been perplexed by Netanyahu and Barak's inability over a number of years to carry out a military operation they seemed to want and one that was consistent with Israeli strategic culture. Netanyahu's critics attributed the inaction to personal character flaws:

> Netanyahu is an overly cautious prime minister with an aversion to military adventurism, for reasons of personal political survival. He knew that if something went wrong with the attack and it then became public that he gave the order despite the recommendations of all of the professionals

in the security services, it would be the end of his political career. At first, he invested enormous energy in trying to convince some of the defense chiefs to adopt his position. [In time,] he finally gave up.

The question that the Israeli right should ask Netanyahu is why he didn't attack Iran in the summer of 2012. As far as Netanyahu was concerned, that summer was seemingly the ultimate moment: The heads of the security forces had left the IDF and were replaced with a new crop of generals lacking experience, charisma or influence among the public ... At the same time, the United States was caught up in a bitter presidential election, in which President Barack Obama was fighting for his second term. Netanyahu was seemingly free to act. There was nothing to prevent him from attacking Iran in July, August or September 2012, but he hesitated and eventually put his dream aside. At the time, however, there was no one to interfere in any significant way.

So why didn't he go through with it? First of all, because Netanyahu was afraid. Second, Barak made a sharp, last minute U-turn and switched to the opponents' side. And there must be other reasons.[49]

Others rationalized that Netanyahu never intended to attack Iran:

Was Netanyahu really totally committed to the attack? Did he really put the maximum pressure on his two most devoted ministers [Steinitz and Ya'alon] to get them to vote the right way? Netanyahu has practically staked his whole political career on the Iran bomb. He has declared many times that the very existence of Israel is involved. How could he allow the private considerations—moral or otherwise—of two ministers he probably does not respect very much to endanger the very existence of the nation? I have a lurking suspicion that Netanyahu had his own secret doubts about the operation, and was unconsciously rather relieved that it was obstructed by his underlings.[50]

Nor was Barak seen as decisive:

Barak is a dangerous kind of person to drive behind. The kind who might signal left, turn the steering wheel in that direction, and still turn right in the end, or the other way around. It's doubtful whether we'll ever know if he really wanted military action, or if he hoped that Netanyahu would back out in the last moment and save him from being responsible for a catastrophe.[51]

The "real" motivations behind Israel's preemption scare of 2009–2013 are thus open to interpretation. A number of realist explanations have been ascribed, ranging from distracting US and world attention from

Netanyahu's intransigence on the Palestinian issue,[52] to frightening the Europeans and Chinese to back tougher sanctions on Iran, to luring Tehran into attacking Israel and thereby dragging the United States into a war against the Islamic Republic:

> The Israeli tail wanted to wag the American dog and start a regional war, one whose end was unknown. If Churchill could recruit Roosevelt into the fight against Hitler, Netanyahu will force Obama into fighting Khamenei. But Obama isn't Roosevelt, Netanyahu isn't Churchill, and Khamenei isn't Hitler.[53]

Still another realist hypothesis was that Netanyahu sought to apply the "Syria model" to Iran's nuclear program, in the way that President Obama's threat of imminent attack persuaded Bashar al-Assad to surrender his chemical weapons in 2013.[54]

STRATEGIC CULTURE INSIGHTS

To these post-mortems, we can add a more systematic treatment from a strategic culture perspective. In that regard, and with the information currently available, we can see that while on the surface a preemptive strike against Iran's nuclear program during 2009–2013 would have been a perfectly reasonable extension of the Begin Doctrine consistent with Israeli strategic culture, in reality there were key cultural thresholds or conditions that were not, or could not be, met. In the end, these cultural inhibitions, combined with other practical considerations, proved insurmountable and made a preemptive strike unacceptable by Israeli standards. Six key factors stand out in this regard:

The last resort/no choice threshold was not satisfied. The Israeli security establishment and key figures in the political echelon did not believe that all other options to avert an Iranian nuclear threat had been exhausted and that the use of force was now justified under Jewish tradition and state practice. Again to quote Mossad chief Dagan in 2011, "An attack on Iran now before exploring all other approaches is not the right way how to do it."[55]

The existential threat condition was not satisfied. Many in the Israeli security establishment believed that in the event Iran managed to acquire nuclear weapons it could be deterred from using them against Israel. This perspective, held by such figures as former Mossad chiefs Dagan and Pardo,[56] and former President Shimon Peres,[57] provided an important counterweight to Netanyahu's messianic diatribes.

The Constitutional process was not satisfied (2010–2011). As Dagan made clear, Netanyahu's 2010 directive to put the IDF on a

"P-Plus" footing was not lawful. In 2011, Bibi did not muster a majority of his Inner Cabinet to support a strike, and so the motion never made it to a forum with the Constitutional authority to order an attack.

Israel's special relationship with the United States could not be preserved. An Israeli preemptive attack against Iranian nuclear sites would not only defy the United States, it would cost US lives in the ensuing Iranian retaliation. No amount of badgering or unprecedented interference in US domestic politics by Netanyahu could change that outcome. Indeed, Dagan noted the severe damage Netanyahu's handling of the Iran issue had done to US-Israeli relations.[58]

The Iranian nuclear problem could not be solved militarily. Even with a perceptual lens and institutional bias favoring military solutions, Israel simply lacked sufficient military capacity to conduct a successful strike with high confidence. Iran had learned the lesson of Iraq in 1981 and Syria in 2007; it had dispersed its nuclear facilities and buried them; in the case of Fordow, deep beneath a mountain. Tasked to come up with a plan, the IDF tried its best, but the distances involved and the operational challenges were enough to make two Iran hawks in the Cabinet, including a former IDF Chief of Staff, "melt." Even if an attack had been launched, Iran would soon recover and then have all the justification it needed to withdraw from the Nuclear Nonproliferation Treaty (NPT) and build the bomb, thus ending Israel's presumed nuclear monopoly and key pillar of national security.

The risk to the Israeli home front was unacceptable. The notion of preventing another Holocaust by preempting Iran's nuclear program collided with the realization that Iranian retaliation against the Israeli populace would have been overwhelming. Unlike Olmert in the Syria case, Netanyahu had been so public about attacking Iran that there could be no hiding it afterward, and to deter him Tehran had been just as outspoken that it would retaliate massively, including against the United States. In preparation, Iran had supplied Hamas to Israel's south and Hezbollah to the north with some 40,000 rockets. In addition, Iran's long-range mobile missiles would present Israel with a three-front war targeting Israeli civilians. A business research company in Israel estimated in 2012 that the financial cost alone of such retaliation to the Jewish State would be over $41 billion.[59]

In a January 2012 interview, Barak posed three key questions by which Israel would decide whether to attack Iran[60]:

1. Does Israel have the ability to cause severe damage to Iran's nuclear sites and bring about a major delay in the Iranian nuclear project? And can the military and the Israeli people withstand the inevitable counterattack?

2. Does Israel have overt or tacit support, particularly from America, for carrying out an attack?
3. Have all other possibilities for the containment of Iran's nuclear threat been exhausted, bringing Israel to the point of last resort? If so, is this the last opportunity for an attack?

From the foregoing strategic culture perspective, the answer to all three questions was a demonstrable "no." Indeed, the failure of Netanyahu and Barak to carry forward their attack plan underscored the robustness of those six cultural criteria.

How Much Influence Did the United States Have on Israeli Decisionmaking?

As former-Israeli Deputy National Security Advisor Chuck Freilich has observed, "'What the Americans think' is the single most important consideration in virtually all [Israeli] policy deliberations, exposing the [Israeli decisionmaking] system to additional approaches and options and setting limits regarding what should and should not be done."[61] As mentioned, one of Prime Minister Olmert's first steps was to take Israel's intelligence on the Syrian reactor to President Bush. He failed to get the Americans to destroy it but found that they would not interfere with Israeli efforts to do so. Netanyahu worked relentlessly for a similar outcome and failed. In the case of Iran, where the stakes for the United States were much higher, President Obama was decidedly opposed to Israeli preemption. Instead, the President worked to reassure Netanyahu that America would invoke its own military option if that became necessary to keep Iran from the bomb. These assurances took many forms, including the dispatch of several high-ranking civilian, intelligence, and military officials to Israel, particularly in 2012; presenting Netanyahu with US contingency plans for an Iran strike to show that President Obama was serious[62]; and, reportedly, joint efforts to sabotage Iran's nuclear program.[63]

Because the United States itself was not sure if Netanyahu was bluffing about an Israeli strike,[64] it would issue warnings, publicly if necessary, that would raise the stakes for Israel. In August 2012, Chairman of the Joint Chiefs of Staff Gen. Martin Dempsey told a group of journalists in London that an Israeli preemptive strike would delay but not destroy Iran's nuclear program, and the sanctions regime that was squeezing Tehran "could be undone if [Iran] was attacked prematurely," famously adding, "I don't want to be complicit if [the Israelis] choose to do it."[65] The implication that a unilateral Israeli strike would be illegal and isolating was not lost on

Israelis who pride themselves on adhering to Just War doctrine.[66] Indeed, whether by design or happenstance, Dempsey's remark effectively used Israel's strategic culture against it, adding a subtle deterrence aspect to the US-Israel relationship.

Netanyahu bristled at the notion that Israel was so beholden to the United States on this issue of vital national security. As if in denial, it seems the more he realized his hands were tied, the more he asserted Israel's right to decide for itself. Perhaps because of the time he spent in America and misplaced confidence in his understanding of it, Netanyahu intervened in US domestic politics in ways that were unimaginable to Israelis of all political persuasions. When Bibi concluded that he could not budge the President, he actively and openly supported Obama's opponent in the 2012 election. The Israeli intelligence community was particularly incensed at Netanyahu's intervention in US domestic politics, fearing the loss of critical intelligence sharing in retaliation. In the view of Dagan, "We are dependent on the Americans for strategic [intelligence and] weapons. When [US] administration leaders say that Israel is acting contrary to the American strategic interest, this is a long-term danger for Israel."[67]

Former Prime Minister Olmert was even more explicit:

What's all this talk, that we will decide alone on our fate and that we won't take anybody else into consideration? Can someone please explain to me with which airplanes we will attack if we decide to attack alone, against the opinion of others—airplanes that we built here in Israel? With which bombs will we bomb, bombs that we made by ourselves? With which special technologies will we do it, those that we made by ourselves or those that we received from other sources?[68]

As noted by Emily Landau, an Iran expert at the Institute for National Security Studies at Tel Aviv University, despite claims from Barak about technical obstacles to carrying out an Israeli strike, in the end, "Netanyahu backed away because he was getting the message that he was going too far and this could do damage [to the special relationship with the United States], this was not helpful either to Israel or to stopping Iran ... Relations with the United States is a much more substantial, real issue, but it's more difficult to give that as your explanation."[69] Thus, when they spoke in September 2012, President Obama and Netanyahu apparently reached an understanding that Israel would not strike Iran on the eve of the US presidential election.[70] In the end, the United States exercised *decisive* influence over Israeli decisionmaking.

How Did Iran Perceive and Influence the Situation?

Iran also acted in ways that constrained Netanyahu and Barak. Tehran's various power centers understood the risks of preemptive attack by Israel and/or the United States and designed their nuclear infrastructure accordingly, hardening and dispersing sites, protecting them with layered air defenses, and so on. As noted above, the Fordow enrichment facility posed enormous planning challenges for the IDF. Barak warned that once Fordow was outfitted, Iran's nuclear program would enter a "zone of immunity," beyond Israel's capacity to destroy it. Abetted by natural advantages like distance and strategic depth, Iran had ensured that a military strike against its nuclear infrastructure would be very costly for the Israelis.

Iran's defensive preparations were not foolproof, however. The introduction of the Stuxnet computer virus into the operating system at the Natanz enrichment facility, which led to the destruction of about 1000 gas centrifuges, caught Iran by complete surprise. Tehran laid the blame for this new form of attack at the feet of the Israelis and Americans.

Tehran combined its defensive posture with a heavy retaliatory component designed to deter an Israeli strike. As mentioned, missiles and rockets provided the means, backed by stern warnings. For example, in September 2010, Iran's Armed Forces Chief of Staff Gen. Hassan Firuzabadi cautioned that if Israel struck Iran's nuclear facilities, Tehran would retaliate against Israel's Dimona reactor, the heart of Israel's nuclear capability.[71] In spite of all these defensive and deterrent measures, Iran remained tense. Large exercises by the Israeli Air Force would be met by Iran's ballistic missile force being put on heightened alert.[72]

Diplomatically, Tehran exploited Netanyahu and Barak's steady drumbeat of attack threats by filing official complaints with the United Nations. This documented series of threats would help generate international sympathy for Iran, particularly among Islamic and developing states, in the event Israel made good on them. Iran also upheld its right to respond, which would help to legitimize retaliation and subsequent withdrawal from the NPT in full-out pursuit of nuclear weapons in the event of Israeli attack.

Tehran was attuned to the debate within the Israeli leadership over whether to strike Iran,[73] but that was not a major feat, given the subject's ample press coverage in Israel and the United States. Still, Iran's close reading of the situation led to a major turning point in the nuclear crisis. In August 2012, while firebrand Mahmoud Ahmadinejad was still president, Tehran started to convert a portion of its 19.75% enriched uranium gas into oxide powder for research reactor fuel rods. In the months prior,[74] Israel had been signaling that it would consider Iran's accumulation of enough 19.75% enriched uranium to supply, with further purification, a bomb's worth of material as its red line for military action. Iran's move to stay below that threshold, as detailed in IAEA reporting, is what led Netanyahu in his UN speech that September to move his red line back a few months; Barak was willing to concede almost a year.[75] Whether or not it proved a convenient excuse for Netanyahu and Barak to postpone a monumental decision they wished to avoid anyway, this shrewd move by Tehran undercut arguments in Israel that Iran was relentlessly moving toward nuclear weapons and had to be stopped militarily.

In short, Iran clearly perceived the risk of preemptive military attack by Israel, as well as the United States. Consequently, Tehran worked assiduously to deny Israel an easy target and raise the cost of attack beyond what Netanyahu ultimately was prepared to accept. Nonetheless, as Bibi's saber rattling brought the nuclear crisis to a crescendo in 2012, Tehran heeded the Jewish State's red line on enriched uranium. This pivotal move bought time for a moderate president to be elected in Tehran, the secret US-Iran back channel to mature, and a comprehensive diplomatic settlement of the Iran nuclear crisis to be reached in July 2015 under the Joint Comprehensive Plan of Action (JCPOA).

POLICY IMPLICATIONS AND RECOMMENDATIONS

The Value of Strategic Culture Analysis

The full story of the Israeli preemption scare of 2009–2013 has yet to be told. What has emerged thus far is largely a tale about the limits of Israel's influence and freedom of unilateral action. This has been a particularly hard lesson to learn for Benjamin Netanyahu and the Israeli right. While realpolitik can address the practical constraints on Israeli conduct, it is through a strategic culture paradigm that we can better appreciate how such ideational factors as identity, values, and norms led Israel's political-military establishment to conclude that an Israeli strike against Syria's nuclear program was appropriate in 2007 whereas in 2009–2013, against Iran's, it was not.

Could the United States have had greater confidence as to Netanyahu and Barak's real intentions and willingness to act vis-à-vis Iran if it had paid closer attention to Israeli strategic culture? Perhaps. As noted, the habitual inscrutability of Israel's top political echelon keeps even senior ministers guessing as to what Israeli policy is at any given moment.[76] Moreover, Israeli military preparations, including large-scale exercises, certainly had the Iranians on edge. Nonetheless, a strategic culture "checklist" of the type presented above could have been a useful indicator of whether key *Israeli* criteria for an attack related to self-identity, values, and norms were or were not being satisfied.

As we have seen, the United States can have tremendous leverage over Israeli political-military decisionmaking under the right circumstances. The prospect of reduced intelligence sharing, curtailed access to strategic weaponry, and political isolation from the United States unnerved top Israeli officials. Notably, Washington can really gain Israel's attention when it plays the Jewish State's own strategic culture, with its emphasis on ethical and democratic conduct, against it.

From a US perspective, the steadfast refusal of the Obama administration to give Israel a "green" or even "amber" light for a unilateral strike against Iran's nuclear facilities averted an unnecessary, highly costly, and unpredictable war. In contrast, on January 16, 2016, the IAEA confirmed that Iran had taken inter alia the following steps in fulfillment of the JCPOA—a deal that Netanyahu proclaimed was his sworn duty to prevent:

- Dismantled 14,000 gas centrifuges, leaving only about 5,000;
- Removed 25,000 lbs of low-enriched uranium from the country, leaving only 660 lbs, an insufficient amount to fuel a nuclear weapon;
- Removed the core from the Arak reactor and filled it with concrete, rendering it useless for producing plutonium;
- Ceased the enrichment of uranium at Fordow, dismantled centrifuges there, and converted the facility to an international scientific center prohibited from any further use of uranium;
- Adopted unprecedented intrusive monitoring arrangements by the IAEA.

In exchange for sanctions relief, these measures pushed Iran's breakout timeline to a first nuclear weapon from 2 to 3 months to a year and holds it there for a decade. In retrospect, Netanyahu's messianic rhetoric seems hollow if not reckless. In August 2015, the IDF publicly laid out its strategy and program for the following five years; Iran's nuclear program was not even mentioned as a threat to Israel.[77]

Israel's Willingness to Use Force Against Iran's Nuclear Program in the Future: Strategic Culture Guideposts

Now that Tehran has very significantly rolled back its nuclear program, international attention is shifting to ensuring Iranian compliance with the JCOPA going forward. This naturally raises questions as to what the 2009–2013 saga tells us about Israel's willingness to use force against Iran's nuclear program in the future. To begin, Tehran's documented compliance with the JCPOA implementation requirements, combined with its compliance under the interim agreement that preceded it, signifies Iran's intent to abide by the nuclear deal. If the threat of a unilateral military strike by Israel against Iran's nuclear program was moot by late 2013, it is even more remote now.

Nonetheless, Netanyahu has been unrepentant in his attitude toward the Iran nuclear deal even upon its implementation, proclaiming that Tehran still "has not relinquished its ambition to obtain nuclear weapons."[78] Moreover, Israel pointedly reserves the right to continue covert action against Iran's nuclear program.[79] What this means is that Israel and the United States will likely remain on edge indefinitely as to whether Iran is cheating on the JCPOA and what to do about it. US coordination with Israel in this regard is essential if Washington is to ensure its vital interests.

With past practice and the "special relationship" as a guide, we can safely assume that Israel will quietly bring to Washington any evidence it develops on Iranian non-compliance, as well as its own recommendations for what should be done about it. For analytical purposes, we are interested in those cases where Israel and the United States disagree on either or both accounts. The presumption will be for Washington to raise the non-compliance directly with Tehran to seek an early resolution, in coordination with the other JCPOA parties. Israel would likely resist such an approach given Iranian "duplicity" and the "demonstrated folly" of negotiations. It will probably still defer to the United States, with the proviso that if Iran does not correct the situation promptly, Israel reserves the right to take matters into its own hands.

In the event, Israel's recourse would likely be to resume covert action against the Iranian nuclear program. Covert action is more likely to pass muster with Israeli values and norms in that it dampens Iranian pressures for massive retaliation, a key constraint for overt military strikes. Israeli covert action would pose an interesting dilemma for the United States, however, as Washington seeks to balance its obligations to the Jewish State with its commitments under the JCPOA.

We can safely assume that serious Israeli consideration of an overt military strike will be limited to extreme cases of Iranian cheating, such as a secret enrichment facility. Netanyahu and Barak, whatever their political fates in the months and years ahead, will likely continue to stoke this danger if for no other reason than keeping up pressure on Iran to comply with the JCPOA. Indeed, Ehud Barak is trying to leverage the nuclear deal to overcome the constraints Israel faced during 2009–2013, advocating that the United States now provide Israel the tools to conduct a successful long-range strike against Iran's nuclear facilities, in effect, making it the enforcer of the JCPOA.[80] Presumably, Washington perceives the moral hazard in such a policy but may be inadvertently enabling it by offering Israel a major arms package as an offset to the Iran nuclear deal, featuring more strike aircraft and V-22 Osprey transports which would make an Israeli commando raid on Fordow more practical.[81]

But in the event of an Iranian "smoking gun," for example, clear evidence that it was in the process of building nuclear weapons, strategic culture tells us Israel's inclination to launch a strike could be quite high. Such brash cheating would underscore to Israeli audiences that diplomacy had patently failed and that there was "no choice" but to use force urgently to prevent Iran from completing the bomb. In such a heightened sense of crisis, the Israeli debate on whether a nuclear-armed Iran posed an existential threat to the Jewish State would be revived and perhaps distorted by the keen sense of urgency.

Iran, for its part, will not be standing still. The long-delayed deal with Russia for sophisticated S-300 air defense missiles has gone forth now that the nuclear deal has been reached. This will enable Tehran to keep up with the forthcoming improvements in Israel's air force. Thus, we may well face a replay of the 2009–2013 stalemate, wherein, despite an infusion of new aircraft, Iranian defenses and retaliatory capabilities are just as formidable and a unilateral Israeli strike remains very risky. This stalemate may well be inescapable in that, despite the Jewish State's presumed nuclear weapons possession, Israel's populace remains vulnerable to retaliation from tens of thousands of rockets in the hands of Iranian proxies, as well as hundreds of Iranian ballistic missiles. As we have seen, the safety of the Israeli public is highly valued within Israeli strategic culture.

Much will depend on the decisiveness of Israel's leadership at the time. The IDF has made clear that, notwithstanding the "P-Plus" controversy in 2010, it will faithfully execute a lawful order to strike Iran's nuclear program irrespective of the risks.[82] Despite his own apparent indecision in 2009–2013, Netanyahu has conceded nothing with respect to the need for a "green light" from the Americans. Responding to Olmert's criticism in November 2012, Bibi remarked:

> If what I just heard is that on this matter which threatens our very existence, we should just say, we should just hand the keys over to the Americans and tell them, 'You decide whether or not to destroy this project, which threatens our very existence,' well, that's one possible approach, but it's not my approach...My approach is that if we can have others take care of it, or if we can get to a point where no one has to, that's fine; but if we have no choice and we find ourselves with our backs against the wall, then we will do what we have to do in order to defend ourselves.[83]

Within Israeli strategic culture, it seems, there is no escaping the "peculiar mixture of fear rooted in the sense that Israel is dependent on the tacit support of other nations to survive, and tenacity, the fierce conviction, right or wrong, that only the Israelis can ultimately defend themselves."[84]

NOTES

1. Howard Arenstein, "Prime Minister Menachem Begin Tuesday Defended the Israeli Raid..." *United Press International*, June 9, 1981, http://www.upi.com/Archives/1981/06/09/Prime-Minister-Menachem-Begin-Tuesday-defended-the-Israeli-raid/5663360907200/
2. This section is based on two key accounts, David Makovsky's, "The Silent Strike," *The New Yorker*, September 17, 2012, http://www.newyorker.com/magazine/2012/09/17/the-silent-strike and Elliott Abrams', "Bombing the Syrian Reactor: The Untold Story," *Commentary*, February 1, 2013, https://www.commentarymagazine.com/articles/bombing-the-syrian-reactor-the-untold-story/
3. Makovsky, op. cit.
4. "The final report of the Winograd Commission, a government-appointed inquiry into the decisions involved in the 2006 war with Hezbollah, was anticipated around the end of the year and was expected to criticize Olmert for his handling of the war and weaken him politically. Olmert worried that Barak would seize upon the report's findings, trigger Olmert's ouster as Prime Minister, and lead the operation against the Syrian reactor himself." Makovsky, op. cit.
5. See, for example, Yoram Peri, *Generals in the Cabinet Room: How the Military Shapes Israeli Policy* (Washington, DC: US Institute of Peace Press, 2006).
6. Charles D. Freilich, "National Security Decision-Making in Israel: Processes, Pathologies, and Strengths," *Middle East Journal*, vol. 60, no. 4, Autumn, 2006, 646, available at: http://belfercenter.ksg.harvard.edu/files/freilich_mej_autumn_2006.pdf

7. See, Gregory F. Giles, "Change and Continuity in Israeli Strategic Culture," in *Strategic Culture and Weapons of Mass Destruction*, Jeannie L. Johnson, Kerry M. Kartcher, and Jeffrey A. Larsen, eds. (New York: Palgrave Macmillan, 2009), 97–116.

8. "Netanyahu's Father Discusses Israeli Arabs, Peace Process: Excerpts from the Exclusive *Maariv* Interview," *Promised Land*, April 4, 2009, http://www.promisedlandblog.com/?p=824

9. Douglas Martin, "Benzion Netanyahu, Hawkish Scholar, Dies at 102," *New York Times*, April 30, 2012, http://www.nytimes.com/2012/05/01/world/middleeast/benzion-netanyahu-dies-at-102.html?_r=0

10. Amy Teibel, "Israel's Netanyahu Hits Back at Iran's Holocaust Claims," *Associated Press*, September 25, 2009. Available at http://www.post-gazette.com/news/world/2009/09/25/Netanyahu-hits-back-at-Iran-Holocaust-claims/stories/200909250190

11. "Full Transcript: Prime Minister Netanyahu Speech to the United Nations General Assembly," *The Algemeiner*, September 27, 2012, http://www.algemeiner.com/2012/09/27/full-transcript-prime-minister-netanyahu-speech-to-united-nations-general-assembly-2012-video/#

12. Yehuda Ben Meir, Olena Bagno-Moldavsky, "Vox Populi: Trends in Israeli Public Opinion on National Security 2004-2009," Memorandum 106, Institute for National Security Studies, November 2010. Available at http://www.inss.org.il/uploadimages/Import/%28FILE%291291193491.pdf

13. Joel Greenberg, "After Years of Sounding the Alarm, Netanyahu Focuses World Attention on Iran," *Washington Post*, February 29, 2012, https://www.washingtonpost.com/world/middle_east/benjamin-netanyahu-invokes-holocaust-in-push-against-iran/2012/02/23/gIQAFKdkhR_story.html

14. Elad Benari, "Netanyahu: I Won't Let Iran Destroy Us," *Arutz Sheva*, August 1, 2012, http://www.israelnationalnews.com/News/News.aspx/158467#.Vpmp5FIWIfM

15. A former national director of the American Jewish Congress attributed this wariness to Obama's early push on the Palestinian issue: "The Israeli reaction to serious peacemaking efforts is nothing less than pathological — the consequence of an inability to adjust to the Jewish people's reentry into history with a state of their own following 2,000 years of powerlessness and victimhood." See Henry Siegman, "Israelis and Obama," op-ed, New York Times, November 1, 2009. Available at http://www.nytimes.com/2009/11/02/opinion/02iht-edsiegman.html?_r=2&hpw

16. Adam Entous, "Spy vs. Spy: Inside the Fraying US-Israeli Ties," *Wall Street Journal*, October 22, 2015, http://www.wsj.com/articles/spy-vs-spy-inside-the-fraying-u-s-israel-ties-1445562074

17. Mazal Mualem, "Has Israel Found Its Savior?" *Al-Monitor*, August 25, 2015, http://www.al-monitor.com/pulse/originals/2015/08/ehud-barak-tapes-attacking-iran-isaac-herzog-bibi-netanyahu.html

18. Jonathan Lis, "The Barak Tapes: Former Defense Minister Calls Netanyahu Weak and Worried," *Haaretz*, August 24, 2015, http://www.haaretz.com/israel-news/1.672624

19. Frelich, op. cit., 652.

20. Given the close political collaboration between them, the Prime Minister's wife, Sara, may be the only exception in this regard. See Ben Caspit, "How Bibi's Wife May Be His Downfall," *Al-Monitor*, December 23, 2015, http://www.al-monitor.com/pulse/originals/2015/12/sara-netanyahu-police-investigation-household-expenses.html

21. "Full Text of Netanyahu Speech to AIPAC 2012," *The Algemeiner*, March 5, 2012, http://www.algemeiner.com/2012/03/05/full-text-of-netanyahu-speech-to-aipac-2012/

22. "The Spymaster: Meir Dagan on Iran's Threat," *60 Minutes*, September 12, 2012, http://www.cbsnews.com/news/the-spymaster-meir-dagan-on-irans-threat-12-09-2012/

23. Barak Ravid, "Barak: Steinitz, Ya'alon Thwarted Iran Strike in 2011," *Haaretz*, August 23, 2015, http://www.haaretz.com/israel-news/1.672335

24. Ibid.

25. Giles, op. cit.

26. Entous, op. cit.

27. "Barak: Netanyahu Wanted to Strike Iran in 2010 and 2011, But Colleagues Blocked Him," *Times of Israel*, August 21, 2015, http://www.timesofisrael.com/barak-netanyahu-wanted-to-strike-iran-in-2010-and-2011-but-colleagues-blocked-him/

28. Yossi Melman, "Hard to Buy Barak's Claim That IDF, Ministers Tied His Hands on Iran Strike," *Jerusalem Post*, August 22, 2015, http://www.jpost.com/Middle-East/Iran/Hard-to-buy-Baraks-claim-that-IDF-ministers-tied-his-hands-on-iran-strike-412935

29. Ravid, op. cit.

30. "The Spymaster: Meir Dagan on Iran's Threat," op. cit.

31. Ethan Bronner, "A Former Spy Chief Questions the Judgment of Israeli Leaders," *New York Times*, June 3, 2011, http://www.nytimes.com/2011/06/04/world/middleeast/04mossad.html?_r=0

32. Jodi Rudoren, "Remarks by Former Official Fuel Israeli Discord on Iran," *New York Times*, April 28, 2012, http://www.nytimes.com/2012/04/29/world/middleeast/yuval-diskin-criticizes-israel-government-on-iran-nuclear-threat.html

33. "Most of Israeli Security Cabinet Backs Iran Strike," *Agence France Presse*, March 15, 2012, available at: http://www.dailystar.com.lb/News/

Middle-East/2012/Mar-15/166774-most-of-israel-security-cabinet-backs-iran-strike-report.ashx

34. *Remarks by Secretary of Defense Leon E. Panetta at the Saban Center,* US Department of Defense Transcript, December 2, 2011, http://archive.defense.gov/transcripts/transcript.aspx?transcriptid=4937

35. "Israel Called Off 2012 Strike on Iran Because It Coincided with Joint US Drill," *Times of Israel,* August 21, 2015, http://www.timesofisrael.com/israel-called-of-2012-strike-on-iran-because-it-coincided-with-joint-us-drill/

36. Emphasis added. *Remarks by President Obama and Prime Minister Netanyahu of Israel,* White House Transcript, March 5, 2012, https://www.whitehouse.gov/the-press-office/2012/03/05/remarks-president-obama-and-prime-minister-netanyahu-israel

37. Ibid.

38. "Israel Asks US for Arms That Could Aid Iran Strike," *Reuters,* March 8, 2012, http://www.reuters.com/article/us-iran-nuclear-israel-usa-idUS-BRE82717220120308

39. Reportedly, the United States had requested that Israel not attack Iran and to provide it notice of its intention to do so. Israel had refused both. See, Ronen Bergman, "Will Israel Attack Iran?" *New York Times Magazine,* January 25, 2012, http://www.nytimes.com/2012/01/29/magazine/will-israel-attack-iran.html

40. "Most of Israel Security Cabinet Backs Iran Strike," op. cit.

41. "Israel Called Off 2012 Strike on Iran Because It Coincided with Joint US Drill," op. cit.

42. Barak Ravid, "Netanyahu and Baraq Clash Ahead of Summit on Iran's Nuclear Program," *Haaretz,* April 9, 2012.

43. Juan Cole, "New Israeli Government Likely Won't Launch Iran Attack," *Informed Comment,* May 9, 2012, http://www.juancole.com/2012/05/new-israeli-government-likely-wont-launch-iran-attack.html

44. Allyn Fisher-Ilan, "Netanyahu's Ex-deputy Appears to Dissent on Iran," *Reuters,* July 23, 2012, http://www.reuters.com/article/us-israel-iran-idUSBRE86M0KX20120723

45. The survey conducted by Tel Aviv University posited that, "According to media reports, Israel's senior security echelon, including the Chief of Staff and the heads of the Mossad and the Israel Security Agency, currently oppose an Israeli attack on Iran. Prime Minister Netanyahu and Defense Minister Barak, however, say that sanctions on Iran are not helping and it is necessary to act before Iran attains nuclear weapons capability. On this issue, on whose judgment do you rely more?" Fifty-seven percent of Israeli Jews said they most trusted the IDF Chief of Staff and the heads of Mossad and Shin Bet on whether to attack Iran, whereas only 27% trusted the judgement of the Prime Minister and Defense Minister. See "The Peace Index – July 2012," Tel Aviv University. Available at

http://www.peaceindex.org/files/The%20Peace%20Index%20Data%20
-%20July%202012%282%29.pdf
46. Entous, op. cit.
47. Ibid.
48. The poll was conducted by the New Wave Research Institute on behalf of
Israel Hayom, Israel's largest circulation daily which generally supports
Netanyahu and the Likud Party. Fifty-five percent of respondents also said
they were satisfied with Bibi's opposition to the nuclear deal. See, "Poll:
Israelis Don't Believe Iran Will Stop Nuclear Program," Israel Hayom,
November 25, 2013. Available at http://www.israelhayom.com/site/
newsletter_article.php?id=13561
49. Ben Caspit, "Why Didn't Netanyahu Attack Iran?" *Al-Monitor*, June 8,
2015,   http://www.al-monitor.com/pulse/originals/2015/06/israel-
jerusalem-post-conference-dagan-ashkenazi-iran-attack.html
50. Uri Avnery, "The Israeli Generals Who Allegedly Spoilt Netanyahu's Plan
to Attack Iran," *Redress*, August, 28, 2015, http://www.redressonline.
com/2015/08/the-israeli-generals-who-allegedly-spoilt-netanyahus-
plan-to-attack-iran/
51. Nahum Barnea, "The Iran Strike That Never Was," *Ynet News*, August 21,
2015, http://www.ynetnews.com/articles/0,7340,L-4693936,00.html
52. Ethan Bronner, "Israel Faces Hard Sell in Bid to Shift Policy," *New York
Times*, May 4, 2009, http://www.nytimes.com/2009/05/04/world/
middleeast/04israel.html?_r=0. See also, Laura Rozen, "Netanyahu Aimed
to Provoke Confrontation Amid 2010 US Peace Push," *The Back Channel*,
November 7, 2012, http://backchannel.al-monitor.com/index.php/
2012/11/3098/netanyahu-intended-to-provoke-us-iran-confrontation-
amid-2010-us-peace-push/
53. Barnea, op. cit. See also, Yossi Melman, "Netanyahu Sought to Provoke,
Not Attack, Iran in 2010," *Al-Monitor*, November 7, 2012, http://www.
al-monitor.com/pulse/originals/2012/al-monitor/israel-secret-seven.
html
54. Ben Caspit, "Netanyahu Supports a 'Syria Model' for Iran," *Al-Monitor*,
October 1, 2013, http://www.al-monitor.com/pulse/originals/2013/
10/netanyahu-obama-un-speech-syria-agreement-nuclear-iran.html
55. Bronner, op. cit.
56. Barak Ravid, "Mossad Chief: Nuclear Iran Not Necessarily Existential
Threat to Israel," *Haaretz*, December 29, 2011, http://www.haaretz.
com/mossad-chief-nuclear-iran-not-necessarily-existential-threat-
to-israel-1.404227
57. "Israel's Peres Sees Containment for a Nuclear Iran," *Reuters*,
April 29, 2009, http://www.reuters.com/article/us-israel-iran-nuclear-
idUSTRE53S78020090429

58. Nahum Barnea and Shimon Schiffer, "There is a Speech. There is No Responsibility," *Yedi'ot Aharanot*, February 27, 2015. Interview with Meir Dagan, translated from Hebrew by the Open Source Center.

59. Rishon Lezion, "Cost of Israeli Iran Attack: $41.4 Billion," *United Press International*, August 21, 2012, http://www.upi.com/Top_News/Special/2012/08/21/Cost-of-Israeli-Iran-attack-414-billion/58171345556685/

60. Ronen Bergman, "Will Israel Attack Iran?" *New York Times Magazine*, January 25, 2012, http://www.nytimes.com/2012/01/29/magazine/will-israel-attack-iran.html?_r=0

61. Freilich, op. cit., 662.

62. Barak Ravid, "US Presented Netanyahu with Contingency Plan for Iran Strike," *Haaretz*, July 29, 2012, http://www.haaretz.com/israel-news/u-s-presented-netanyahu-with-contingency-plan-for-iran-strike-1.454235

63. David Sanger, "Obama Ordered Sped Up Wave of Cyberattacks Against Iran," *New York Times*, June 1, 2012, http://www.nytimes.com/2012/06/01/world/middleeast/obama-ordered-wave-of-cyberattacks-against-iran.html

64. "'Whether this [Israeli posturing about attacking Iran] was all an effort to try to pressure Obama, or whether Israel was really getting close to a decision, I don't know,' said Michéle Flournoy, who at the time was undersecretary of defense for policy." Entous, op. cit.

65. Richard Norton-Taylor, "Israeli Attack on Iran 'Would Not Stop Nuclear Programme,'" *Guardian*, August 30, 2012, http://www.theguardian.com/world/2012/aug/30/israeli-attack-iran-not-stop-nuclear

66. See, for example, Chemi Shalev, "General Dempsey Is 'Complicit' in Goading Israel to Attack Iran," *Haaretz*, September 2, 2012, http://www.haaretz.com/blogs/west-of-eden/general-dempsey-is-complicit-in-goading-israel-to-attack-iran-1.462230

67. Barnea and Schiffer, op. cit.

68. Rudoren, op. cit.

69. Ibid.

70. Entous, op. cit.

71. "Iran Says to Strike Israel Nuclear Site If Attacked," *Reuters*, September 3, 2010, http://www.reuters.com/article/uk-iran-nuclear-israel-idUKTRE6821DO20100903

72. Even before Netanyahu returned to the premiership, Iran responded to an unusually large Israeli air force exercise by moving its Shahab-3 ballistic missiles into their launch positions. "Iran Missiles Target Israeli Nukes," *Press TV*, June 30, 2008.

73. See, for example, "IRGC Journal Refers to Internal Dispute in Israel Over Attack on Iranian Nuclear Facilities," *Iran Daily Brief*, August 27, 2012,

http://www.irandailybrief.com/2012/08/27/irgc-journal-refers-to-internal-dispute-in-israel-over-attack-on-iranian-nuclear-facilities/

74. See, for example, David Makovsky, "Friendship Under Fire," February 22, 2012, *Foreign Policy*, February 22, 2012, http://foreignpolicy.com/2012/02/22/friendship-under-fire/

75. David Blair, "Israel Says Iran Has Pulled Back from the Brink of Nuclear Weapon—For Now," *Telegraph*, October 30, 2012, http://www.telegraph.co.uk/news/worldnews/middleeast/iran/9643647/Israel-says-Iran-has-pulled-back-from-the-brink-of-nuclear-weapon-for-now.html

76. Freilich, op. cit., 652.

77. Ben Caspit, "New IDF Strategy Dismisses Iran Nuclear Threat," Al-Monitor, August 17, 2015. Available at http://www.al-monitor.com/pulse/originals/2015/08/israel-new-strategy-eizenkot-terror-hezbollah-hamas-is-iran.html

78. "World's Response to Implementation of Iran Historic Nuclear Deal," *Press TV*, January 17, 2016, http://www.presstv.ir/Detail/2016/01/17/446068/world-response-jcpoa-implementation-/

79. Entous, op. cit.

80. Robert Satloff, "A Candid Conversation with Ehud Barak," December 8, 2015, Washington Institute for Near East Policy, https://www.youtube.com/watch?v=VDIJyz3Q5jI

81. Gili Cohen, "Israel, US Agree on Arms Supply in Wake of Iran Deal," *Haaretz*, November 9, 2015, http://www.haaretz.com/israel-news/.premium-1.685071

82. "Israeli Decision-Making in Turbulent Times," US National Defense University Symposium, September 30, 2015, conducted under Chatham House rules.

83. Rudoren, op. cit.

84. Bergman, op. cit.

CHAPTER 6

Cultural Underpinnings of Current Russian Nuclear and Security Strategy

Dmitry (Dima) Adamsky

This chapter highlights cultural factors that have left significant imprints on Russian military innovations, nuclear and conventional, over the last decade. In doing so, this chapter enables better understanding of current and prospective Russian strategic behavior, in the nuclear realm in particular, and demonstrates the analytical virtues of the cultural mapping method.

This chapter presumes that Russian national security style since the collapse of the Soviet Union demonstrates more continuity than change. This assumption enables us to elaborate on the existing corpus of knowledge about Russian strategic culture and to apply it to the contemporary issues of Russian foreign and security policy. This chapter argues that the cultural topography method enables better understanding of the Russian art of strategy in conventional and non-conventional realms, and promotes this argument by linking several innovative traits in Russian strategic behavior with several characteristics of Russian strategic culture.

To discuss past, present, and future Russian strategic behavior in theoretical terms, this chapter employs the lenses of the cultural topography approach outlined in the methods chapter of this book. Specifically, this chapter utilizes four main categories of the Cultural Topography Analytic

D. (Dima) Adamsky (✉)
Lauder School of Government, Diplomacy and Strategy, Interdisciplinary
Center Herzilya, Herzilya, Israel

© The Author(s) 2018
J. L. Johnson et al. (eds.), *Crossing Nuclear Thresholds*,
Initiatives in Strategic Studies: Issues and Policies,
https://doi.org/10.1007/978-3-319-72670-0_6

Framework (CTAF): norms, values, identity, and perceptual lenses. This chapter traces these categories within five aspects of Russian strategic culture: (1) the balance of moral-psychological and material factors in the culture of war, (2) a holistic approach to strategy, (3) theory-driven military innovations, (4) management and learning style, and (5) siege mentality.

Following the introduction, this chapter's first section describes current Russian geopolitical threat perceptions. The second section discusses Russia's nuclear community, and the third section outlines the evolution of Russian nuclear and cross-domain coercion strategies over the last two decades. The next section discusses five basic characteristics of Russian strategic culture, linking them to the tendencies in recent Russian strategic behavior, and situates these insights within the categories of the CTAF. Finally, the conclusion summarizes this chapter's findings and offers policy-relevant insights.

Two methodological disclaimers are due. First, this chapter does not cover all aspects of Russian strategic culture, as it does not discuss all aspects of the Russian art of strategy. It is confined, rather, to the main issues related to Russian strategic conduct and focuses on those cultural and behavioral aspects where the correlation of the former and the latter is evident. Second, the same traits of behavior may manifest different aspects of strategic culture and different categories of the CTAF. When this is the case, the discussion demonstrates how these aspects are organically interconnected within Russian strategic behavior.

RUSSIAN IDENTITY AND CURRENT GEOPOLITICAL THREAT PERCEPTIONS

To grasp contemporary Russian military theory and practice, and the accompanying thinking about nuclear coercion, it is essential to situate the discussion in the context of Russian strategic culture, and within the broader ideational milieu informing its geopolitical threat perception.

The inception of current Russian military thought emerged during a period of peculiar and enormous strategic frustration, often overlooked by the West. What matters in this strain of thought is the narrative that the Kremlin has been telling itself, its citizens, and the world for the past two decades, even if it sounds to Western ears like a counterintuitive conspiracy theory. Overall, the discourse within the strategic community demonstrates that, in keeping with the traditional Russian siege mentality, many in the Kremlin and within the entourage of Russian leadership genuinely perceive Russia as operating under a long-lasting encirclement which aims to undermine and ultimately destroy it in geopolitical terms. Its current behavior, in its eyes, is a defensive counterattack following Western aggression across various domains—in international, military, economic-energy, and internal affairs.[1]

On the global geopolitical level, Moscow perceives the United States as a usurper that has been unfairly exploiting the unipolar moment since the collapse of the Soviet Union. Washington, in its view, has manifested double standards and hypocrisy in international politics worldwide, expanding the North Atlantic Treaty Organization (NATO) eastward—first to incorporate former Warsaw Pact countries, then former Soviet republics—and then intervening in the rest of Moscow's "zone of privileged interests," thus threatening Russian sovereignty. Feeling betrayed and exploited, Moscow found supporting evidence bolstering its perception of Western aggressive intentions in the arms control sphere. Moscow saw New START (Strategic Arms Reduction Treaty), supplemented by the deployment of ballistic missile defense (BMD) and the prospect of conventional prompt global strike (CPGS) capability, as a unified counterforce concept targeting Russia's shrinking nuclear forces and aimed at nothing less than the degradation of its deterrence potential: the main guarantor of Russian national security against the backdrop of its fundamental conventional military inferiority.

Despite shared concern over global jihad, the US Global War on Terror policy following the 9/11 terrorist attacks has given Moscow more fears than solutions. Moscow has been anxious about US military influence in Central Asia and the Caucasus: Washington's Middle Eastern policy, by default or by design, gradually dismantled parts of Russia's alliance architecture and was seen as threatening the rest of it. In Moscow's view, under the smokescreen of democratization, Washington carefully orchestrated regime changes across the region, seeking to subordinate regional actors into its own sphere of influence, and away from Russia's. From Moscow's point of view, the Arab Spring and the Color Revolutions have been links in the same chain, instigated by the United States and serving its aspiration for global dominance.

In the energy sphere, where Moscow seeks to secure uninterrupted demand and supply, it also feels under attack. US competitive strategies in regional energy markets aimed at gaining access to and cultivating non-Russian regional energy sources have encouraged local actors to build energy pipelines and transit corridors outflanking and bypassing Russia, thus preventing it from realizing its energy weapon potential. These perceived battlefields with the West extend to the domestic sphere as well. Washington's continuous critique of the Kremlin's return to an authoritarian political and economic course and the curtailment of liberal democratic principles and freedoms is seen as attempted intervention into internal affairs. Moscow views US funding and support of pro-democracy activities and opposition groups as strategic subversion, not only against the ruling regime but also against Russia as a strong state. US desire to undermine the Kremlin's power at home aims, in its view, to limit Russia's ability to compete in the international arena.

From the 2008 Georgia War onward through the events of the Arab Spring, what is seen as a Western offensive incursion into the zones and spheres of privileged interests has been steadily increasing, infringing upon an area where Moscow considers itself to have hegemonic rights. In Moscow's view, Western escalation started to gather momentum in the early 2000s and reached its culmination in Ukraine in 2014, directly catalyzing Russia's rise from its knees. Yet when Moscow, which perceives itself as a great power (*derzhava*) with a historical role in the international arena, started to regain its due status as a respected and indispensable actor after being sidelined into a subordinate role in international politics during the "unipolar moment," the West redoubled its efforts to contain it. Consequently, the Kremlin started to see the current world order not only as unfavorable and unjust but also dangerous. Around the same time, Moscow crystallized its view of how the West operationalizes its aggressive aspirations in the military realm and formulated its own countermeasure: a cross-domain, asymmetrical, non-linear confrontation frequently dubbed in the West as Russian "hybrid warfare" (HW). In Moscow's eyes, however, at this moment of maximum tension, its *modus operandi* is a strategically defensive counteroffense.

THE NUCLEAR COMMUNITY AND ITS DECISIONMAKING ARCHITECTURE

The Russian nuclear community is a comprehensive set of institutions and organizations organically integrated into the broader Russian strategic architecture. A detailed outline of the whole nuclear community, its dynamics and processes, is beyond the scope of this chapter. Here, for the sake of the thematic discussion of this book, it is sufficient to identify the following key actors and organizations involved in the process of nuclear policy formulation and implementation.

The Russian nuclear triad consists of Strategic Missile Forces, operating intercontinental ballistic missiles; Long Range Aviation, operating long-range bombers; and the Navy, operating submarine-launched ballistic missiles. In addition to the strategic nuclear triad, operational-tactical nuclear capabilities are operated by the dual-use platforms of the Russian general purpose forces. In terms of the arsenal and the organization responsible for it, Russian experts lack a single opinion and consensual definition of what are tactical, operational-tactical, or non-strategic (sometimes sub-strategic) nuclear weapons—the most frequently and interchangeably used terms in the Russian professional lexicon. In various works, including military dictionaries, the classification refers to target and mission (a tactical vs. an operational level of warfare), scale of combat (regional vs. global), yield (destructive power), range, delivery platform and corps affiliation (General Purpose Forces vs. Strategic Missile Forces or Long Range Aviation), type of subordination (commanders in the theater of operations vs. high command authority), or exclusion (not part of SALT and START). Similarly, in the West, the most frequently used dividing line designates all weapons not covered by strategic arms control treaties as non-strategic.

According to this division, Russian strategic nuclear forces counted under the START treaty include intercontinental ballistic missiles or ICBMs (SS-18M3, SS-19M6, SS-25, and SS-27) operated by the Strategic Missile Forces, submarine-launched ballistic missiles or SLBMs (SS-N-18M1, SS-N-23M1, SS-N-32) operated by the Navy, and heavy, long-range bombers (Tu-95MS6/16, Tu-190) operated by Long Range Aviation. According to the "definition by exclusion," the Russian inventory of non-strategic nuclear warheads contains a variety of delivery platforms and weapon types that are assigned to the Russian General Purpose Forces. Air and Anti-Ballistic Defense forces operate S-300/400 air, coastal, and antiballistic defense systems. The Air Force operates Su-24 and Su-34 fighter bombers that only deliver bombs, whereas Tu-22M bombers deliver both missiles and bombs. Ground-launched non-strategic warheads are earmarked for use by SS-21 and SS-26 surface-to-surface missiles operated by Ground Forces. The naval non-strategic arsenal includes land-attack cruise missiles, anti-ship cruise missiles, anti-submarine rockets, anti-air missiles, torpedoes, and depth bombs. All delivery systems and platforms of the above-mentioned services are dual use for conventional and nuclear munitions and thus are operated, except for the Tu-22M, by the general purpose forces. For this reason, they are referred to here and elsewhere as non-strategic delivery systems or platforms as opposed to ICBMs, SLBMs, and Long Range (Strategic) Aviation, which are strategic nuclear platforms or weapons.[2]

The 12th Main Directorate of the Ministry of Defense, also known as the nuclear custodians, is a separate institution directly subordinate to the Minister of Defense. The directorate is responsible for the storage and maintenance of the nuclear warheads, controlling their operational-technical conditions and the provision of the arsenal, upon demand, to all legs of the nuclear triad and to the nuclear-capable general purpose forces.

Presumably, the President, the Minister of Defense, and the Chief of the General Staff (GS) are all plugged into the "nuclear football portal" and have the highest nuclear authority and sole release authority. Since the late 1980s, this senior leadership could employ, in a crisis or threatening period (*ugrazhaiustchii period*), either automatic or semi-automatic nuclear command-and-control modes.[3] Early warning system architecture providing the leadership with the decisionmaking window for nuclear use may also be seen as part of the architecture.

During peacetime and wartime, senior commanders of the nuclear triad are subordinate directly to the Chief of the GS, and to the GS itself, as the main organ responsible for the planning and execution of military operations. In 2015 the National Defense Management Center was introduced as an additional supervisory organ overseeing military and defense policy in both peacetime and wartime. As the main platform for orchestrating all national security activities, it is on par with or even above the GS in the realm of national defense policy integration and implementation.

The nuclear industry is also a very important player in designing force buildup, concept of operations, and overall strategy for the nuclear arsenal. The two most important nuclear arsenal design bureaus loom large as institutions that, together with the military and civilian brass of the above-mentioned organizations, generate policy. The first one is RFIaTs VNIIEF: the Russian Federal Nuclear Center's All-Russian Research Institute of Experimental Physics of the State Atomic Energy Corporation (ROSATOM), headquartered in Sarov (formerly Arzamas-16). The second one is RFIaTs VNIITF: the Russian Federal Nuclear Center's All-Russian Research Institute of Technical Physics of the State Atomic Energy Corporation (ROSATOM), headquartered in Snezhinsk (formerly Cheliabinsk-70). Their work is not only confined to the design of the weapons prototypes but is also directly linked to strategy, doctrine, and policy formulation. In addition, several central scientific research institutes of the Ministry of Defense which design and produce means of delivery, command and control, and early warning capabilities for the nuclear triad are also directly involved and have significant influence on strategy generation in the nuclear realm. Finally, last but not least, are several defense intellectuals, retired senior officials, and think tank experts who are not necessarily officially affiliated with the government but advise and consult on an occasional basis. These influential defense intellectuals develop strategic-theoretical concepts that can be later traced in official doctrinal documents.

Several institutions are not part of the nuclear community per se, but are systematically involved in its central process. The two most visible actors are the National Security Council and the Ministry of Foreign Affairs. Both organizations are involved in formulating national nuclear policy. The National Security Council is responsible for the staff work and publications of the main nuclear-related white papers, such as the national security strategy and its classified appendices for internal consumption. The Foreign Ministry publishes the National Foreign Policy Strategy that also reflects the Russian position on arms control and executes actual policy in this regard. The staff work on Military Doctrine takes place within the GS, which also publishes it. Segments of the intelligence community, both military and civilian, provide data and estimates underpinning threat perception formulation, directions of force buildup, and formulation of operational concepts. To a certain extent, several committees of the Russian Parliament approving budget allocations for defense and nuclear-related issues may be counted and mentioned as well. However, the most specific and up-to-date data on strategic and non-strategic nuclear forces, their state, and development programs is not transparent. This highly classified data is not presented even at closed sessions of the Russian Parliament.[4]

The Evolution of Russian Nuclear Strategy

The scope of this chapter focuses on the evolution of Russian views on the art of coercion, and on the role of nuclear weapons in it, from the post-Cold War "regional nuclear deterrence" (RND) thinking to the current "Gerasimov Doctrine." Often labeled as "hybrid warfare," this "New Generation War" is waged across several domains (nuclear, conventional, informational, etc.). Cross-domain coercion operates under the aegis of the Russian nuclear arsenal and aims to manipulate the adversary's perception, to maneuver its decisionmaking process, and to influence its strategic behavior while minimizing, compared to the industrial warfare era, the scale of kinetic force use. Current Russian operational art thus involves a nuclear dimension that can only be understood in the context of a holistic coercion campaign: an integrated whole in which non-nuclear, informational, and nuclear capabilities can be used in the pursuit of deterrence and compellence. The evolution of the Russian art of coercion involving nuclear capabilities can be divided into two periods. The first one dates from the Soviet collapse and lasted until the publication of the 2010 military doctrine. The second began in 2009, when the wave of "New Generation Warfare" (NGW) thinking started to gather momentum and remains in effect today. The first period is characterized by a strong emphasis on the role of nuclear weapons in regional deterrence. The second one is characterized by an effort to harmonize a nuclear tool of coercion, without diminishing its role, with other tools of influence across the domains, specifically with non-nuclear and informational coercion.

"Regional Nuclear Deterrence" (1991–2010)

Since the Soviet collapse, two strategies of nuclear deterrence have emerged in Russian military theory and practice. The first nuclear weapons strategy, based on a threat of massive launch on warning and retaliation strikes, aimed at deterring nuclear aggression. The second strategy, which is based on a threat of limited nuclear strikes, aims at deterring and terminating a large-scale regional conventional war. In most of the references, global deterrence rests on a strategic nuclear arsenal, and a regional one supported by non-strategic nuclear weapons (NSNW), although Russian thinking on this matter is incoherent. The causal mechanism underlying the RND concept is also unelaborated. Implicitly, it assumes that regional conventional wars would not involve values for which the adversary would tolerate the risk of even a single nuclear strike. Consequently, limited nuclear use would deter or terminate conventional hostilities, without escalation to a massive nuclear exchange. Scenario vignettes from the Russian military exercises of the last 20 years demonstrate that Russian authors believe that after a counterattack by NSNW has restored the status quo, the adversary does not turn to a nuclear retaliation and terminates hostilities.[5]

"New Generation Warfare" (2010–Present)

A body of ideas is emerging in Russian professional discourse under the rubric of "New Generation Warfare" (NGW). Western experts often dub it "Hybrid Warfare" (HW), implying that Moscow incorporates non-military, informational, cyber, nuclear, conventional, and sub-conventional tools of strategic influence in an orchestrated campaign.[6] In the center of NGW is a holistic informational (cyber) campaign, waged simultaneously on the digital-technological and cognitive-psychological fronts, which skillfully merges military and non-military capabilities across nuclear, conventional, and sub-conventional domains. Essentially, this is not a brute force strategy, but coercion that aims to manipulate the adversary's perception, to maneuver its decisionmaking process, and to influence its strategic behavior while minimizing the use of kinetic force. The nuclear component is an inseparable part of NGW, but cannot be analyzed as a standalone issue, as was the case until recently, and can be understood only in the context of this holistic coercion campaign.

The Western term *cross-domain coercion* is probably the best description of the Russian art of orchestrating *non-nuclear, informational,* and *nuclear* influence within a unified program. This art, not yet doctrinally outlined, has manifested itself during the recent standoff in Ukraine and in the Middle East and seems rather straightforward. Informational struggle choreographs all threats and moves across both conventional and nuclear, military and non-military domains to produce the most optimal correlation of trends and forces. Nuclear weapons in this concept are a coercion "master of ceremonies": by nuclear manipulations, Russia can construct a *cordon sanitaire* that gives it an immune maneuver space, a sphere of the possible, within which other forms of influence can achieve tangible results with, or preferably, without the use of force. Ideally, the image of unacceptable consequences produced by this cross-domain coercion should paralyze Western assertiveness and responsiveness. Uninterrupted informational deterrence waged on all possible fronts against all possible audiences, augmented by nuclear signaling and supplemented by intra-war coercion, constitutes an integrated cross-domain campaign. The main rationale of this enterprise is to de-escalate, or dissuade, the adversary from aggression, and impose Russia's will with minimal violence. Until the Russian operation in Syria, given the state of the Russian arsenal, and despite a quest for non-nuclear deterrence, experts agreed that regional and massive conventional conflicts could be deterred and de-escalated only through threat of, or actual, nuclear use.[7] Non-nuclear means of coercion can only enable Russia to achieve limited political goals over the enemy in the local conflict. Any form of influence above that, to effect either political goals or operational moves of a higher order, will demand nuclear coercion, at least until Russia equips itself with reconnaissance-strike complexes,[8] enabling strategic coercion with conventional, non-nuclear, means of influence.

However, this assumption may be revisited. As the contours of Russian campaign design in Syria are slowly emerging, one may assume that it may also draw from the NGW concept outlined above. In terms of threat perception, Moscow perceived the situation in Syria as the result of a US effort, albeit one which failed to conduct HW against the incumbent regime along the lines of the Libyan scenario. Moscow's demarche, driven by the interplay of several factors, manifested sophisticated orchestration of hard and soft power across military, diplomatic, and public domains. Intensive informational and active measures and a diplomatic campaign were synchronized with the military buildup, which enabled the generation of tangible operational results through sophisticated reflexive control. As such, the campaign design, at least at the initial stage, seems to reflect the NGW guideline of a 4:1 ratio of non-military and military activities. Synchronized air and informational struggle strikes that started in late September sought to prepare optimal conditions for the forthcoming ground operation led by non-Russian forces of the Moscow-led coalition.

The use of precision-guided munitions (PGMs), air power, and dual-use long-range precision strikes that the campaign has already demonstrated is unprecedented for Russia and confirms the feasibility of conventional coercion. This demonstration of performance counterbalances the skepticism of Russian commentators who argued in recent years that pre-nuclear deterrence is not a feasible option for the Russian military, since it lacks sufficient IT-RMA era capabilities and thus cannot function as a reconnaissance-strike complex. Russian operation design in Syria corresponds with characteristics of cross-domain coercion, both in terms of informational struggle (digital-technological and cognitive-psychological) and in terms of nuclear muscle flexing. Moscow operated the range of informational struggle capabilities (electronic and cyber) for the purpose of a military-diplomatic anti-access/area denial operation against adversarial activities. Establishing such an electromagnetic-cyber cordon sanitaire around the operational environment of the pro-Assad coalition can disrupt reconnaissance-strike UAVs, PGMs, aerial operations, and political-diplomatic demarches. Furthermore, dual-use platforms, both aerial and naval, existed in the theater of operations and conducted limited conventional strikes. Although these conventional strikes produced some limited battlefield effects, the main expected utility was an informational/public relations effect that enables Russian coercion signaling for regional and global purposes in current or future tensions with the West in European and Atlantic theaters.

What are potential and primary policy concerns with regard to Russian decisionmaking and potential nuclear thresholds? Three issues loom large. First is the arms race issue. While there are no indications whatsoever suggesting that Moscow may initiate any horizontal proliferation, it is safe to assume that Moscow is likely to continue to expand a vertical one—that is, to resume a nuclear arms race and further sophisticate its arsenal. The second concern relates to the fact that although Moscow currently possesses probably the lowest threshold of nuclear use worldwide, it seems that its decisionmakers, strategists, and operators encounter several serious methodological-procedural difficulties in calculating the battlefield damage inflicted on Russia that should trigger actual nuclear use. Finally, the issue of Russian cross-domain coercion that will be discussed below encapsulates the high risk of inadvertent escalation brought primarily by crisis miscalculations. In addition, this assertive nuclear doctrine may undermine, under specific circumstances, global and regional strategic stability.

CULTURAL UNDERPINNINGS OF RUSSIAN STRATEGIC BEHAVIOR

Moral-Psychological vs. Material Factors in the Culture of War

Values and norms in the Russian culture of war tend to emphasize cognitive-psychological factors over material ones. Russian military tradition has been first and foremost preoccupied with outperforming the enemy qualitatively, and its theory of victory emphasized moral superiority and fighting for a higher cause as the main sources of power. According to the Russian culture of war, battles are won by men, by spiritual and psychological power, and not by machines, technology, or material factors. With the transformation of warfare following the revolutions in military affairs, the Russian military never became techno-centric, notwithstanding its technological procurement and military modernization.[9] Even in the framework of the Russian attempts to increase the technological quality of warfare, the soft aspects of strategy and the components of morale were always *primus inter pares*, and they maintain similar status in Russian military tradition to this very day. This contrasts with the cultural inclination of the US theory of victory to build more technologically sophisticated war machines. As before, during the current nuclear and cyber eras Russian military tradition continues to perceive cognitive-psychological components as the main center of gravity of the enemy system. In keeping with this norm of Russian strategic culture, the current Russian theory of victory in recent military innovations, in a nutshell, emphasizes the soft side of strategy.

This inclination of Russian strategy is evident within the current Russian art of strategy, described above as "cross-domain coercion." Better known as the Gerasimov Doctrine, or in Russian professional parlance, "New Generation Warfare" (NGW), it manifests the inclination to the softer side of strategy in the following domains. It targets the adversary's perception and is centered around affecting the opponent's will and manipulating his strategic choices. Consequently, the role of informational struggle looms unprecedentedly large in it. Since, according to NGW, the main battlefield is consciousness, perception, and the strategic calculus of the adversary, the main operational tool is informational struggle, aimed at imposing one's strategic will on the other side. Perception, consequently, becomes a strategic center of gravity in the campaign. It is difficult to overemphasize the role that Russian official doctrine attributes to the defensive and offensive aspects of informational struggle in modern conflicts. In the framing of the NGW, nuclear and non-nuclear aspects of strategy are integrated in a holistic campaign aimed primarily at shaping, influencing, and manipulating the perceptions and decisionmaking processes of the adversary. The informational strike is about breaking the internal coherence of the enemy system—not about its integral annihilation.

In the ideal type NGW campaign, the "informational-psychological struggle" first takes a leading role, as the moral-psychological-cognitive-informational suppression of the adversary's decisionmakers and operators assures conditions for achieving victory. Informational struggle, in its turn, in the Russian interpretation, comprises both technological and psychological components designed to manipulate the adversary's picture of reality, misinform it, and eventually interfere with the decisionmaking processes of individuals, organizations, governments, and societies to influence their consciousness. Sometimes referred to as "reflexive control," it forces the adversary to act according to a false picture of reality in a predictable way, favorable to the initiator of the informational strike, and seemingly independent and benign to the target. Moral-psychological suppression and manipulation of social consciousness aims to make the population cease resisting, even supporting the attacker, due to the disillusionment and discontent with the government and disorganization of the state and military command-and-control and management functions. The end result is a desired strategic behavior.[10]

Holistic Approach to Strategy

One way to examine the Russian perceptual lens is through cognitive style. Cultural psychologists exploring Russian social interactions and communication styles define the objects of their query as a high-context culture. Similar to other cases in which collectivist, high-context, polychronic cultures exhibit a stronger degree of cognitive field dependency, scholars usually define Russian society as one with a strong inclination toward a "holistic-dialectical" cognitive style. Inferential processes of individuals from a Russian sociocultural environment have a tendency to attend to the context or field as a whole, to focus on and to assign causality to the relationships between a focal object and the field, and to explain and to predict events on the basis of such relationships. These conclusions of cultural psychologists are supported by evidence from the history of ideas and science in Russia. For centuries, intellectual circles in Russia cultivated a concentration on holistic theories as the most appropriate goal for scientific inquiry. This belief produced norms which demanded that science be multidisciplinary and that it generate a synthesis of all the possible subjects. An opposite approach was regarded as a radical fallacy of thinking.

The Russian approach to scientific inquiry is symptomatic of the mentality that influenced Soviet, and today Russian, thinking in military affairs. Scholars emphasize innate Russian cultural ability to see the big picture, with an evident impact of this grasp on theory making, military planning, and procurement. For example, in keeping with this inclination, Soviet military thought, which still serves as the main conceptual foundation to contemporary Russian strategic thinking, was multidimensional, counting intangible assets such as coherence and active measures as an integral part of the correlation of forces. As such, it was a more holistic approach than the Western one. The cognitive maps of the Soviet and American leaders during Cold War strategic interactions demonstrate that the Soviets were driven by a holistic-dialectical thinking style with a strong predisposition toward declarative knowledge. Russian military thought still adheres to the synthetic and holistic method of analysis, which guides it in developing concrete military concepts.[11] The recent Russian National Security Strategy demonstrates this inclination to a holistic grasp of reality in terms of threat perception (seeing threats as interrelated) and in terms of countermeasures (seeing them in a complex and systemic manner).[12]

A holistic approach to military thought is a predisposition that keeps with traditional Russian cognitive style and manifests itself in a consistent set of norms within the following three aspects of the Russian cross-domain coercion. First examined is the Russian approach to informational struggle. This approach is *holistic* (*kompleksnyi podhod*) as it merges digital-technological and cognitive-psychological attacks. While digital sabotage aims to disorganize, disrupt, and destroy a state's managerial capacity, psychological subversion aims to deceive the victim, discredit the leadership, and disorient and demoralize the population and the armed forces. Second, it is *unified* (*edinstvo usilii*), in that it synchronizes informational struggle warfare with kinetic and non-kinetic military means and with effects from other sources of power; and it is *unified* in terms of coopting and coordinating a spectrum of government and non-government actors—military, paramilitary, and non-military. Tools of informational struggle merge psychological-cognitive and digital-technological components of strategy. Informational struggle includes EW, computer network operations (CNO), psychological operations (PSYOPS), and *maskirovka* activities that enable an integrated informational strike (*informatsionnyi udar*) on the adversary's decisionmaking. Digital-technological and cognitive-psychological components of this informational strike are synthetically interconnected and mutually complementary.[13] Finally, the informational campaign is an *uninterrupted* (*bezpriryvnost'*) strategic effort. It is waged during "peacetime" and wartime, simultaneously in domestic, the adversary's, and international media domains and in all spheres of new media. The online "troll" armies wage battles on several fronts: informational, psychological, and, probably, digital-technological. This enables the creation of managed stability-instability across all theaters of operations.[14]

Second, NGW perception of modern warfare is interdisciplinary and multidimensional. In keeping with the holistic approach, the boundaries between internal and external threats are blurred, the threat is perceived as a cohesive whole, and the military is expected to address it in a holistic manner. The rising importance of pressuring adversaries by non-military means results in an unorthodox multidimensional merge of soft and hard power, operating non-military activities in conjunction with military (conventional and non-conventional), covert and overt operations, special forces, mercenaries, and internal opposition to achieve strategic outcomes.[15] NGW is an amalgamation of hard and soft power across various domains, through skillful application of coordinated military, diplomatic, and economic tools. In terms of efforts employed in modern operations, the ratio of non-military and military measures is 4:1, with these forms of non-military strategic competition being under the aegis of the military organization. Regime change brought by Color Revolutions, and especially by the Arab Spring (and recent events in Ukraine), is seen, within the NGW theory, as a type of warfare capitalizing on indirect action, informational campaigns, private military organizations, special operations forces, and internal protest potential, backed by the most sophisticated conventional and nuclear military capabilities.[16]

Finally, nuclear strategy is not a class in itself but a component integrated across the domains. As vignettes of Russian military exercises of the last years demonstrate, Moscow incorporates nuclear capabilities, both strategic and non-strategic, in a variety of scenarios: nuclear, conventional, and sub-conventional. Moreover, as the annual (2015) nuclear command-and-control exercise demonstrated, Moscow tends to merge strategic and non-strategic nuclear capabilities in the frame of one integrated arsenal. This emerging tendency may look like a deviation of the practice established in the last two decades, when NSNW were seen as a separate arsenal; however, it is a clear continuity from Soviet times when both strategic and non-strategic nuclear capabilities were seen as a unified arsenal.

Theory-Driven Military Innovations

In contrast to the Western approach, theory has traditionally in Russian (Tsarist and Soviet) military innovations been valued and promoted as the necessary precursor to practice and force buildups, more than the other way around. In keeping with the Russian culture of war, Soviet military science developed a distinct field that addressed the "interrelation between human being and military technology" and proved the superior role of the former over the latter. In accordance with the overriding principle that practice should be driven by theory, doctrines and concepts of operations were formulated first, and appropriate force structures were subsequently designed. Only at the end of that process was it identified what sort of technology the industry should develop and produce to satisfy the demands of the military. This deductive approach was, for the most part, fundamentally different from the American practice in this area, and has preserved itself into the present. Military science has been and is an all-encompassing discipline with several subfields that regulate professional practice from strategy and doctrine on the national level to tactics on the battlefield. In the Soviet times it was believed to have discovered the objective, almost natural, laws of war and to have developed stratagems for military operations. Like in many militaries worldwide, combat experience was considered the essential ingredient of professionalism in the Russian military. However, the primacy of developing theory had been established by the Soviet tradition as a key value and norm and has been preserved until today. Remarks of the current Chief of the GS, Gerasimov, calling to foresee and forecast the emerging change in the character of war, clearly indicate that.

Following the Great Patriotic War, a systematic thinking approach in military affairs was consciously formulated and promoted by the Soviets. The "culture of military thinking" consisted of numerous detailed methodologies and scientific postulates that regulated all aspects of intellectual activity in military affairs. It was the methodological polestar for how to think about war in a scientific fashion. To envision the nature of future war was the primary goal of Soviet military science. Specifically, it obliged Soviet military theoreticians to attend primarily to emerging discontinuities in military affairs: those fundamental changes taking place in operations and organizations under the impact of the new technologies. Soviet military science treated these qualitative leaps in warfare development as manifestations of the emergence of a new military regime. To conceptualize the scientific-technological breakthroughs that bring radical shifts in ways and means of waging war, the terms *Revolution in Military Affairs* and *Military-Technological Revolution* were introduced in Soviet military science. Applying the methodology of forecasting and foreseeing, the Soviets systematically analyzed emerging technologies to identify them as either revolutionary or evolutionary with regard to the nature of war. This "scientific" prediction, in fact, constituted the starting point for all military activity.[17]

The valuing of strategic and military theory is so pronounced within Russian strategic culture that on some occasions theory has outstripped actual capabilities, which may be non-existent at the moment in the Russian arsenal; a pattern manifest in the following aspects.

First, Russian pre-nuclear (conventional) deterrence theory was developed for more than a decade while the Russian military actually lacked operational capabilities supporting this theoretical construct. Since the mid-2000s, Russian defense intellectuals, in conjunction with staff work by the Russian military on nuclear deterrence, have been popularizing a pre-nuclear deterrence theory. A prelude to nuclear use, the concept suggests improving deterrence credibility by increasing the number of rungs on the escalation ladder. It was based on a threat of launching long-range conventional PGMs against targets inside and outside the theater of operations. Selective damage to the military and civilian infrastructure should signal the last warning before limited low-yield nuclear use. However, given the slow procurement of advanced capabilities, Russian experts then envisioned the "pre-nuclear deterrence" only as a distant prospect and did not see any non-nuclear alternative to deterring conventional aggression. In the 2010 doctrine, "non-nuclear deterrence" received a passing reference, but back then, Russia lacked a unified system of strategic deterrence that would include conventional options (codified theory, methodological apparatus, and procedures supporting it), as well as a coordinating organ orchestrating it across all domains. The 2014 doctrine codified these ideas circulating in the Russian expert community. Non-nuclear deterrence, a complex system "of foreign policy, military, and non-military measures aimed at preventing aggression by non-nuclear means," is the doctrine's main innovation. Although Russian conduct in Syria demonstrates maturation of several capabilities that may support non-nuclear coercion, practice and capabilities are still lagging behind the advanced theoretical outlines.

Second, one may observe similar tendencies in the theoretical activism of the Russian nuclear industry during the 1990s and 2000s around the notion of a new generation of nuclear weapons. Analysis of statements by the Russian nuclear industry's senior officials suggests that the fundamental scientific research of low-yield nuclear weapons with tailored effects has generated another strand of thought about nuclear deterrence of conventional aggression. Several figures from the Russian nuclear industry have been engaged in research and popularization within the Russian strategic community of conceptual products that had nothing to do with the policy outlined in white papers or with actual capabilities.[18]

Finally, the set of Russian RND ideas has often been detached from the arsenal which should supposedly support it, making it a vague notion not calibrated among different parts of the strategic community. Contradictory white papers neither reflect nor frame intellectual and professional dynamics within the nuclear and broader strategic communities. The lack of tight integration between strategy, theoretical conceptualization, and operational concepts that is evident in the Russian case is not unique. Flexible response demonstrates that establishing a coherent theater nuclear posture and streamlining it with national deterrence strategy has been a demanding and frequently unfulfilled task. Thus, the Russian case is unique, not so much when compared to other states, but primarily when observed from the perspective of Russian strategic tradition. Tsarist and Soviet military innovations demonstrated that it is not unusual for Russian doctrine to outpace actual capabilities, but not the other way around, as in the present case when the NSNW arsenal was disconnected from the strategic theory on the subject.[19]

Several factors may explain why the set of Russian RND ideas has been detached from the arsenal that should supposedly support it. First, the Western theory of deterrence was a novelty for Russian strategic studies when that intellectual activity started in the 1990s. The latter started to coopt the former systematically only during the last decade and the concept of deterrence remains under construction. Second, Russian national strategic declarations have minor bearing on the actual force posture. Contradictory white papers neither reflected nor framed intellectual and professional dynamics within the nuclear and broader strategic community. Internal norms including a lack of coordination of national security priorities and threat perceptions, coupled with bureaucratic parochialism, produced a chronic inconsistency between official nuclear policies, procurement, military-technical decisions, and theoretical thinking. Finally, historical evidence suggests that one should not set the bar too high and expect more nuclear coherence than that observed in the Russian case. Orchestrating policy, science, strategy, procurement, and execution is a challenging enterprise for any country, and particularly a nuclear power. States' national security and military policies are frequently saturated with mismatches between declarations and implementation, bureaucratic parochialism, organizational complexities, and varying views on the "theory of victory," especially during defense transformations. This is particularly relevant in the discussed case. Indeed, Russian defense spending and reforms have changed several times in the past two decades, which certainly have had some effect on coherent development of any kind of strategic plan or doctrine.

Culture of Management and Military Innovations

Identification with authority and the wish for a strong leader have characterized the Russian people over the centuries. The population saw authoritarian power as the antidote to helplessness and as a means of guarding against chaos. The inclination to be guided by strong leadership has had significant influence on the organizational and managerial culture of Russia and the USSR. Power, authority, and initiative in Russian or Soviet organizations, military and civilian alike, came from the top of the organization. In Soviet society everything was controlled, integrated, and organized hierarchically. The authoritarian center was the primary agent initiating social, economic, and technological change. Military writings, plans, innovations, and international negotiations nearly always began with a "top-down" argument. This cultural legacy of authoritarian norms was fully manifested in the role the GS played in Russian and Soviet military traditions, dubbed the "brain of the military."

In keeping with the authoritarian cultural legacy and centralist Russian mindset in management, Soviet institutions were controlled, integrated, and organized top-down. The GS, accordingly, executed the highest authority in all existing aspects of Soviet military affairs. It played a pivotal role in developing a new theory of victory and created the institutional framework for generating knowledge on the Revolution in Military Affairs. The "brain of the military" has been charged with planning and executing operations, but first and foremost its mission has been to synthesize insights of military science and develop fundamental military knowledge. The role given to the GS in the Soviet military system, the professional approach of the GS officers, and the intellectual atmosphere in its directorates enabled this brain of the military to capitalize on its intellectual potential and to develop constantly fresh military ideas about the future of war and then to distill from them strategy, doctrine, and weapons development. The GS possessed a unique triumvirate of absolute authority: to forecast future trends in the theory and practice of war, to experiment with new operational and organizational concepts, and to initiate the innovation from the top of the organizational pyramid through all the branches and services of the Soviet military. It played a far more central role in initiating military innovations than did similar organizational institutions in the West.[20]

The managerial tradition of a centralized mode of command left an imprint on the Russian approach to military innovations. As a rule, Russian military innovations originate in a top-down and not in a bottom-up manner, in a deductive rather than in an inductive manner. The resultant Russian military norms predispose Russian experts and professionals to innovate more by anticipation rather than by adaptation. Anticipation emerges in a deductive manner, and innovation, in that case, evolves in the top-down mode. This is primarily a peacetime effort that involves a great deal of imagination, systematic exploration, and a holistic grasp of the current character of war. Adaptation is primarily a wartime effort that builds on the insights produced by battleground friction and on the lessons learned from the best practices.[21]

Recent Russian military innovations and management style in military affairs do overall correspond with this cultural inclination. That said, a reality check offers a more complex picture.

During its operations in Crimea, Eastern Ukraine, and currently in Syria, Moscow has demonstrated an aptitude for organizational and conceptual learning and transformation, and a scale of improvisation that is rather unorthodox if judged by the standards of Soviet and immediate post-Soviet Russian military practice. Available sources suggest that, at least until recently, the Russian strategic community lacked a clear division of labor in the sphere of cross-domain coercion in general, and as pertains to informational struggle in particular. It seems that the lack of regulations does not constrain but stimulates Russian military theory development and operational creativity in the theaters of operations. Being in the midst of conceptual learning, and with multiple actors competing for resources and responsibilities, especially in the field of informational (cyber) warfare, the Russian strategic community manifested the coexistence of institutional incoherence and relative operational effectiveness during the recent standoffs.

Although the military exercises of the last couple of years indeed have emphasized non-nuclear forms of warfare, and military reform since 2008 has focused on improving NCW, C4ISR, and EW capabilities, the impressive performance in Crimea was not based on exercises simulating Gerasimov's doctrine and seems to be more of an improvisation rather than a preplanned strategic-operational design along NGW lines. In the subsequent operations in Ukraine, Moscow tried to replicate its success, but probably learned hard lessons about the limits of force, as additional military involvement and mechanical application of earlier practices has not enabled it to settle the situation in Donbass once and for all. Indeed, it has only drawn Russia further into a battle it neither expected nor desired. The Russian strategic community continues its learning process, transforming its doctrine, and conceptualizing a new theory of victory. The standoff in Ukraine is just one of the cases from which Russian experts are learning lessons, in keeping with Gerasimov's call in 2013 to explore new forms of struggle, to come up with military innovations, and to shape the armed forces accordingly. The current Russian campaign in the Middle East offers to the Russian defense establishment a subsequent laboratory to further refine the Russian art of strategy and demonstrates a relatively high Russian aptitude for battlefield adaptation.

Indeed, the levels of improvisation, coordination efforts' orchestration, and operational learning have been more characteristic to Israel or to the United States, to the extent that one may assume a discontinuity in the traditional Russian approach. That said, current Russian performance, in terms of a remarkable level and scale of coordination, and in terms of operational learning and adaptation, does resemble the functioning of the Soviet military during the Great Patriotic War. Also, this trait is one of the virtues of operational art: a field of knowledge and sphere of theoretical and practical activity that Russian military tradition invented and introduced into the discipline of military science worldwide. Thus, an intellectual and practical predisposition to this type of conduct is natural to Russian military tradition. Moreover, it seems that recent Russian operational and strategic effectiveness is also partially owed to the newly established National Center of Defense Management. Headed by the Minister of Defense, the center started to fulfill the function of the main strategic and operational management organ of national security, military and non-military, affairs in all theaters of operations. In a way, it plays the central management role in national security affairs while incorporating the GS—the brain of the military. In any case, the tradition of one unified organ running and orchestrating military policy stays intact.

Siege Mentality

Similar to the Israeli and Iranian cases, a key feature of the Russian strategic perceptual lens and resultant behavior is siege mentality. It incorporates a sense of inferiority, reflecting a feeling of persecution and oppression, coupled with a feeling of superiority and grand strategic aspirations. Similarly, Soviet foreign and defense policy, in rhetoric and in action, often expressed a puzzling combination of these contradictory attitudes. In the framing of the security context, in the Russian strategic mentality "both an inferiority complex and a superiority complex can be simultaneously on display: defensiveness bordering on paranoia, on the one hand, combined with assertiveness bordering on pugnacity, on the other."[22] Accordingly, to grasp contemporary Russian military theory and practice, and the accompanying thinking about nuclear coercion, it is essential to situate the discussion within the broader ideational milieu informing its geopolitical threat perception. Representing reality as it is seen from Moscow is essential in order to explain the perceptions driving Russian strategic behavior, even if this analytical disposition and Russian perception may sound counterintuitive, confusing, and contradictory. This particularly relates to discussing Russian threat perceptions and countermeasures to perceived challenges.

CONCLUSION

In keeping with the central questions explored in this book, in conjunction with findings of the other chapters, and based on the analysis offered here, what are potential trajectories of prospective Russian strategic behavior in the nuclear realm in general and with regard to crossing nuclear thresholds?

It seems that in the Russian case, the chances for horizontal proliferation are low. As of the present moment, it seems highly unlikely that Russia will seek to transfer nuclear capabilities even to allies or assist them in crossing the threshold of nuclear acquisition. Moreover, Moscow is likely to follow closely potential proliferators, both on the initiating end—such as North Korea, China, Pakistan, or Ukraine—and on the receiving end—such as Iran, Turkey, Saudi Arabia, Egypt, and the Gulf States—and to invest significant strategic energy to prevent the eventuality of the expansion of the nuclear club. That said, vertical proliferation in the form of the arms race is likely to continue further. In the context of the current Russian strategic mentality and threat perception that it generates, the chances for further reductions and new arms control treaties in the nuclear realm seem low.

Moreover, the Russian approach to arms control negotiations is likely to continue to be comprehensive and holistic, not singling out nuclear capabilities, but interconnecting them with negotiations on other strategic capabilities. From Moscow's point of view, under the most recent START, Russia's problem is not to reduce forces but to bring them up to the treaty ceilings. Moscow has started to see NSNW as a means of compensating for falling behind the United States in strategic weapons. Moscow does not take at face value declarations that BMD and PGS are intended to counter terrorists and rogue states, and deems the US justification to be a smoke-screen for its main goal: the degradation of Russian strategic nuclear deter-rence. Moscow views BMD and PGS as a unified counterforce concept targeting its shrinking strategic forces. NSNW are emphasized as a peace-time deterrent and as a wartime operational countermeasure. This threat perception is amplified by the emerging concerns about the US R&D programs on hypersonic glides. Thus, it is likely that Moscow will seek linkages between several negotiations tracks if the arms control issue becomes prominently relevant in the near future.[23]

This chapter has offered systematic insight into current and prospective Russian strategic thinking and *modus operandi* in the nuclear realm. Given strategic norms, values, identity, and perceptual lenses that Russian strate-gic behavior has recently manifested, what insights and questions may actors engaging Moscow through various competitive strategies wish to consider? Policymakers engaging Moscow on a host of geopolitical issues and charged with formulating short-, mid-, and long-term policies and competitive strategies vis-à-vis the Kremlin may wish to consider the fol-lowing three issues.

First, practitioners may benefit significantly from further employing the cultural approach to diagnose Russian strategic behavior. This chapter concurs with the premise that, emerging in a specific ideational and cul-tural context, "theories of victory," operational art, and coercion are social constructions, and their conceptualization, consequently, is not universal, but varies across strategic communities, has national characteristics, and may differ from Western strategic theory. Consequently, a "one-size-fits-all" non-tailored approach for examining operational art and coercion styles of different actors may result in strategic blunders. Scholars should examine and measure the Russian *modus operandi*, especially in the fields of nuclear and conventional coercion, in a much more idiosyncratic man-ner. The ability to explore and understand the interplay between national security aspirations, strategic culture, and military tradition in the frame-work of the emerging version of Russian operational art is crucial to any-one seeking to engage Moscow on a host of geopolitical issues.

Second, practitioners formulating policy vis-à-vis Moscow may benefit from considering the "the culminating point of deterrence." Inspired by the logic of the Clausewitzian term "culminating point of victory (attack)," the "culminating point of deterrence" refers to a moment after which additional threats may become counterproductive; instead of leading to an actor's restraint, they will provoke escalation. When the "culminating point of deterrence" is crossed, a threat becomes more likely to incite the opponent rather than to back them down. After this point, credible threats become so convincing that the adversary feels cornered with nothing to lose, assuming that the enemy is about to strike anyway, and therefore decides to preempt, thus overreacting. It is when force employment is seen as becoming this dangerous that it incites the adversary to escalate. In peacetime, this may stimulate dangerous and undesired military innovations; for example, development in the field in new generations of nuclear weapons. In both cases more is lost than gained and the deterrence program becomes a self-defeating overreaction. While practitioners lack a mechanism to diagnose this under-theorized tipping point, scholars are somewhat skeptical about the ability to determine deterrence culmination in advance—or in the midst of fighting. Although the gap between theory and practice on this matter seems difficult to bridge, the "culminating point" problem's recognition and conceptualization may enhance strategic performance. Acknowledgment by policy planners of the limitations in identifying the culminating point of deterrence calls for caution with competitive strategies.

Finally, there is an issue concerning the moments of maximum danger. Russian siege mentality, coupled with the inclination to accept conspiratorial theories, might condition Russian reality perception and crisis behavior. Imagined threat perceptions might encourage Moscow to interpret particular events through the lens of past associations, draw flawed conclusions from connecting unrelated events, and attribute non-existent aggressive intentions and capabilities to its adversaries, consequently resulting in overreaction. The fundamental distrust produced by a siege mentality and traumatic formative experiences will make it difficult to reassure Russia that the counterpart bargains in good faith and means what it says. This inclination may increase blunders at a time of strategic signaling and analysis of the enemy's actions. Russia might take genuine proposals to cooperate as fake and genuine threats as bluff. The nuclear signals sent by adversaries might be unnoticed, misunderstood, or misinterpreted, thus generating an undesired escalation. The lack of set norms or an explicit methodology in Russia for identifying when to cross the nuclear threshold of use further complicates the situation. The 2014 military doctrine reconfirmed the first use policy in response to conventional aggression that threatens territorial integrity and sovereignty. However, as of summer

2015, Russian strategic planners lack a codified procedure to estimate the conditions under which they would recommend senior leadership to de-escalate non-nuclear aggression by nuclear means. No methodology for calculating what would be an unacceptable level of damage to Russia or Russian interests, justifying crossing the nuclear use threshold, has been established. Thus, it seems that any decision concerning crossing the nuclear use threshold in response to conventional aggression would be very subjective; thus affected, possibly, by siege mentality.[24]

NOTES

1. See Dmitry (Dima) Adamsky, "Cross-Domain Coercion: The Current Russian Art of Strategy," *IFRI Proliferation Papers*, no.54, November 2015; Bobo Lo, *Russia and the New World Disorder* (Washington, DC, Brookings Institution Press with Chatham House, 2015); Anthony Cordesman, *Russia and the Color Revolution: Russian View of a World Destabilized by the US and the West* (Washington, DC, CSIS, 2014).
2. Dmitry (Dima) Adamsky, "Nuclear Incoherence: Deterrence Theory and Non-strategic Nuclear Weapons in Russia," *Journal of Strategic Studies*, vol. 37, no.1, 2014.
3. David Hoffman, *The Dead Hand* (New York: Doubleday, 2010).
4. Adamsky, 2014.
5. Ibid.
6. "Hybrid" categorization is inaccurate. The current Russian thinking and waging of war is different from HW, even if similar in some regards. Ironically, the Russian strategic community envisions its NGW, which it wages across several domains, as a response to what it sees as a Western "hybrid campaign" directed against Russia.
7. Adamksy, 2014; V.Poletaev and V. Alferov, "O neiadernom sderzhivanii," *Voennaia Mysl'*, July, no.7, 2015, pp. 3–10.
8. In Russian military terminology, reconnaissance-strike complex stands for the system that integrates long-range precision-guided munitions (strike) with the host of intelligence, surveillance and reconnaissance sensors, and command and control capabilities into one operational architecture.
9. See Dima Adamsky, *The Culture of Military Innovation: the Impact of Cultural Factors on Revolution in Military Affairs in Russia, the US and Israel* (Palo Alto: Stanford UP, 2010), pp. 42–45.
10. See Adamsky, 2015, pp. 25–27.
11. Adamsky, 2010, pp. 40–42.
12. For examples, see the complex view of threats and countermeasures in *Russian National Security Strategy*, 31 December 2015.

13. Adamsky, 2015, p. 29.
14. Ibid., p. 29.
15. Ibid., p. 25.
16. Ibid., p. 23.
17. Adamsky, 2010, pp. 44–47.
18. Adamsky, 2014.
19. Ibid.
20. Adamsky, 2010, pp. 48–50.
21. See Dmitry (Dima) Adamsky and Kjell Inge Bjerga, *Contemporary Military Innovation* (New York: Routledge, 2012).
22. Adamsky, 2010, p. 40.
23. Adamsky, 2014.
24. The problem partially rests in the inability of the Russian early warning systems to provide the leadership with the reliable notice on the incoming massive precision-guided strikes by groups of conventional low-altitude cruise missiles on military and civilian infrastructure targets. The problem is also due to the absence of criteria for defining or calculating unacceptable damage, prospective and actual, to critical social-military-economic infrastructure or to political-military command-and-control systems, by means of conventional aggression. O. Aksenov, Iu. Tret'jakov, E. Filin, "Osnovnye principi sozdaniia sistemy ocenki tekucshego I prognoziruemoga uscherba," *VM*, no. 6, 2015, pp. 68–74.

CHAPTER 7

Ukraine's Nuclear Culture: Past, Present, Future

Ekaterina Svyatets

Traditional theories of international relations, including both realism and liberalism, have somewhat overlooked the role of culture in important policy decisions. This chapter helps fill this gap and move one step closer to deciphering the role of identity, norms, values, and perceptual lenses as they are applied to nuclear proliferation and nonproliferation issues. Sociocultural factors are extremely influential in policy decisionmaking—even more so than pure power calculations.

As a case study, Ukraine in particular benefits from a cultural mapping approach. Since giving up its nuclear arsenal after the dissolution of the Soviet Union, Ukraine has not made any attempt to develop its own nuclear weapons, despite its nuclear capability. To explain Ukraine's nonproliferation, analysis of Ukraine's social circles and values related to nuclear issues helps isolate key cultural influences as explanatory factors. Additionally, such research identifies which personalities and groups in Ukrainian society may be crucial for maintaining its non-nuclear status quo.

Ukraine can be described as a young state striving to become a Western state. This identity leads to norms that prescribe cooperative initiatives

E. Svyatets (✉)
University of Southern California, Los Angeles, CA, USA

© The Author(s) 2018
J. L. Johnson et al. (eds.), *Crossing Nuclear Thresholds*,
Initiatives in Strategic Studies: Issues and Policies,
https://doi.org/10.1007/978-3-319-72670-0_7

with the West. However, the perceptual lens through which Ukrainians currently view the world and their threat matrix have largely focused on its defense against Russia. Another part of Ukraine's identity—the memory of the Chernobyl catastrophe, which has shaped the Ukrainian perceptual lens for the past two decades—is to a degree fading, and it is facing competition from the rising geopolitical concerns of its relations with Russia.

As a result of Ukraine's conflict with Russia since 2014, Ukrainian leaders and the public have started to discuss Ukraine's capacity to create nuclear weapons. Still, the government has not pursued a nuclear path, partially due to its fear of becoming a pariah state and partially because of its desire to be a part of the West. Moreover, the Ukrainian nuclear scientific community sees itself as a leader in the nonproliferation movement, and this position has become an identity that is deeply valuable to Ukrainians.

As a small state that is still struggling with its self-conceptualization, Ukraine historically has seen itself as a diplomatic, norm-abiding society. Currently, the Ukrainian government is actively pursuing the goal of economic integration with the West. However, Ukraine wants above all to be a sovereign state, keeping its post-Soviet territory intact. As Ukraine's territorial integrity has become threatened in the conflict with Russia, its leadership has started to question the norm of nuclear non-acquisition. Consequently, as one potentially effective lever or diplomatic approach to encourage the maintenance of Ukraine's non-nuclear status quo, the West should continue integrating Ukraine into the European economic space and supporting its civil society as a sovereign state. To do so, a knowledge of Ukraine's key decisionmakers and influencers is vital to the United States. This chapter looks at several key actors and how they affect the course of Ukraine's nonproliferation future. Some of these include major political figures, such as Arseniy Yatsenyuk, Leonid Kravchuk, Petro Poroshenko, and Yulia Tymoshenko; as well as the military, the eastern Ukrainian separatist movement, the nuclear scientific community, and grassroots civil movements. Additionally, this chapter explores elements of popular culture as it shapes public opinion about nuclear issues.

METHODOLOGY AND SOURCES

Ukraine is a unique historic case of a young state that is asserting its place in the international system, including the nonproliferation regime. Having survived an unprecedented nuclear tragedy—Chernobyl—the

Ukrainian case strongly benefits from a cultural approach in order to explain the country's path. Nuclear questions are very closely connected in Ukraine with the issue of nationalism, and being a non-nuclear-weapon state has become a part of Ukraine's national ideology. Analysis of this ideology and the state's norms and narratives requires a historical and sociocultural approach.[1]

Increasingly, strategic culture scholarship transcends disciplinary boundaries. Studies have not remained confined to international relations literature and traditional international relations theories but have grown to incorporate related disciplines, including nuclear engineering, philosophy, sociology, and anthropology in order to shed light on countries' nuclear decisions. Drawing on these seemingly distant disciplines may provide frameworks for analyzing nuclear weapons in light of grassroots organizations, popular culture, and media and folklore. In the particular case of Ukraine, for example, folklore can deliver novel insights by offering understanding of the public's perceptions of drastic historical events, whether positive or devastating. The Chernobyl nuclear meltdown is one such devastating event for Ukraine. Today, the topic of Chernobyl is reflected in multiple aspects—"rumors, personal narrative, children's games, short rhyming *chastushkas*, parodies of popular songs, and jokes"— forming what has been described as "nuclear" folklore. Unlike traditional government rhetoric, this folklore depicts "distrust of official actions and statements, and enumeration of the disaster's cataclysmic effects on living systems."[2]

In order to unearth Ukraine's nuclear narratives and the aspects of identity, norms, values, and perceptual lens that compose them, this chapter employs an interpretive case study method founded on the premise that social decisions are "guided in part by social constructions of meaning, and so social knowledge is contextual, dynamic, and pluralistic."[3] This approach does not look for "generalizable causal explanations but contextual understanding of the meaningfulness in human experience."[4] The research conducted here employs the interpretive tool set of the Cultural Topography Analytical Framework (CTAF) to analyze media products, statements of politicians and social figures, academic sources, and popular culture elements: books, video games, and movies as sources of cultural information. Together, they provide a window into the social context which frames security decisionmaking in contemporary Ukraine.

FACTORS STRENGTHENING NUCLEAR NONPROLIFERATION IN UKRAINE

In Ukrainian strategic culture, the country's position on nuclear weapons is simultaneously influenced by two sets of factors: those that help prevent nuclear proliferation and those that encourage it. The first set of factors, those inhibiting nuclear proliferation, is outlined in this section. These include Ukraine's lack of control over the Soviet nuclear weapons that were positioned on Ukrainian territory; the extensive Ukraine–West cooperation on nuclear matters; the legacy of Chernobyl, reflected in popular culture and survivors' accounts; the efforts of environmental nongovernmental organizations (NGOs); poor financial conditions and the economic crisis; and finally, Ukraine's identity as a young diplomatic state that considers itself a leader in the global nonproliferation movement.

Ukraine's Lack of Control of the Soviet Nuclear Arsenal

Ukraine has never been a nuclear state in the full sense. During the Soviet era, Ukraine did not exercise control over the Soviet nuclear weapons positioned on its territory, but rather simply hosted the warheads while the nuclear launch controls were located in Moscow. After the dissolution of the Soviet Union in the early 1990s, the newly sovereign state of Ukraine inherited 1,600 nuclear warheads.[5] Ukraine later "gave up" these weapons, an act of nonproliferation attributable to a mix of reasons. On one front, because of international pressure, the Kravchuk government did not have the serious option of keeping the weapons, as Russia and other guardians of the international nonproliferation regime would have been very unlikely to allow it. On another front, the Ukrainian government at the time expressed a lack of any nuclear ambition: Ukrainian Foreign Minister Anatoly Zlenko—a key decisionmaker over nuclear issues at the time—repeatedly stated that even though the nuclear warheads were still located on Ukrainian territory, the control over them was solely in Russia's possession.[6]

As a result, Ukraine transferred its Soviet-era nuclear arsenal to Russia as early as 1991, on condition of Ukraine's independence from other former Soviet states.[7] A year later, the Ukrainian government ratified the START I treaty and joined the Nuclear Nonproliferation Treaty (NPT), adopting a seven-year timeline for complete nuclear weapons elimination from Ukrainian territory. Ukraine fully kept its commitments: in October

2001, in the presence of US and Ukrainian officials, the last nuclear missile silo was destroyed in Pervomaisk by a controlled explosion.[8] In addition to removing the nuclear warheads, by 2012 Ukraine had also eliminated its entire stock of highly enriched uranium.[9]

The crucial steps in the 1990s toward becoming a non-nuclear-weapon state would not have been possible without the cooperation of Ukrainian President Leonid Kravchuk (1991–1994), who declined a belligerent nuclear proliferation route in favor of cooperation with both Russia and the West—a course Kravchuk assessed would hold greater benefit for Ukraine than pursuing independent nuclear capacity. Post-Soviet Ukraine had no production facilities for warheads, and committing to a nuclear weapons program would have required an investment of 80 billion USD. Furthermore, most of the Soviet warheads had been targeted against the United States, and keeping warheads pointed at the United States was not the newly independent Ukraine's strategy, which, on the contrary, was pursuing very friendly relations with the West in the 1990s.[10]

Ukraine's lack of control over the Soviet nuclear warheads once hosted on its land continues to affect the Ukrainian perceptual lens: nuclear weapons were never an integral part of Ukrainian national identity. As a result, key Ukrainian decisionmakers informed the public via the national media that Ukraine did not have any intention to unlawfully keep the Soviet nuclear weapons. The majority of the public agreed that the nuclear arsenal needed to be surrendered, and as a result, Ukrainian strategic culture remained nuclear-free. It must be noted (and is explained in detail below) that not all Ukrainian nuclear scholars and political leaders instantly agreed to give up the nuclear warheads—some of them did so reluctantly. Ultimately, however, the sentiment of the majority favored a non-nuclear-weapons path, and the country firmly committed to this course.

Ukraine's Identity as a Leader in the Global Nonproliferation Movement

Far from being a proliferating state, Ukraine's identity post-1991 adopted an opposite angle: Ukraine became a full cooperator with the West in global nuclear threat reduction. Such cooperation instantly provided a sense of belonging to the Western community of states and established Ukraine's place as a new player in the global nonproliferation movement. In light of the recent UN effort to ban nuclear weapons, Ukraine's early commitment to nonproliferation appears especially progressive.[11]

Beginning in the 1990s, Ukraine became involved in multiple bilateral and multilateral nuclear nonproliferation initiatives:

- Collaborating with the US Nunn–Lugar Program for dismantling Ukrainian intercontinental ballistic missiles
- Hosting the multilateral Science and Technology Center in Ukraine (STCU) and engaging over 20,000 Soviet scientists who had previously worked on Soviet weapons[12]
- Adopting IAEA safeguards (in 1995) and later signing the Additional Protocol (in 2000)
- Joining the Global Partnership against the Spread of Weapons of Mass Destruction (in 2005)
- Joining the Global Initiative to Combat Nuclear Terrorism (in 2007)
- Participating in Nuclear Security Summits (in 2010 and 2012)
- Extending the US–Ukraine Cooperative Threat Reduction Umbrella Agreement to increase safety and risk reduction at civilian nuclear facilities (in 2013)
- Building Chernobyl's $337-million landmark shelter, sponsored by the United States
- Completing the joint US–Ukraine construction of the Neutron Source Facility at the Kharkiv Institute for Physics and Technology (in 2014)[13]

Traditionally, Ukraine's civilian nuclear energy generation relied heavily on Russia's technology, but in recent years Ukraine has turned progressively to the West. The Ukrainian government's 2015 purchase of a passive hydrogen control system for the Zaporizhia nuclear power plant and announcement of plans to acquire nuclear fuel from Westinghouse (USA) instead of Russia illustrate this point. Additionally, Ukraine's EnergoAtom (also known as the National Nuclear Energy Generating Company of Ukraine) is currently working on two multibillion-dollar projects with Western partners: one is the Central Spent Fuel Storage Facility, undertaken jointly with Holtec International (USA); the second, the Sarcophagus in Chernobyl, is supported by the European Bank for Reconstruction and Development (EBRD), Vinci (France), and Bouygues S.A. (France).[14] These and other multibillion-dollar joint projects with Western organizations greatly reduce the financial risk for the Ukrainian nuclear industry and bring Ukraine more deeply into the orbit of Western influence. In addition, these projects have provided Ukraine's nuclear scientific community with relevant and important opportunities within their native economy.

The nonproliferation stance, however, of the nuclear scientific community in Ukraine should not be taken for granted. When initially confronted with the dissolution of the Soviet nuclear program, these scientists harbored fears of becoming irrelevant, and by the logic of self-preservation some argued in the 1990s in favor of Ukraine keeping its Soviet nuclear arsenal. Leading Ukrainian scientist Yakov Eisenberg proposed in 1993 that Ukraine and Russia create a dual key system for the nuclear missiles based in Ukraine, meaning that any launch of these missiles by Russia would require Ukrainian President Leonid Kravchuk's consent.[15] Eisenberg's proposal was anchored in his professional interests—as the one in charge of Kharton, a large nuclear institute in Ukraine which employed approximately 11,000 people, maintaining a nuclear weapons program seemed a valid course not only for national security but also for personal and economic security.[16] Notwithstanding the entrenched interests of the Ukrainian nuclear community, Eisenberg's proposition was abandoned, and to the relief of Western governments Kravchuk chose the path of nonproliferation. Despite the economic collapse of the 1990s, Ukraine has gradually implemented other economic incentives to keep these scientists employed, including the international projects mentioned above. Such initiatives have not only contributed to the advancement of global nuclear safety but also provided Ukrainian nuclear scientists and technicians with employment and stable income, avoiding an economic collapse among a subpopulation with a potentially dangerous knowledge base that, unchecked, could degenerate into rogue-state type nuclear proliferation.

In the 1990s and early 2000s, concern about this type of proliferation turned Western experts' attention to the safety of Ukraine's uranium stockpile and the question of whether Ukrainian personnel had sufficient economic motivation to resist selling the nuclear resources in their possession to rogue states or nonstate actors. US reports concluded that some of the nuclear material at the Kharkiv Institute of Physics and Technology (KIPT) was "secured by nothing more than an underpaid guard sitting inside a chain-link fence,"[17] and fears built among US officials that the uranium the institute possessed for civilian research might be sold to Iraq to address KIPT financial shortfalls. Concerns were fueled when one such deal became public, confirming that Yuri Orshansky, the head of Montelekt business confederation (which included several of the KIPT's sister institutions in Kharkiv), indeed tried to sell nuclear materials to Iraq in order to make ends meet for his organization. Yet due to the aforementioned political decisions made by the Ukrainian government, the institute ultimately took a less problematic course, and began to allow visits by Western inspectors and to participate in joint projects with the West instead of selling nuclear material on the black market.[18]

Ukrainian scientists came to see cooperation with the West as a major source of funding and the key to their economic prosperity. While limited cooperation with Middle Eastern countries continued even after 2002— such as participation in the Iranian Bushehr nuclear power plant construction up until 2012—Ukraine was much more in favor of protecting working relations with the West.[19] Though Khartron is still a leading enterprise for "development and production of control systems for launch vehicles, spacecraft, and orbital stations,"[20] the scientists at Khartron and other Ukrainian nuclear facilities consider themselves a part of the global scientific community and demonstrate no public intention to "go rogue" and build a nuclear weapon. The result has been the achievement of an important milestone at the UN General Assembly: in 2013, Viktor Yanukovych celebrated "the 20th anniversary of Ukraine's accession to the Treaty on Nonproliferation of Nuclear Weapons as a non-nuclear-weapon state."[21]

Unlike nuclear weapons, peaceful nuclear technology is a source of national pride for Ukraine, and the country seeks to play an important international role in the nuclear safety regime. After the Fukushima nuclear disaster, Ukraine stepped in to provide its guidance and expertise to the Japanese government. In April 2012, the secretary of the Ukrainian National Security and Defense Council (NSDC), Andriy Kliuyev, announced plans to expand nuclear safety cooperation between Ukraine and Japan, stating: "Countries that have experienced such terrible disasters at nuclear power plants are quite naturally attempting to coordinate efforts not only in tackling their consequences, but also in preventing them in future."[22] Additionally, Ukraine is cooperating with France on nuclear contamination research.[23] To legitimize its leadership status, Ukraine is trying to become an associate member of the European Organization for Nuclear Research (CERN).[24]

Nuclear safety is very important for Ukraine in no small part because of the legacy of the Chernobyl nuclear disaster, which plays a major role in Ukraine's thinking. Since 1986, when the catastrophe occurred, the Chernobyl area has remained dangerous and requires continuous attention. In 2013, Ukraine built a new repository in the Chernobyl exclusion zone for nuclear waste that came as a leftover after the decommissioning of the Chernobyl facility and other nuclear plants. The construction of the facility, which also collects radioactive waste from laboratories, hospitals, and different scientific and technical institutions, was sponsored by the EU, contributing 2 million EUR, and the United Kingdom, offering 8 million GBP. It is unlikely that Ukraine would be able to build the necessary repositories without European financial help. This repository is extremely important for nuclear waste storage, and dozens more still need to be constructed because of the large volume of nuclear waste produced annually.[25]

Keeping nuclear waste safe is also essential in preventing nuclear smuggling. In 2013, Yanukovych signed an agreement with Russia and Hungary about the transportation of nuclear materials between these countries through the territory of Ukraine, in compliance with the Vienna Convention on Civil Liability for Nuclear Damage (1963).[26] Efforts to prevent the loss of nuclear materials have further strengthened Ukrainian anti-nuclear-weapon norms and the sense of national pride related to civil nuclear technology.

Ukraine's desire to join NATO has also been an important factor in the Ukrainian anti-weapon position. In 2015, Prime Minister Arseniy Yatsenyuk, in a meeting with NATO Secretary-General Jens Stoltenberg, underscored that "… [Ukraine's] joint position with NATO allies is the key to restore the territorial integrity of the Ukrainian state and to prevent further breach of international law, international stability, and the loss of territories by independent states because of Russian military aggression."[27] Despite the lack of any assurances from NATO, Yatsenyuk emphasized that NATO membership was "very necessary for Ukraine." More than just a short-lived political sentiment, the potential for NATO membership has already become a part of Ukrainian political culture. Since pursuing acquisition of nuclear weapons would firmly eliminate whatever small chance Ukraine has of joining NATO, the desire to become part of the alliance may help reinforce Ukraine's nuclear non-acquisition norms. Given that Yatsenyuk has repeatedly stated that "full NATO membership" is "unquestionably" what the Ukrainian people want,[28] the desire to become a NATO member—however unlikely that potential is in reality—will continue to act as a stabilizing factor within Ukraine's nonproliferation culture.

Nuclear Narratives in Popular Culture: The Fear of Another Nuclear Disaster

Most of the nuclear events above, and the concept of nuclear technology in general, have found reflection in Ukrainian popular culture (jokes, movies, books, and video games), in which the Chernobyl legacy and Ukraine's hosting of Soviet nuclear weapons are two prominent elements. Far from being pro-nuclear weapons, Ukrainian popular culture focuses more readily on the dire side of nuclear technologies: the dangers of a nuclear detonation and the horrific consequences of nuclear meltdown. There is almost no glorification nor positive accounting of nuclear technologies in Ukrainian popular culture.

Popular narratives played a critical role in forming national perceptions of the Chernobyl event. Information about the tragedy was not announced by the official government media until the fourth day after the meltdown, and even then the state assured the Soviet people that the situation was completely under control and they had "nothing to worry about." The public instantly named government spokespeople "the nightingales," with the connotation in Russian culture of someone not telling the truth. In such an atmosphere, rumors were deemed by the public as more reliable than official statements.[29] Over time, other expressions of popular culture combined with early rumors to make sense of the Chernobyl disaster: short stories based on real-life events; interviews with witnesses conducted by writers and researchers; and rhymes, songs, children's games, and jokes. A typical folkloric piece strikes a somber tone:

> Votosi sedeiut (The hair is getting gray)
> Na gohvke detskoi. (On the child's head)
> Khorosho zhivetsia vsem ... (O how well everybody lives)
> Ekh, v strane sovetskoi! (In the Soviet land!)[30]

While at first glance such folklore elements might seem peripheral to political decisions, they are indicative of the deepened distrust in the government which resulted from the Chernobyl tragedy and which served to accelerate the breakdown of the Soviet Union from within. In the Ukrainian people's minds, the humanitarian disaster of Chernobyl was connected with the dysfunctional character of the Soviet system. The meltdown affected the Ukrainian people so deeply that the memory of the disaster is still important for the Ukrainian mentality as a nation. In the words of a US official memorializing the 25th anniversary of the Chernobyl incident:

> As clouds of radioactive smoke billowed across large portions of the western Soviet Union and Europe, these men and women struggled valiantly around the clock to mitigate a humanitarian disaster. Their heroic sacrifice—and the abandoned town of Pripyat—together serve as a powerful reminder that the events of Chernobyl must never be forgotten.[31]

Popular culture in post-Soviet countries (including in Ukraine) has acquired significance beyond entertainment value. *Anekdots* (jokes), for example, have become an expression of public opinion within populations that do not have a multiplicity of other outlets for free speech.[32] In Ukraine, people often use *anekdots* to express their opinion about nuclear weapons and nuclear strikes. The main themes in *anekdots* are the aversion to a first nuclear strike as an act of war, Russia's great power status and its possession of nuclear weapons, and the consequences of Chernobyl. There is almost no glorification of nuclear weapons. Outside of *anekdots*, the Chernobyl disaster is a strong theme in other avenues of Ukrainian popular culture, especially in well-known books and movies. One such movie *Chernobyl Diaries* (2012) is about tourists arriving to the city of Pripyat near the Chernobyl site. The movie shows tourists shocked at the deserted and degraded state of a formerly booming city—one to which inhabitants have not returned. The tone of the movie is somber and provides a warning to its audience that such catastrophes might easily happen again.[33]

Nuclear issues are often reflected in Ukraine's popular literature, both in fiction and in nonfiction. One such book, *Voices from Chernobyl: An Oral History of a Nuclear Disaster* by Svetlana Alexievich, became famous in Ukraine and internationally after the book was translated into English and won the 2005 nonfiction prize from the National Book Critics Circle in the United States. Alexievich later received the 2015 Nobel Prize for Literature. The book especially resonated with the readers because of the author's devastating description of how "her sister was killed and her mother was blinded" during the Chernobyl accident—providing a poignant narrative of the great potential danger of nuclear technologies.[34] Five years earlier, another novel, *The Sky Unwashed* by Irene Zabytko, had focused on the lives of Chernobyl's survivors who were facing increased rates of cancer and other health consequences as a result of the nuclear disaster. International literary critics highly praised the book as a reminder that behind the blur of statistics and sterile academic discussions, there were real people who were living and dying proof of Chernobyl's lasting legacy.[35]

Literature on this topic was published even as early as the 1990s. *The Nuclear Century: Chernobyl*, by Vladimir S. Gubarev, describes in detail how the Chernobyl meltdown happened and how it was dealt with by the government, providing a sobering account of what can go wrong with nuclear energy production.[36] Only 3,000 copies of the book were published, but the volume became so popular that the author wrote two more related books: *Nuclear Century: The Bomb* and *Nuclear Century: Plutonium*. All of these works relate the historic account of nuclear development, and especially the negative consequences of such development. Books such as Alexievich's, Zabytko's, and Gubarev's serve as a reminder in Ukrainian popular literature about the perils of nuclear technologies, maintaining the narrative that behind the nuclear bravado there are human tragedies and ruined health—a narrative powerful enough that there have been almost no books in Ukraine that instead promote the opposite concept of the "glory" of nuclear proliferation and the "need" to develop nuclear weapons again.

It is a common belief that young people read fewer books than in the past, relying more on the gaming industry for entertainment. Computer games in Ukraine are another slice of popular culture featuring artifacts that showcase the dangers of housing nuclear weapons on Ukrainian soil. An example is the popular game "Stalker," made by the Kiev-based company GSC Game World, whose installments include "Call of Pripyat," "Shadow of Chernobyl," and "Clear Sky." The games realistically recreate such aspects of the Chernobyl area as the Exclusion Zone, the Red Forest, and abandoned cities such as Prypiat and the nuclear power plant itself, "portraying the zone as a land of creepy people and mutated animals." It is possible that the game's extraordinary success—thousands of fans turned out on Kiev's Independence Square when GSC Game World hosted a launch party[37]—could be taken as a sign that a sort of paradoxical nuclear legacy has started to emerge in Ukraine, wherein the younger generation which has not witnessed nuclear meltdown and its aftereffects first-hand has developed a sort of pride in the dark legacy of Chernobyl. However, the physical damages and lasting aftereffects of the nuclear disaster graphically depicted in the game still bring the narrative of the risks of nuclear technology prominently into the sphere of the younger generation, albeit in a manner that young people may relate to differently than older generations.

Non-governmental Organizations as Drivers of Ecological Awareness and Nonproliferation Norms

Ukrainian NGOs focused on environmental and economic development are especially interested in and active on nuclear issues, and play an important role as influencers in the public opinion domain. Among the most active such NGOs are the Chernobyl's Children Centre, the Children of Chernobyl Relief Fund, Greenpeace Ukraine, the National EcoCentre of Ukraine, the "Naturalist" League for Protection of Rights for Life and Balance in Nature, and the Ukrainian Society for Sustainable Development. Also playing a prominent role are the Ukrainian Youth Environmental League, Ecological Education Publishing House, Donetsk Environmental Council, Podolsk Ecological Society, Eco-Centre K, the Committee for Global Environmental Issues and International Tourism, the Odessa Socio-Ecological Union, and the Young Ecologist Club.[38] While NGOs are not directly consulted by the Ukrainian government in political decisionmaking, the work of these organizations on the topical focus of nuclear and environmental issues creates a "spillover effect" as those involved in these organizations share their agenda in Ukrainian civil society.

In addition, similar to Ukraine's scientific community, Ukrainian NGOs have actively worked to integrate themselves with European civil society. A coalition of leading Ukrainian NGOs have organized themselves into the Ukrainian Think Tanks Liaison Office in Brussels, whose mission is to "build a permanent and independent center of a joint action of the Ukrainian think tanks community in order to support and advance European integration of Ukraine."[39] It is notable that notwithstanding the development of affairs in Crimea and east Ukraine, none of these NGOs have been seen to advocate a breakout from the European path of nonproliferation, and most in fact are anti-nuclear. The efforts of Ukrainian NGOs to keep Ukraine a non-nuclear-weapon state have not faced a significant challenge thus far, as Ukraine has not yet made any visible attempts to "go nuclear."

NUCLEAR "ENABLING" FACTORS POTENTIALLY WEAKENING UKRAINE'S NON-NUCLEAR STATUS

The conditions identified in the previous section which support a narrative of nonproliferation in Ukraine are experiencing a measure of counterinfluence by nuclear "enabling" factors. These influences, potentially pressuring the Ukrainian state to depart from its 26-year course as a non-nuclear-weapon state, include the presence of latent nuclear skills and technology, the ongoing conflict with Russia, emerging pro-nuclear sentiment by leading public figures, and an overall increase in pro-nuclear public opinion. Notwithstanding Ukraine's established adherence to the nonproliferation regime, this norm could be weakened by a chain of events and disappointments experienced in recent years by the Ukrainian government and population.

Nuclear Weapon Technology Latency

Due to its Soviet nuclear past, Ukraine retains significant nuclear expertise, fuel cycle capability, and a large civilian nuclear power program. Some experts and commentators accentuate the elements of reluctance that existed during Ukraine's transfer of Soviet nuclear weapons to Russia, even asserting that in 1993 the Ukrainian government was "on the brink of declaring Ukraine an interim nuclear weapons state and of postponing accession to the NPT" because the government had not received enough financial assistance and security guarantees from the Russian government. To ease these concerns and facilitate the disarmament process (Ukraine had about 670 bomber warheads on its territory at the time), the United States agreed to purchase 500 metric tons of highly enriched uranium from the former Soviet arsenal, providing Ukraine with financial motivation to dismantle the warheads.[40] It may be argued that there was also an element of intellectual ownership over the Soviet nuclear weapons, as scientific institutions such as the Kharkiv Institute for Physics and Technology (formerly known as the Ukrainian Institute for Physics and Technology—UIPhT) contributed to the creation of Soviet nuclear weapons and to the fundamental design for the atomic bomb.[41]

A central perception of Ukrainian pro-nuclear circles in this period was that nuclear weapon possession was a symbol of equality with Russia. Even then-President Leonid Kravchuk stated that "Ukraine's nuclear ownership did not contradict the NPT since the country did not aspire to operational control over its weapons."[42] As of 2017, Ukraine's relationship with Russia is still a factor in nuclear debates, becoming an especially important issue after Russia's annexation of Crimea following the referendum of March 16, 2014, which took place in response to Ukrainian President Viktor Yanukovych's ousting and the 2014 Maidan demonstrations in favor of joining the EU economic cooperation treaty. Though the Crimean referendum was deemed illegitimate by the Ukrainian government and most Western governments,[43] the peninsula moved firmly under Russian control.

After the annexation, officials and experts in east European states started to voice opinions about how nuclear deterrence could have been potentially helpful in protecting Ukraine's territorial integrity, arguing that "[t]he message received over the past few months by countries bordering the Russian Federation is: If you have nuclear weapons, never give them up; if you don't, try to get the Americans to shield you with theirs."[44] Such sentiments have surfaced in Ukraine in the form of public bitterness about surrendering the Soviet nuclear stockpile in the 1990s, but even several Russian experts have supported this view. Andrei Illarionov, former economic adviser to Russian President Vladimir Putin, noted that "Iran, North Korea, and other prospective nuclear countries will conclude that the only way to guarantee their own territorial integrity is by being nuclear powers." He continued that "if Ukraine had not given up its nuclear weapons, Russia would never have dared interfere in Crimea."[45] In 2014, Ukraine's National Security and Defense Committee considered a "bill to reestablish Ukraine as a nuclear power and demand financial compensation for Russia's violation of its territory," although this proposal did not become law.[46]

The global nuclear community has been divided on whether it is technologically and financially possible for Ukraine to restore nuclear weapons if the Ukrainian government chooses to follow that path. Scholarly debate surrounding Ukraine's nuclear weapon latency, which is defined in the literature as "the expected time to be taken by a non-nuclear weapons state to develop a conventionally deliverable nuclear weapon given the state's position on a path toward or away from a nuclear weapon and accounting for the state's motivations and intentions,"[47] has led to a variety of predictions concerning Ukraine's future course. Notwithstanding Ukraine's nuclear past, some experts such as Joseph Cirincione of the Ploughshares Fund argue that "fears of nuclear fallout from the Ukraine crisis are unfounded."[48]

In the meantime, the nuclear technology that Ukraine heavily relies upon is in the form of nuclear energy, an area in which the country has extensive scientific talent. The share of nuclear power in the country's electricity generation is about 50% (8.234 GW), and Ukraine's official energy strategy has stated that "nuclear power will continue to play a significant role in Ukraine's energy portfolio for the foreseeable future."[49] Ukraine's recent economic downturn, however, has negatively affected the country's nuclear energy sector. Utilities in Ukraine (Energoatom and Turboatom) are state-controlled and financed from the national budget, and the economic crisis of 2014–2015 led to diminished infrastructure spending, as the state budget itself had been on the decline and the national currency (hryvnia) had collapsed in value. Financing in the energy and utilities sector dropped by 17% in 2015, and the decrease in financing and value continued in 2016.[50] According to Ukrainian Energy Minister Volodymyr Demchyshyn, 5 of the state's 15 nuclear power units were shut down for repairs in 2015.[51]

Nevertheless, the share of nuclear energy in the country's electricity supply continues to expand. For example, in 2015, the Ukrenergo plant announced a plan to build a new 220 kV power transmission line to the Luhansk region from Russia's Novovoronezhskaya nuclear power plant and Ukraine's Zaporizhia.[52] Ukraine also plans to build six new nuclear power units (including two new reactors at the Khmelnitsky power plant) by 2020 worth 5.3 billion USD. A difficult politico-economic complication is presented, however: since Ukraine's finances are in disarray, the construction will be mostly financed by Russia. This dependence creates a rift among those who are comfortable continuing to rely on Russia for power plant expansion and those who want to become more self-sufficient in nuclear technology.[53]

In sum, Ukraine's potential nuclear capability does exist, both in civilian applications and in nuclear weapon design, and therefore the state's nonproliferation path is based mostly on political will, rather than on the lack of technology.

The Perceptual Lens of the Conflict with Russia

Ukraine as a society currently views the world largely through the lens of the conflict with Russia. Although the 2014 Crimea crisis is hardly the first time Russia's and Ukraine's economic and cultural interests have clashed—previous areas of conflict include Ukraine's hosting the Russian fleet, natural gas price disputes, and the Orange Revolution—the current ongoing conflict tips the tension in the relationship between the two countries to a new level. Russia is again seen as a threat to Ukraine's existence as an independent sovereign state,[54] and grievances and bitterness against "the big neighbor" (Russia) have become deeply embedded in Ukrainian culture and popular sentiments.

After Crimea joined Russia, key Ukrainian politicians made emotional statements about Russia's disregard of the Budapest Memorandum, which guaranteed Ukraine's territorial integrity. Key influencers within Ukrainian society have fostered public resentment over Ukraine's relinquishing of its nuclear weapons in the 1990s, repeating the implied refrain that had the weapons still been in Ukraine, they would have served as a powerful deterrent against Russia's actions. Historical revisions have also played a role leading up to the current conflict: perceptions of current events by the Ukrainian public are informed by the historical memory of such events as the mass starvation in the 1920s, the Soviet cruelty to Don Cossacks, the Banderovtsy movement of WWII, and Nikita Khrushchev's gift of Crimea to Ukraine. These historical events are a source of national grievances both in Ukraine and in Russia. Ukrainian key decisionmakers have also been concerned for years about the expansion of Russia's military influence via the Collective Security Treaty Organization (CSTO), as Russia "has invested tens of billions of dollars in upgrading its army."[55]

A key point in Ukraine's current tenuous relations with Russia began when a separatist movement in eastern Ukraine emerged in 2013 after Ukrainian President Viktor Yanukovych backed out of an association agreement with the European Union. The association agreement, which had been a "priority" for the Ukrainian government, was supposed to integrate the Ukrainian economy with the European Union's (short of the EU membership) and create a free trade zone.[56] Yanukovych's decision not to sign the Agreement created a huge wave of disappointment and anger among Ukrainians eager to become closer to Europe. In early December 2013, more than 350,000 people took to the streets to protest Yanukovych's decision and to call for his resignation, concentrating their actions on Kiev's Independence Square. Yanukovych's government attempted to stop the protests by issuing a court order to disperse the crowds, but the pro-European protesters refused to vacate the streets.[57]

While reviled in parts of the country, Yanukovych's decision not to pursue closer relations with the EU and instead to keep the economy more closely integrated with Russia (via a customs union and other measures) was welcomed in the Russian-speaking provinces of eastern Ukraine. The pro-European protests, known as the "Euromaidan protests," created a backlash in the provinces of Donetsk and Luhansk, in which people were afraid that their right to speak the Russian language and their political rights would be threatened after Yanukovych's departure. A strong pro-Russian separatist movement started, with a subsequent military response from Kiev. The separatist movement also highlighted and utilized certain extremist and nationalist ideas. The so-called Anti-Maidan movement has exposed three overlapping agendas: some have been driven to it by "social grievances," others have pushed the idea of Ukraine as a "federal state," while yet others have been extreme pro-Russia nationalists who would like to secede from Ukraine and join Russia in the future.[58]

The current cultural prism in Ukrainian society is mostly focused on the Crimean and eastern Ukrainian conflicts, holding implications for Ukraine's nuclear future—particularly if an eastern separatist movement at some point succeeds in gaining full independence from Kiev. The leadership of the breakaway provinces have been strong supporters of nationalist ideas. Pavel Gubarev, a key influencer and former member of the far-right Russian National Unity party, became the self-proclaimed "People's Governor of Donetsk Oblast," and branches of other Russian-speaking nationalistic parties (e.g., the International Eurasianist Movement, the Russian National Unity, the National Bolshevik Party, and the Russian Image) in the eastern provinces have also become influential in the region.[59] The main concern from the nonproliferation point of view is whether eastern Ukrainian separatists will decide to pursue nuclear weapons of their own to give them added leverage in their fight, especially since there is radioactive waste in a storage facility at the Donetsk Chemical Factory that might easily be stolen. So far, the separatist movement has not expressed any intention to break with the nonproliferation regime in Ukraine, but little guarantees this from changing.[60] In the theoretical scenario of eastern Ukraine gaining full independence and choosing to pursue acquisition of nuclear materials or weapons as a power play against Ukrainian or Western intervention, ultranationalist Crimean leader Sergey Aksyonov, who was voted into power with strong Russian support after the Crimean annexation, represents the sort of political figure dispositioned to act as an enabler of a nuclear program of the separatist region.[61]

International nuclear experts are divided in two schools of thought on how dangerous such a theoretical scenario could be. Some highlight the low-tech threat presented by separatists choosing to smuggle nuclear materials in order to create a dirty bomb, while others argue that the risk of dirty bomb creation is low and that insurgents are unlikely to follow this path because the destructive advantage of a dirty bomb is not sufficient to outweigh the risks of dealing with the low-enriched material. Many experts agree that the separatists have no actual capability to create nuclear weapons, and their appetite to do so seems low: in their official declarations, the eastern Ukrainian self-proclaimed governments of Donetsk and Luhansk announced the union combining both People's Republics as "a nuclear-free zone."[62]

Nevertheless, simmering conflicts in Donbass, Luhansk, and Donetsk may potentially affect the security arrangements in the region, including the location of Russia's and NATO's nuclear weapons. An uptick in trafficking of nuclear materials by separatist groups and placement of nuclear weapons by Russia and Western powers in the Black Sea region is not out of the realm of possibility. Experts point out that the newly placed tactical nuclear weapons by Russia and NATO "are not covered by the New START regime,"[63] and since Crimea joined Russia, the Russian government has repeatedly hinted that additional nuclear weapons may be deployed in Crimea. NATO, so far, has officially abstained from increasing the nuclear arsenal in the Black Sea region despite appeals by Poland and the Baltic States for more military presence, but this balance could change in the future.[64]

Nuclear Terrorism and Cyber Terrorism Threats

Because of its geographic location, Ukraine has been used as a transit state for smuggling nuclear material from Russia and the Transnistria region. Even though nuclear materials belonging to Ukraine are sufficiently secure, smuggling of nuclear matter that belongs to other states across Ukraine's territory means that the region needs to be monitored by international anti-nuclear smuggling authorities, as any nuclear material stolen by (or from) smugglers could potentially be used for a dirty bomb. Between 1991 and 2012, experts reported 630 nuclear trafficking incidents; in some of the incidents, Ukraine has been a transit state, especially in the Odessa harbor.[65] As recently as August 2015, it has been reported by the BBC that there was an attempt to smuggle radioactive material from the Ivano-Frankivsk region of Ukraine to Romania.[66]

During the recent unrest in eastern Ukraine, the international nuclear community started to be especially concerned about potential dangers of nuclear terrorism in the separatist provinces. The US government emphasized that "[a]ny state which possesses one of the two substances that can be used to produce nuclear weapons—highly enriched uranium (HEU) or plutonium—could be the victim of theft or diversion by those seeking to create a nuclear device, leading to the use of nuclear weapons by nonstate actors."[67]

Another community very much concerned with nuclear security in Ukraine is cyber specialists. With the rising incidence of cyberattacks globally, nuclear plants are becoming increasingly vulnerable to interference on the cyber front. The automated controlling systems at nuclear plants in Ukraine in particular are potentially vulnerable to cyberattacks. According to cybersecurity experts, "because both weapons systems and critical infrastructure use computers and networks to run and operate, they are much more than legitimate targets."[68] The Ukrainian State Special Communications and Information Protection Administration, a government agency charged with cybersecurity, has recently published a number of resolutions on this issue, using an "American model" as a template for addressing this issue.[69] Ukrainian state agencies—the National Commission for State Regulation of Communications and Information (NCSRCI) and the National Commission for State Energy and Public Utilities Regulation (NCSEPUR)—implement these regulations on the ground. The threat of cyber-interference, leading to the remote hijacking of a nuclear facility, substantially broadens the range of perils related to a potential nuclear incident.[70]

KEY POLITICAL ACTORS AND INFLUENCERS OF UKRAINIAN NUCLEAR CULTURE

A number of key influencers and decisionmakers have had a significant effect on the political culture in Ukraine and the country's nuclear decisions in recent years. The key politicians below, via their statements and policy decisions, have brought the discussion of nuclear weapons back into the limelight and must be taken into account when considering Ukraine's current posture on nuclear decisionmaking.

Petro Poroshenko. In March 2015, Ukrainian President Petro Poroshenko wrote a bitter op-ed in the *Wall Street Journal*, explicitly addressing the issue of the nuclear weapons that Ukraine gave up in the 1990s. In his words, by "illegally annexing" and "occupying" Crimea, as well as "supporting an insurgency led by Russia in eastern Ukraine," Russia broke the Budapest Memorandum on Security Assurances of 1994, which was supposed to protect the territorial integrity of Ukraine. As a result, he continued, "other nations may now determine it is better to acquire the bomb than risk foreign guarantees."[71]

Although President Poroshenko never explicitly discussed whether Ukraine might consider in the future acquiring nuclear weapons for protection, his comments may represent a thought that Ukraine could potentially join those "other nations."

Yulia Tymoshenko. Ukraine's Prime Minister in 2005, as well as in 2007–2010, Yulia Tymoshenko is another vocal leader who has made several pronouncements about Ukraine's decision to give up nuclear weapons. In a March 2014 interview to Western media, Tymoshenko underscored that the Budapest Memorandum guaranteed Ukraine's territorial integrity "in exchange for it giving up its Soviet-era nuclear weapons"[72] and urged the US government to intervene in the Crimean affair based on this guarantee, ensuring that the peninsula remains in Ukraine and doing "everything that will stop the aggressor [Russia]. Period."[73] It is possible that since the West did not prevent the Russian government from annexing Crimea, Tymoshenko, among other prominent Ukrainian politicians, may be frustrated with Ukraine's inability to ensure its own territorial integrity and may regret not having a nuclear deterrent—regret which could potentially steer future policy decisions.

The 2014 interview was not the first time that Tymoshenko expressed her frustration with the West's lack of support. In 2010, Tymoshenko lamented that "Ukraine's independence and stability were being put at risk by Russia's dash to strike energy and security deals with President Yanukovych,"[74] and she expressed concern about a possible fracturing of Ukraine. Even at that point, worry was voiced about threats to the country's "political sovereignty," as some government officials had mentioned a possibility for Crimea to rejoin Russia in the future. Referencing the political divisions between the western and eastern parts of Ukraine, Tymoshenko stated: "When Ukraine surrendered its nuclear weapons [after the collapse of the Soviet Union] it received guarantees that its territorial integrity would be protected. I would like to believe that these guarantees are still in force."[75] As a result of this and other disagreements with then-President Yanukovych, Tymoshenko and other opposition leaders established the People's Committee to Defend Ukraine.[76]

Tymoshenko's sensationalist comment in a leaked March 2014 video showed part of her conversation with Nestor Shufrych of Ukraine's National Security Council, in which she declared that "the 8 million Russians living in Ukraine should be killed with nuclear weapons."[77] Even though such a clearly hyperbolic quip is far from an official statement—and the *Washington Post* reported after the incident that the video was publicized by Russian state-controlled media—it is unclear whether such a comment might be an indication that while nuclear weapons in general are considered taboo by most Ukrainian politicians, their use in a possible tactical setting is not entirely proscribed. The line here, of course, is blurred in terms of which of these comments are real political opinions and potential policy options, and which constitute little more than empty demagoguery and emotional outbursts.

Arseniy Yatsenyuk. In September 2015, Ukrainian Prime Minister Arseniy Yatsenyuk expressed a sentiment similar to those of Petro Poroshenko and Yulia Tymoshenko: "We have never asked for offensive weapons. But we have to defend our country. We must defend peace, tranquility, and stability, in Europe as well."[78] He added that "Russia repeatedly gets away with violating international law," implying Russia's possession of nuclear weapons as a reason for its impunity in such violations. Yatsenyuk further highlighted that Ukraine depends on NATO members "who will ensure restoration of our territorial integrity and independence."[79]

Nuclear scholars have already noted that the disappointment and weakening of confidence by the Ukrainian government in protections from the West may lead to the erosion of the country's dedication to the nonproliferation regime. Even though Ukraine's nonproliferation norms might not be weakening in a meaningful way yet, harsh political rhetoric by politicians could potentially shift the wider public opinion on this issue away from its quarter-century commitment to being a nuclear-free state. Ukrainians remember that Russia, the United States, and the United Kingdom were guarantors of Ukraine's territorial integrity in the 1994 Budapest Memorandum. When Crimea was annexed to Russia, Ukrainians faced a strong negative example of Russia's non-compliance and the West's non-intervention to ensure these terms—seeding doubt not only for Ukraine but also for other non-nuclear-weapon states in such international guarantees.[80]

Ukrainian Military Leaders. Lastly, the service chiefs of Ukraine's military may also be influential actors in the question of Ukraine's nuclear future. In one interesting case, Ukraine's Defense Minister Valeriy Heletey at the September 2014 NATO summit in Wales stated that "…Ukraine would return to the issue of restoring its nuclear status if it fails to receive western support in resisting Russia … If the world does not help us, we will be forced to return to the creation of nuclear weapons to defend ourselves against Russia."[81] Shortly after the incident, Heletey, who had served as defense minister for only three months, was forced to resign. The official reason for his resignation was his unsuccessful military operation in eastern Ukraine, and he was replaced with Colonel General Stepan Poltorak.[82] Though it is evident that his pro-nuclear sentiments did not help him keep his position, there was no indication that his pro-nuclear statement had led to the resignation, and the nuclear attitudes of future military and defense officials may shape Ukraine's nuclear posture.

CONCLUSIONS AND POLICY LEVERS

The analysis of Ukraine's strategic culture related to nuclear nonproliferation points toward the conclusion that Ukraine's current norms and values are dominantly pro-Western, and that many Ukrainians see their nation as a European state. Closeness to NATO and the EU in cultural, economic, and political terms creates a strong nonproliferation incentive, especially in the areas of nuclear energy security and nuclear waste research. Though leading Ukrainian politicians, who are major influencers and decisionmakers, have heatedly addressed the security crisis presently facing Ukraine and intimated that it might be playing out differently if Ukraine had a nuclear arsenal, observation over time demonstrates that these leaders value their friendly relations with the West—likely more than whatever potential security gain could come from nuclear weapons acquisition, which would be extremely costly and make Ukraine a pariah state.

The cultural factors discussed in this piece have collectively impacted the Ukrainian perceptual lens regarding nuclear facilities and have especially impacted the view of acquiring weapons. The Chernobyl accident in particular contributed to the non-nuclear-weapon identity and norms that have been cultivated in Ukraine since the tragedy and which have endured through the subsequent turning over of Soviet nuclear warheads in the 1990s. Popular opinion in Ukraine blends together the risks of nuclear energy production and the dangers of hosting nuclear weapons, making the legacy of Chernobyl a resilient factor in Ukrainian public memory that still deters nuclear weapons acquisition.

However, these norms are now coming into conflict with the perceptual lens of the conflict with Russia. Some Ukrainian politicians and military officials have made pro-nuclear statements, reflecting their bitterness about Russia's actions in Crimea and pointing to Ukraine's giving up of its Soviet nuclear arsenal as a reason for losing Crimea. Though these statements have thus far been limited to emotional outbursts that have not been reflected in policy decisions, the conflict with Russia is clearly threatening Ukraine's identity as a relatively young sovereign state and may hold potential power to shift Ukrainian nuclear norms.

The central policy recommendation produced by these insights in order to keep Ukraine a non-nuclear-weapon state is to more fully integrate Ukraine into Western organizations and associations (economic, nuclear, political, and cultural) to increase the state's stake in adhering to the non-proliferation regime. In particular, the West needs to continue encouraging major enablers (Ukrainian politicians) and doers (nuclear scientists) to participate in cooperation with NATO and the EU as a deterrent for nuclear proliferation. Furthermore, the West can foster continued Ukrainian public wariness of nuclear proliferation by providing financial aid to Ukrainian NGOs and possible grants for new books, movies, and documentaries about the dangers of nuclear proliferation. The identity of being a leader in the global nonproliferation movement is highly valued by Ukraine, and the West must continue to encourage Ukraine's leadership role in the nonproliferation scheme, finding new incentives and levers to support and strengthen Ukraine's norms as a non-nuclear-weapon state and a young champion of the NPT.

NOTES

1. English, Robert, Ekaterina Svyatets, and Azamat Zhanalin. "Nationalism and Post-Communist International Relations." In *The International Studies Encyclopedia*, edited by Robert Denemark, 5279–301: Blackwell Pulishing Ltd., 2010.
2. Fialkova, Larisa. "Chornobyl's Folklore: Vernacular Commentary on Nuclear Disaster." [In English]. *Journal of Folklore Research*, 38, no. 3 (May 2001): 181–204.
3. Greene, Jennifer C. "Toward a Methodology of Mixed Methods Social Inquiry." [In English]. *Research in the Schools*, 13, no. 1 (Spring 2006): 93–99.
4. Ibid.
5. Johnston, Bruce. "International: Ukraine Denies Nuclear Ambition." *The Daily Telegraph*, December 2, 1993, 13.
6. Ibid.
7. Blair, Bruce. "Ukraine's Nuclear Backlash." [In English]. *The Brookings Review*, 11, no. 3, 46.
8. Dinmore, Guy, and Tom Warner. "Black Market Anxieties Revived on Ukraine Arms: Tom Warner on Claims That Missiles Were Sold to Iran and China." *Financial Times*, February 4, 2005, 7.

9. "Nuclear Security Survives Ukraine Issue." *Oxford Analytica Daily Brief Service*, April 10, 2014, 1.
10. "Security and Nukes." *Ukrainian Weekly*, January 10, 1993, 6.
11. Peltz, Jennifer. "US Leads Major Powers in Protesting UN Effort to Ban Nuclear Weapons." *St. Louis Post—Dispatch*, March 28, 2017.
12. The STCU was founded by Canada, Sweden, Ukraine, and the United States on October 25, 1993, and the Center's projects are funded by Canada, the European Union, and the United States.
13. "Science and Technology Center in Ukraine." http://www.stcu.int/
14. "Ukraine Infrastructure Report—Q4 2015." 1–65. London: Business Monitor International, 2015.
15. Meek, James. "Fingers on the Buttons Ukraine's Leading Nuclear Scientist Tells James Meek Why His Country Should Have Dual Control over the 176 Missiles Left after the Cold War." *The Guardian (pre-1997 Fulltext)*, July 24, 1993.
16. Ibid.
17. Warrick, Joby. "Nuclear Terrorism Focus Shifting to Research Facilities." *The Washington Post*, November 28, 2002.
18. Ibid.
19. "Ukrainian Nuclear Scientists Cooperate with Iranian Colleagues at Bushehr Npp—Iranian Ambassador." [In English]. *Interfax: Ukraine Business Weekly* (February 15, 2012).
20. "State Space Agency of Ukraine." http://www.nkau.gov.ua/nsau/nkau.nsf/indexE
21. "Yanukovych: Ukraine to Initiate Holding of Conference on Further Non-Proliferation of Nuclear Weapons." *Interfax: Ukraine General Newswire*, September 25, 2013.
22. "Ukraine to Strengthen International Cooperation in Nuclear Safety, Says Kliuyev." *Interfax: Ukraine Business Daily*, April 23, 2012.
23. "Europe Energy: France and Ukraine Co-operate on Nuclear Contamination Research." [In English]. *Europe Energy*, (April 16, 2000): 1.
24. "Ukraine to Strengthen International Cooperation...."
25. "Ukraine Builds Nuclear Waste Repository in Chernobyl Using UK, EU Money." *BBC Monitoring Former Soviet Union*, October 6, 2011.
26. "Yanukovych Signs Law on Ratification of Ukraine-Russia-Hungary Agreement on Transportation of Nuclear Materials." *Interfax: Ukraine General Newswire*, November 14, 2013.
27. "Ukraine Needs Defense Capabilities against Nuclear Power Intimidating Today the Entire Civilized World." [In Eng]. *MENA Report* (September 23, 2015).
28. Ibid.

29. Fialkova, 2001.
30. Ibid.
31. Gottemoeller, Rose. "US Official's Remarks on the 25th Anniversary of Chornobyl." *Ukrainian Weekly,* May 1, 2011, 20.
32. Weitz, Richard. "Nuclear Non-Proliferation Regime on a Tightrope." [In English]. *Jane's Intelligence Review,* 27, no. 10 (October 1, 2015).
33. Laws, Roz. "Thriller Deals Nuclear Blow to Poor Ukraine." *Birmingham Mail,* June 22, 2012, 36.
34. Reardon, Patrick. "Non-Fiction Book Prize May Boost Fortunes of Small Illinois Publisher." *Chicago Tribune,* March 8, 2006, 8–5.8.
35. Kuzma, Alex. "Maddening Uncertainty." *Ukrainian Weekly,* April 23, 2000, 8.
36. Gubarev, Vladimir. *Yaderny Vek: Chernobyl (Nuclear Century).* Moscow, Russia: Nekos, 1996.
37. Kuzma, 2000.
38. "List of Certified NGOs." SGS Group, http://www.sgsgroup.com.ua/en/Public-Sector/Monitoring-Services/NGO-Benchmarking/List-of-Certified-NGOs.aspx
39. "Our Story." Ukrainian Think Tanks Liaison Office in Brussels, https://ukraine-office.eu/en/about-us/our-story/
40. Blair, 1993.
41. Ibid.
42. Budjeryn, Mariana. "Ukraine's Nuclear Predicament and the Nonproliferation Regime." [In English]. *Arms Control Today,* 44, no. 10 (2014): 35–40.
43. Svyatets, Ekaterina. *Energy Security and Cooperation in Eurasia: Power, Profits and Politics.* Routledge, 2016.
44. Braw, Elisabeth. "After Ukraine, Countries That Border Russia Start Thinking About Nuclear Deterrents." *Newsweek,* April 25, 2014.
45. Ibid.
46. "Ukraine: Ukraine Crisis Stirs Fears of New Nuclear Arms Race." *Asia News Monitor,* May 16, 2014.
47. Sweeney, David J. "Nuclear Weapons Latency." Ph.D., Texas A&M University, 2014.
48. "Ukraine: Ukraine Crisis...."
49. "Ukraine Infrastructure Report...."
50. "Ukraine Infrastructure Report...."
51. "Ukrainian Power Stations Unable to Stock up on Coal—Minister." *Interfax: Kazakhstan Mining Weekly,* August 17, 2015.
52. "Ukraine Needs Defense Capabilities against Nuclear Power Intimidating Today the Entire Civilized World." [In Eng]. *MENA Report,* (September

23, 2015); "Ukrenergo to Build New Power Line to Feed in Northern Luhansk Region." *Interfax: Ukraine General Newswire*, August 17, 2015.

53. "Ukraine Infrastructure Report...."

54. Svyatets, 2016.

55. "Ukraine Needs Defense...."

56. "Yanukovych Says Signing Association Agreement Priority for Kyiv at Current Stage of Relations with EU." *Interfax: Ukraine General Newswire*, February 15, 2013.

57. Svyatets, 2016.

58. "Ukraine: Ukraine Crisis Stirs Fears of New Nuclear Arms Race." *Asia News Monitor*, May 16, 2014.

59. "Ukraine Crisis: Crimea's Troubled History Is Dictating Modern Day Events." *Telegraph.co.uk*, March 7, 2014.

60. "Nuclear Security Survives Ukraine Issue." *Oxford Analytica Daily Brief Service*, April 10, 2014, 1.

61. Socor, Vladimir. "Political Implications of Russia's Annexation of Crimea." *Ukrainian Weekly*, March 30, 2014, 3.

62. Weitz, Richard. "Nuclear Non-Proliferation Regime on a Tightrope." [In English]. *Jane's Intelligence Review*, 27, no. 10 (Oct 1, 2015).

63. Peterfi, Carol-Teodor. "Proliferation of Weapons of Mass Destruction in the Black Sea Region—New and Old Challenges." Bucharest, 2017.

64. Ibid.

65. Peterfi, 2017.

66. Dinmore, Guy, and Tom Warner. "Black Market Anxieties Revived on Ukraine Arms: Tom Warner on Claims That Missiles Were Sold to Iran and China." *Financial Times*, February 4, 2005, 7.

67. "Nuclear Security Survives...."

68. Conte, Andrew. "Experts: Infrastructure 'Legitimate Target' in Battle for Cyber Supremacy." *McClatchy—Tribune Business News*, February 15, 2015.

69. "Ukraine to Implement American Approach to Cyber Security." *BBC Monitoring Former Soviet Union*, May 2, 2015.

70. Ibid.

71. Barker, Thorold, and Alan Cullison. "Ukraine President Petro Poroshenko: 'Sanctions Are Working' on Russia." *Wall Street Journal*, January 20, 2015.

72. Taylor, Adam. "In Latest Wiretapping Leak, Yulia Tymoshenko Appears to Say 'Nuclear Weapons' Should Be Used to Kill Russians." Washington: WP Company LLC d/b/a *The Washington Post*, 2014.

73. Danilova, Maria. "Tymoshenko Urges West to Stop Russian Aggression." *The Epoch Times*, March 6, 2014, 1.

74. Ibid.

75. Halpin, Tony. "Moscow's Embrace Will Crush Our Nation, Says Tymoshenko." *The Times*, May 19, 2010, 28.
76. Ibid.
77. "Ukraine Infrastructure Report...."
78. Halpin, 2010.
79. "Ukraine Needs Defense...."
80. Ibid.
81. "NATO Members 'Start Arms Deliveries to Ukraine'." *Asia News Monitor*, September 16, 2014.
82. "Defense Minister Replaced Again." *Los Angeles Times*, October 14, 2014.

CHAPTER 8

North Korea's Strategic Culture and Its Evolving Nuclear Strategy

Shane Smith

To date, North Korea has conducted six nuclear tests and a series of missile launches that suggest that sooner or later it will be able to target South Korea, Japan, and the US homeland with nuclear weapons. North Korea is now estimated to possess enough fissile material to build dozens of nuclear weapons and is poised to expand the quantity, quality, and diversity of weapon systems in its arsenal over the coming years.[1] Indeed, Kim Jung Un has long stated his intention to do just that, by "increas[ing] the production of precision and miniaturized nuclear weapons and the means of their delivery and ceaselessly develop[ing] nuclear weapons technology to actively develop more powerful and advanced nuclear weapons."[2]

To be sure, North Korea has already crossed several nuclear thresholds and appears bent on developing and deploying an operational nuclear weapons capability. If it continues down that path, it will face a number of decisions about the shape, size, and character of its arsenal that could profoundly impact US and international security. Those choices can be

Analysis and findings are that of the author and do not necessarily reflect the views of National Defense University, the Department of Defense or any other part of the US government.

S. Smith (✉)
National Defense University, Washington, DC, USA

© The Author(s) 2018
J. L. Johnson et al. (eds.), *Crossing Nuclear Thresholds*,
Initiatives in Strategic Studies: Issues and Policies,
https://doi.org/10.1007/978-3-319-72670-0_8

divided between those that have to do with nuclear doctrine and those that concern strategic command and control.[3] Nuclear doctrine tends to reflect the purposes that nuclear weapons serve and consists of plans about when and how they might be used. Command and control relate to how nuclear weapons are incorporated into a state's broader military structure to ensure that they are used only when and how government leaders decide that they should be used. North Korea's unique strategic culture offers some insight into how its leaders might think about such questions.

THE SUPREME LEADER: ULTIMATE DECISIONMAKER AND EMBODIMENT OF NORTH KOREAN NATIONAL IDENTITY

In 2009, Joseph Bermudez wrote that "More than any other nation today, the strategic culture of the Democratic People's Republic of Korea (DPRK) is the product of the personal dreams and ambitions of a single individual— Kim Il Sung."[4] This is probably still true today. Kim reigned over North Korea for 26 years, from its establishment in 1948 until his death in 1994. During that time, his power was near limitless within the North's borders and he ruthlessly wielded that power to shape North Korea's government and society to protect his and his family's rule. In doing so, Don Oberdorfer and Robert Carlin argue, "Kim created an impermeable and absolutist state that many have compared to a religious cult. No dissent from or criticism of Kim Il Sung, his tenets, or his decisions was permitted."[5]

Kim Il Sung's influence can be found in nearly every facet of modern North Korea, especially in the identity, norms, values, and perceptual lenses under investigation here that continue to bind its ruling elite, legitimize their power, and guide state decisionmaking. Nowhere is this more visible than in the *Suryong*-dominant (leader-dominant) system of governance that he left behind, which bestows the Supreme Leader with ultimate authority and enshrines the Kim family dictatorship. All power and legitimacy flow from the leader, be it Kim Il Sung, Kim Jong Il, or Kim Jong Un, who is generally portrayed as godlike—omnipotent, omniscient, and omnipresent—and the sole source of national self-actualization. As one typical piece of North Korean propaganda illustrates: "the *Suryong* is an impeccable brain of the living body, the masses can be endowed with their life in exchange for their loyalty to him, and the Party is the nerve of that living body."[6]

This monolithic system is also intensely personal. It is built around and deeply intertwined with the Kim family. The preamble to the North Korean constitution makes that abundantly clear when it stipulates that

"The constitution of the DPRK is the constitution of Kim Il-sung and Kim Jong-il that codifies the thought of self-reliant national construction and achievements of national construction of the Great Suryong and comrade Kim Il-sung and the Great Leader and the comrade Kim Jong-il." So engrained is the Kim family in the national identity of the North (discussed further below) that it is nearly impossible to imagine that North Korea, as we know it today, could survive with an alternative leader outside of the Kim family. "The naturalization of the Kim family at the heart of conceptions of national identity," Hazel Smith argues, "is one reason for the maintenance of a member of the Kim family as official leader of the state."[7]

Today, Kim Jung Un is the ultimate decisionmaker and sole source of legitimacy for the regime but there has been debate among North Korea watchers about his ability to consolidate power.[8] While his bloodline and position as Supreme Leader confer an inherent legitimacy, he is thought to lack the unquestioned, absolute, and enduring loyalty of the elite and mass population that his father and grandfather enjoyed. Indeed, he is farther removed from the revolutionary credentials of his grandfather and, as the third-generation leader, he cannot necessarily rely on partisan loyalties cast long ago. Kim Jong Un also did not have the decades that his father had to burnish his cult of personality and image as a powerful, shrewd, and legitimate leader before he was given the reins of control. To the contrary, he and his father only had a few years to lay the ground for succession. Kim Jung Un is young and relatively inexperienced. He did not serve in the military but rather grew up in the lavish comforts of the Kim family while much of the nation struggled to survive during the 1990–2000s. He even went to school in the West for a period of that time, suggesting that he was somewhat removed from his own generation of revolutionaries with whom he could have forged loyal and trusted relations.

It would be imprudent, however, to suggest that Kim Jong Un's dominance or authority is in question. As Supreme Leader, he faces no challenge for authority and he simultaneously holds positions atop all of the major bodies of leadership in North Korea. He is the First Secretary of the Korean Workers' Party (KWP) and Presidium Member of the KWP Politburo, Chairman of the KWP Central Military Commission (CMC), Chairman of the National Defense Commission (NDC), and Supreme Commander of the Korean People's Army (KPA). All members of the political and military elite who serve in and benefit from their positions do so at the pleasure of Kim Jong Un. To lose favor and confidence of the

Supreme Leader can result in the loss of everything, even one's life. That said, Kim Jong Un cannot effectively govern by fiat and make policy on a whim despite the prerogatives he is officially bestowed as the Supreme Leader. Even in North Korea, governance requires adhering to the protocols and boundaries of what is viewed as appropriate by a wider cross-section of those who would safeguard and carryout state policy. Doing so likely means hewing to widely shared notions of national identity and the norms, values, and perceptual lenses that have long guided North Korean decisionmaking. This may be especially true for Kim Jong Un, even if he holds a distinctly different worldview, at least until he garners a level of legitimacy and loyalty on par with that of his predecessors.

North Korea's peculiar brand of government, which places so much authority in and attributes deity-like qualities to the Supreme Leader, has implications for its nuclear policies. For instance, there should be little doubt about who in North Korea has sole authority to launch nuclear weapons. The Supreme People's Assembly (SPA) promulgated the Law on Consolidating Position of Nuclear Weapons State in 2013, which is the most authoritative statement on North Korean nuclear policy. It makes clear that "nuclear weapons of the DPRK can be used *only* by a final order of the Supreme Commander of the Korean People's Army"—a position that has been held only by members of the Kim family. Who else could be trusted with such a grave responsibility? It is difficult to imagine North Korean leadership placing nuclear weapons, which it calls "the nation's life" and "a national treasure," in the hands of lower-echelon political and military authority. Doing so would seem to run counter to the one overarching rule of North Korean governance and national identity: There is only one ruler. Putting these weapons in the custody of another military commander or political leader with pre-delegated launch authority could serve to identify, at least symbolically, a suitable successor to the Supreme Leader.

Reluctance to relinquish authority over its nuclear weapons could constrain North Korea from adopting operationally complex command and control systems involving forward deployed weapons and issuing launch-on-warning type of authority. Such constraints would likely impact its doctrinal options. For instance, nuclear doctrine that is aimed at deterring adversaries from launching disarming or decapitating first-strikes or a warfighting doctrine that can be used to compel adversaries is thought to be more credible if the state is able to rapidly disperse and use nuclear weapons without centralized authority. Without that ability, North Korean doctrine might be limited to maintaining an existential deterrent with comparatively low credibility against high-end attacks on its leadership and strategic assets.[9]

NORTH KOREAN IDENTITY AND NUCLEAR WEAPONS

An extraordinarily isolated country, North Korea's identity is shaped by extreme forms of a "national solipsism," militarism, and ethnocentrism that borders xenophobia. Its historiography and internal propaganda propagate the view that North Korea is the decisive element in the world system, if not the center of the universe. Bruce Cummings captures this internal narrative when he writes that "Korea is [thought to be] the center, radiating outward ... the world tends toward Korea, with all eyes on Kim Il Sung or Kim Jong Il."[10] It is not only that North Korea is the decisive element in the world. It also is the decisive element in history, as state media even proclaims the *Taedong* river basin to be "the cradle of mankind" based on suspect archeological findings dating back one million years.[11]

North Koreans trace their political lineage over 5000 years to the mythical founder of the Korean state, *Tan'gun*. They claim to have dug up his remains at a site near Pyongyang, proving that "there is a distinct Korean race and that the foundation of the first state of the Korean nation by *Tan'gun* was a historic event ... about 3000 BCE, which centered around Pyongyang."[12] State propaganda goes on to link the Kim dynasty to *Tan'gun* and imply that the regime is the rightful successor to the founder of Korea. However, as Hazel Smith writes, North Koreans are effectively told that "it was only with the advent of the Kim family onto [this] historical stage that the ethnically distinct Korean nation gained the opportunity to fulfill historic aspirations" of a unified Korea that is free from foreign domination.[13]

Nuclear weapons have become central to this narrative in a number of ways. They are seen to offer the prestige that is befitting a historically great, if not the most important, country. For instance, following North Korea's launch of a *Taepo-dong*-1 in 1998, state media declared it "a great pride of the *Tan'gun* nation."[14] Nuclear weapons also are often characterized in sweeping historical terms, helping North Korea claim its central place in the world and securing its destiny for all time. In 2016, North Korean TV announced its fourth nuclear test this way:

There took place a world startling event to be specially recorded in the national history spanning 5,000 years ... The spectacular success made by the DPRK in the H-bomb test this time is a great deed of history, a historic event of the national significance as it surely guarantees the eternal future of the nation ... By succeeding in the H-bomb test in the most perfect manner to be specially recorded in history the DPRK proudly joined the advanced ranks of nuclear weapons states possessed of even H-bomb and the Korean people came to demonstrate the spirit of the dignified nation....[15]

Two ideas that flow from North Korea's self-conceptualization are essential to understanding its political culture. *Juche* is the dominant North Korean precept that Kim Jong Il once called the quintessence of Kimilsungism. It emphasizes self-importance, self-determination, and unquestioned loyalty to the Supreme Leader. On the one hand, *Juche* is an organizing principal of both state and society. As Kim Il Sung instructed in 1968:

The government ... will thoroughly implement the line of independence, self-subsistence, and self-defense to consolidate the political independence of the country ... ensuring the complete reunification, independence and prosperity of our nation, and increase the defense capabilities of the country so as to reliably safeguard its security on the basis of our own forces, by excellently materializing our Party's idea of *Juche* in all fields.[16]

On the other hand, it is much more than an ideology. *Juche* is fundamental to modern North Korean identity. There is no individual identity but through the nation and the goal of national self-determination. It permeates all of North Korean life, with constant visible reminders like the *Juche* Tower in Pyongyang that is a 170-meter monument constructed with 25,550 blocks of white granite, one for each day of Kim's life from birth to his 70th birthday.

Songun or "military-first" politics was introduced by Kim Jong Il to restructure government and society in a manner that serves military interests above all else. It is only through *Songun* that *Juche* can be realized. In part, this was no great departure for an already military-centered North Korean society. It is a nation that has long seen itself as under constant siege. Having suffered hundreds of incursions from more powerful neighbors over millennia, Korean identity has been shaped by a historic vulnerability to outside predators. Indeed, the modern North Korean nation rose out of conflict against Japan's brutal colonization of Korea from 1911 until the end of World War II. The Korean War, or what it calls the Great Fatherland Liberation War, failed to unite the Peninsula due to US intervention and nuclear threats, according to official history. Since then, it has held that the imperialist Americans are bent on destroying North Korea and the distinct Korean identity. As such, *Songun* is justified internally by the argument that only through "preparing an unconquerable army to forestall the aggressive attempt of the forces of imperialism and domination and continuing to advance socialism by relying on the powerful army is his [Kim Jong Il's] far-sighted political strategy."[17] Under *Songun*, all matters of state and society, even the party, are subordinate to the military as the guardian of the Korean nation and its revolution.

Nuclear weapons are often held as both an expression of and essential to *Juche* and *Songun*. In 2012, North Korea revised its constitution to declare that it is a nuclear weapon state this way:

> Amid the collapse of the world's socialist system and the vicious anti-Republic oppressive offensive by the imperialists' joint forces, Comrade Kim Jong Il honorably defended the gains of socialism which is Comrade Kim Il Sung's lofty legacy through military-first politics; changed our fatherland into a politically and ideologically powerful state that is invincible, a nuclear state, and a militarily powerful state that is indomitable....

Again, North Korean announcements following its fourth nuclear test illustrate just how the two concepts animate its nuclear developments. For example, it released images of the cover pages of two documents related to the test with written guidance from Kim Jong Un. One read: "Let the whole world look up to the *Juche* socialist Chosun, a nuclear power, the great Worker's Party of Korea by opening up the year of 2016, a victorious and glorious year in which the 7th party congress will be held, with the thrilling sound of the first H-bomb blast!"[18] An official statement claimed that the test was part of an "all-out charge to bring earlier the final victory of the revolutionary cause of *Juche*, true to the militant appeal of the Workers' Party of Korea." Calling the United States a "gang of cruel robbers," it goes on to argue:

> [T]he present-day grim reality clearly proves once again the immutable truth that one's destiny should be defended by one's own efforts. Nothing is more foolish than dropping a hunting gun before herds of ferocious wolves ... The army and people of the DPRK will steadily escalate its nuclear

deterrence of justice both in quality and quantity to reliably guarantee the future of the revolutionary cause of *Juche* for all ages.[19]

So embedded are nuclear weapons with all that makes North Korea North Korea, that one longtime student of the country suggests that "the nation itself and nuclear weapons have been combined in a condensed symbol of intention."[20] For this reason, it is increasingly difficult to imagine that North Korea will ever give up its nuclear ambitions. To the contrary, it is likely to continue to do just as it says: build bigger, better, and more nuclear weapons as a manifestation of national purpose. Because nuclear weapons have become central to North Korean identity and the regime's legitimacy, however, its leaders may be inclined to exaggerate nuclear accomplishments and capabilities. In fact, international analysts have long been skeptical of hyped North Korean nuclear claims. For North Korean leaders to admit otherwise, however, might reflect poorly on the Supreme Leader and, in turn, the nation itself for failing to live up to national ideals. That said, we should also expect North Korea to attempt to demonstrate through continued missile and nuclear testing that it is an advanced nuclear power equal to other modern nuclear states.

A third and final element of its national identity also has potential implications for its nuclear decisionmaking. For North Korea, ethnicity and nation are one and the same. It is one of the most racially homogenous countries in the world. Its leaders regularly employ ethnocentrism in support of maintaining the integrity of North Korean society as pure, undiluted by foreign blood, and the vessel of the "true Korea." In a 2006 article of the *Rodong Sinmun*, for instance, the tolerant attitude of the South Korean government toward multiracial and multinational marriages was compared to treason against the interests of the Korean nation.[21] To be sure, North Korean identity and officialdom hold Korean blood—both in the North and South—to be sacrosanct. Kim Jong Il once declared that "the Korean nation is a homogenous nation that has inherited the same blood and lived in the same territory speaking the same language for thousands of years." People in the North and South share the "same blood and soul of the Korean nation" and are "linked inseparable with the same national interests and a common historical psychology and sentiment."[22] The South, according to the North Korean narrative, has simply been led astray if not enslaved by US imperialists.

How would North Korean ethnocentrism impact decisions over nuclear doctrine or operations? It might be reluctant to use nuclear weapons against the South, with which it has strong blood ties and a shared sense of both national history and destiny. That brand of horrible might be reserved for foreigners. But, it would be foolish to ignore repeated North Korean threats to turn Seoul into a "sea of fire," which have become almost commonplace. As the sole vessel of the "true Korea" and the center of all that is important, North Korea would unlikely show restraint even for its fellow Koreans in the South should it feel threatened. As Radio Pyongyang boldly declared in 2003, "the world without North Korea is meaningless, and it should be destroyed."[23]

NORTH KOREAN VALUES AND NUCLEAR WEAPONS

The symbiotic relationship between the Kim family dictatorship and national identity translates into one core value above all others: the survival and veneration of the Kim family. As the highest ranking North Korean defector and former International-Secretary of the KWP, Hwang Jang Yop, once wrote, "the highest moral value [in the North] is dedicating one's body and soul to the Great Leader."[24] It is of course now quite common for analysts to note that regime preservation is the primary motivation behind North Korea's nuclear program. How this might impact doctrinal and command and control type of decisions, however, is uncertain. On the one hand, it suggests that nuclear weapons might be used only when the regime believes that it has no other option. That is to say, it would use nuclear weapons only as a final bid to save the Kim family in the last throes of conflict. To do otherwise carries the risk of actually hastening the destruction of the regime. On the other hand, a sense of fatalism among North Korea's leadership could be triggered without a decisive military defeat or with United States and South Korea forces approaching the gates of Pyongyang. Some observers believe that the regime is brittle—outwardly rigid and hard but if struck in the right spot, like a partial but humiliating military defeat, it could shatter or unravel. Early but limited use of nuclear weapons might be seen by North Korea's leaders as the best way to stave off that fate. Indeed, the North's "declaratory policy" suggests an ambiguous and potentially low threshold for nuclear use, when it states that nuclear weapons "serve the purpose of deterring and repelling the aggression and attack of the enemy against the DPRK."[25]

Obedience, solidarity, and commitment also are highly regarded values in North Korea. Not only are these values institutionalized and imposed by its *Suryong*-dominate system, where contrary behavior is harshly punished, North Koreans are instructed from childhood to "model [themselves] after the traits of soldiers" in accord with *Songun*. They "should put the interests of society and the collective above their own."[26] All forms of media and popular entertainment stress the duty to praise the Kim family, to submit one's life to the Supreme Leader, and to constantly prepare for war with a readiness to obey orders without question.[27]

This demand for unity of effort no doubt helps explain how North Korea has been able to build a nuclear weapons program despite being one of the world's poorest and least developed countries. However, these values also might impact its nuclear decisionmaking with regard to doctrine and command and control but could do so in different ways. On the one hand, North Korean leadership could trust lower-echelon political and military authority to faithfully carryout orders and to jealously guard the rights of the Supreme Leader as the sole individual with nuclear launch authority. Under such conditions, North Korea might implement an operationally complex command and control system involving forward deployed weapons and pre-delegated launch authority that would allow it to adopt an array of nuclear doctrines. On the other hand, North Korea's notoriously brutal imposition of such rigid hierarchical values suggests that those values are not fully accepted across society. To the contrary, the need to brutally impose those rules suggests a manifest concern about the potential for disobedience and the lack of commitment even within the military. Under these circumstances, we would expect the Supreme Leader to maintain tight, centralized control both over the custody of nuclear weapons and the authority to use them, which would limit North Korea's nuclear strategy.

As with most military-centered cultures, North Korean propaganda also emphasizes strength and resolve as core national values while weakness and vacillation are seen as abhorrent. Nuclear weapons are clearly a symbol of strength and resolve against outside forces for North Korea, as previous quotes make clear. Abandoning its nuclear ambitions would seemingly run counter to its Spartan-like values. Its brand of militancy, however, is also informed by its partisan guerrilla struggle for independence against Japanese colonial rule. The guerrilla tradition—as exemplified in Kim Il Sung's guerrilla experience—is widely idolized in North Korean society. Dating back to 1946, there is evidence that the guerrilla tradition has significantly influenced not only North Korean military thinking and organization but the broader North Korean state and society.[28] Kim Jung Un even recently implored his athletes to adopt "guerrilla-style tactics" in international competitions.[29] Two relevant values stem from this guerrilla tradition.[30] One is the will to endure and persevere against tremendous odds for the sake of redeeming the nation. The other is the creative use of unconventional tactics, brinksmanship, and unpredictability to prevail against superior forces. As Scott Snyder summarizes, North Koreans see "little benefit to be gained and much danger to be faced if one plays strictly by the [stronger] opponent's rules."[31]

North Korea has a long history of using unorthodox tactics and threats ostensibly to convey its willingness to both impose and accept far greater costs than the United States or South Korea, and to also impart a sense of unpredictability in how it might respond to even the slightest infraction. For instance, in the days following its seizure of the USS *Pueblo* in 1968, when it took hostage 82 US sailors, it threatened "genocidal blows" in response to a kinetic US response. In 1994, North Korea first threatened to turn Seoul into a "sea of fire," which it has repeated on a number of occasions. After US President George Bush included North Korea as part of an "axis of evil" in 2002, Pyongyang said that it would "mercilessly wipe out the aggressors." In 2015, it said that it would use nuclear weapons "at any time" against the United States. In 2017, the Korea Asia-Pacific Peace Committee, which handles the North's external ties and propaganda, released a statement through KCNA that "The four islands of the [Japanese] archipelago should be sunken into the sea by the nuclear bomb of Juche. Japan is no longer needed to exist near us." Such threats now seem routine. The problem today is that North Korea can actually make good on these threats as its nuclear capabilities grow. It is reasonable to expect that as its threats become more credible, Pyongyang will continue if not increase its use of nuclear brinksmanship to challenge what it contends to be objectionable political and territorial arrangements.

It is impossible to know with certainty what is behind North Korean nuclear threats: Are they for internal consumption, playing on values in the guerrilla tradition? Do North Korean leaders really believe that they could endure and survive a nuclear war? Or, are they bluffs that are intended for deterrence purposes? Many analysts treat the North's threats as mere bluster and more for domestic purposes than for communicating serious military threats but there are good reasons to take them seriously. For one, North Korea's leadership has shown in the past a willingness to impose extreme deprivation on its own people and to call on them to make great sacrifices. For decades, North Korea has reportedly been building tunnels for its leadership and military to ride out a nuclear war only to reemerge to fight and prevail.[32] The people and army of North Korea are continuously told to prepare for a final war against imperialism, such as when *The Pyongyang Times* wrote in 2011 that the "DPRK's revolutionary armed forces are in full preparedness for launching a do-or-die battle against any act of military provocation."[33] North Koreans have so often repeated to themselves that their military is more courageous, spirited, and resilient than that of their opponents and that using nuclear weapons is the surest way to defeat its enemies that they may actually come to believe this statement and become emotionally committed to an irrational optimism about the prospects of waging and prevailing in a nuclear conflict.[34]

In line with the guerrilla tradition, North Korea might think about using nuclear weapons in limited ways to surprise, shock, and/or degrade enemy forces. For instance, it might use nuclear weapons for psychological effects during a conflict by firing a demonstration shot; for area denial effects by targeting access points to North Korea or military ports in the South, such as the Port of Busan, where the United States might otherwise disembark forces; or for operational effects by targeting military bases away from civilian population centers, such as air bases at Kusan and Osan, to reduce US air sorties.[35] The guerrilla tradition in North Korea might also impact how North Korea thinks about different delivery methods, including the use of highly trained special operations forces to penetrate lines of defense. In fact, North Korea showed off what it claims to be an atomic backpack unit in a 2013 military parade. A limited use doctrine and an operational system involving individually portable weapons would have both command and control as well as technical hurdles that North Korea may be unable to surmount. But, given the influence of guerrilla warfare on shaping North Korean values, it is not unreasonable to assume that it is exploring such options.

North Korean Norms and Nuclear Weapons

In 1958, well-known Sovietologist Betram Wolfe wrote that "There is a principle of selection in personal despotisms which surrounds the despot with courtiers, sycophants, executants, yes-men, and rules out original and challenging minds."[36] North Korea's style of personal despotism likely exceeds that of Stalin's Soviet Union and any other country in modern times. It is a country where citizens are arrested and sent to gulags for defacing or sitting on a newspaper photograph of the Supreme Leader or member of the Kim family. Reports abound of inhumane treatment, torture, public execution, and imprisonment of those who fail to sufficiently conform to Kimism both at the mass and at the elite levels.[37] For instance, Jang Song Thaek, Kim Jong Un's uncle, vice chairman of the NDC, and often thought to have been second-in-command among Pyongyang watchers, was publically executed and labeled a traitor in 2013.[38] In 2015, Hyon Yong Chol, the minister of the People's Armed Forces, was purged (some suggest that he was executed for treason) for insubordination and sleeping during formal military rallies, including one that was attended by Kim Jong Un.[39] Later that year, Choe Ryong Hae, senior WPK Secretary and member of the Politburo's Presidium, was reportedly sent away for "re-education."[40] There is no dissent, no loyal opposition, and no "conversation" with the Supreme Leader in North Korea. One only receives orders and instructions. This is often illustrated in pictures released by state media, which show Kim Jong Un surrounded by top military and party officials with pen and pad in hand eagerly awaiting the next nugget of "benevolent wisdom."

Either through favor or fear, the North Korea system likely habituates conformity, deference, and an unwillingness to bear bad news. This norm could cloud information flows to leadership that results in what Bermudez calls a "lens of self-deception."[41] This could have a number of implications for North Korea's nuclear decisionmaking. One implication focuses on the types of actors involved in nuclear decisionmaking, particularly the closest advisors that surround Kim Jong Un. Inclined to tell the Supreme Leader what he wants to hear or to embellish their own accomplishments, senior advisors may be reluctant to be completely truthful about actual capabilities. That was the case in Iraq, as records show that Saddam Hussein was repeatedly misinformed by senior military and party officials about military capabilities that did not exist and especially about the strength and readiness of the WMD arsenal that Iraq had amassed.[42] The same may be true in North Korea. During a 2013 crisis on the Korean Peninsula, Pyongyang issued a nuclear threat and released photos of Kim Jong Un surrounded by top military generals. The images showed a map in the background that was marked "US mainland strike plan" with missile trajectories targeting Hawaii, Washington, DC, Los Angeles, and Austin, Texas.[43] While widely seen among analysts as bluster or regime propaganda, it is possible that the Korean military was actually telling Kim Jong Un a lie about their capabilities to bolster their own standing. Similarly, Kim Jong Un announced that North Korea had a hydrogen bomb in

December 2015 and a couple of weeks later stated that the country had successfully tested a H-bomb despite all evidence to the contrary. This only raises further the question of exactly what Kim Jong Un knows about the country's actual nuclear capabilities. As a result, it is not clear that North Korean decisions about nuclear doctrine would be tied to reality.

Senior advisors might also be reluctant to fully inform the Supreme Leader about operational progress, limitations, and risks. This is a particular concern during crises. For instance, the 1999 India–Pakistan Kargil crisis appeared to be veering toward nuclear war when US intelligence found that Pakistan's military was moving nuclear weapons toward its border with India. When confronted by US President Bill Clinton, Pakistani Prime Minister Nawaz Sharif was reported to be genuinely surprised by the supposed missile movement. He later claimed that he was not informed about the movements and that the entire crisis was the result of misadventure on part of General Musharraf, who later revealed that Pakistan's nuclear delivery systems were not even operational during the conflict.[44] While perhaps not a perfect analogy for North Korea because the seamlessness between civilian and military rule there suggests that the prospect of a "rogue" general is unlikely, it does highlight a principal-agent problem that can be exasperated by misinformation or poor communication out of fear of informing Kim Jong Un about facts on the ground. How sure could he be in establishing an effective command and control system that guarantees nuclear weapons are used when and only when he intends them to be used?

North Korean Perceptual Lens and Nuclear Weapons

North Korea's perceptual lens is shaped by a historical sense of vulnerability to outside predators. Korea is surrounded by more powerful and, at times, expansionist neighbors. It has suffered centuries of being coveted, colonized, and paying tribute to outsiders. From 1392 to 1897, it was a vassal state of China. The Russo-Japanese War of 1904–1905 was fought over the conflicting imperial ambitions those countries had over Manchuria and Korea. When Japan won, it became the dominant power in Asia and annexed Korea in 1911. It brutally ruled over the Korean people until the end of World War II. North Korean historiography and entertainment media often retell the humiliation at the hands of its neighbors with the promise of "never again." Nuclear weapons are portrayed as the means for keeping that promise and overturning the traditional hierarchy of regional geopolitics. International aid, assistance, and diplomatic concessions that it has gained through nuclear threats have even been presented domestically as "tribute."[45] More concerning is that the tone of humiliation that is often spread through propaganda connotes a requirement for retribution.

To be sure, Korea has long likened itself to a "shrimp among whales" to illustrate its historical position in Asian geopolitics. For North Korea today, its position is even more precarious. Its relevancy is in decline compared with its modern and economically superior neighbors, save for its nuclear weapons. It has fewer vested interests in a stable regional status quo that unevenly benefits others. Its leaders might look at trend lines in the region and decide that particularly bold actions are necessary to reassert control over their ability to shape future political outcomes. It would thus be unsurprising if the North used nuclear threats and provocations in an effort to generate instability that, in turn, might open opportunities to advance its interests. Statements out of Pyongyang suggest that its leaders are in fact thinking about how to exploit nuclear weapons to "dictate" international trends and regional relations.[46]

While its geopolitical position certainly shapes the North's perceptual lens, it is South Korea and the United States that are seen to be more immediate and existential threats. Since the Korean War, leaders in Pyongyang and state propaganda have portrayed South Korea as a "puppet" of the United States. In fact, North Koreans are taught that the South colluded with the United States to invade the North in 1950. Without US intervention in Korea's domestic affairs, the story goes, the victory of the "people's revolution" would have been complete.

For decades, the North held conventional military superiority over the South. The KPA is still the world's fourth largest military. Its thousands of artillery tubes, potentially filled with chemical weapons munitions, could devastate Seoul and therefore pose a credible deterrent against South Korea. However, this superiority has eroded over the past generation. The KPA primarily fields legacy weapon systems built by China and the Soviet Union in the 1950s, 60s, and 70s.[47] Its capabilities and resources have dwindled along with the country's economy and its international isolation. Meanwhile, South Korea has become one of the world's largest economies with a modern society and a modern military. Faced with relative and dramatic decline, John Park argues that North Korea has viewed nuclear weapons as a way "to restore a semblance of balance on the peninsula."[48] Indeed, statements out of Pyongyang suggest that the North is looking to augment if not supplement its waning conventional forces. The CMC released a report one day before the SPA Law on Consolidating Position of Nuclear Weapons State was adopted, directing the military to begin to more fully integrate nuclear weapons into its broader doctrine: "The People's Army should perfect the war method and operation in the direction of raising the pivotal role of the nuclear armed forces in all aspects concerning the war deterrence and the war strategy, and the nuclear armed forces should always round off the combat posture."[49]

With lost confidence in its conventional capabilities vis-à-vis South Korea, nuclear weapons offer the North an attractive substitute. Some, such as Peter Hayes and Scott Bruce, argue that the target of its nuclear doctrine has in fact shifted since 2009 from the United States to a multidirectional and flexible strategy that has South Korea as its main focus. Recent nuclear threats from Pyongyang might reflect such a change. In December 2010, the North threatened "the south Korean puppet forces" with "a sacred war of justice Korean style based on the nuclear deterrent" in response to South Korean military exercises. Moreover, nuclear weapons may have emboldened North Korean leaders to launch low level provocations like the ones in 2010—the sinking of the Cheonan and shelling of Yeonpyeong-do—because they were confident that the specter of nuclear war would deter South Korean escalation.

While South Korea represents a growing threat to the North's ambition to unite the peninsula and, in turn, to the part of the regime's legitimacy that is pegged to the stated goal of unification, Pyongyang has been and continues to be obsessed with the threat from the United States. Its leaders have consistently justified developing nuclear weapons as a deterrent primarily against US aggression. In 2002, Pyongyang defended its nuclear work as self-defense against US nuclear threats.[50] When it announced that it had nuclear weapons in 2005, the Ministry of Foreign Affairs declared:

> The US disclosed its attempt to topple the political system in the DPRK at any cost, threatening it with a nuclear stick. This compels us to take a measure to bolster [our] nuclear weapons arsenal in order to protect the ideology, system, freedom and democracy chosen by [our] people. We had already taken the resolute action of pulling out of the NPT and have

manufactured nukes for self-defense to cope with the Bush administration's evermore undisguised policy to isolate and stifle the DPRK. [Our] nuclear weapons will remain [a] nuclear deterrent for self-defense under any circumstances.[51]

Ahead of its first nuclear test in 2006, the Foreign Ministry similarly explained:

[A] people without [a] reliable war deterrent are bound to meet a tragic death ... [North Korea's] nuclear weapons will serve as [a] reliable war deterrent for protecting the supreme interests of the state and the security of the Korean nation from the US threat of aggression....[52]

Under Kim Jong Un, North Korean propaganda has called the United States its "sworn enemy" and even released a dreamscape film in 2013 depicting an attack on New York and Washington, DC, stating:

It appears that the headquarters of evil, which has had a habit of using force and unilateralism and committing wars of aggression, is going up in flames it itself has ignited. Just imagine riding in a Korean spaceship. One day, my dream will come true. No matter how hard the imperialists try to isolate and stifle us, they will not stop our people's path toward our final victory of achieving a unified, strong and prosperous Korea.[53]

Not only does North Korea see the United States as its greatest threat and primary nuclear target, its state media also continuously warn of pre-emptive US strikes against its "supreme interests," suggesting that the United States would launch a decapitating first-strike on its leadership or a disarming first-strike on its strategic nuclear assets ("national treasures"). Such concerns could incentivize North Korea to adopt nuclear operations that emphasize survivability, such as the dispersal of forces, and tiered launch authority to ensure that others will retaliate in the event that the Supreme Leader is removed. As previously suggested, this would come with significant risks. For a regime that might be concerned about internal rivals or maintaining a tight grip on the levers of power, relinquishing authoritative control over weapons that it calls "the nation's life" and "a national treasure" could expose internal vulnerabilities. Of course, there would also be external risks. For instance, there would likely be international political and economic consequences as well as increased military tensions, since the United States and South Korea could be expected to respond with their own heightened defenses. Putting nuclear weapons in the hands of lower levels of authority could also lead to unintended escalation during crises and even the loss of command and control. North Korea may be willing to accept these costs and risks, but it is unclear whether it can ever overcome the inherent obstacles, even if it aspires to develop such capabilities.

Policy Implications and Recommendations

Nuclear weapons are tightly intertwined with all that makes North Korea North Korea. They have become integral to its national identity and both an expression of and fundamental to its national aspirations of self-determination, reunification, and historical significance. For this reason, it is increasingly difficult to imagine that North Korea will give up its nuclear weapons program. Any hope to slow, halt, or reverse its nuclear program will require four elements.

First, the United States must redouble its efforts to build broad diplomatic and economic pressure to oppose North Korea's nuclear ambitions. It must demonstrate to leaders in Pyongyang that nuclear developments will result in increasing international isolation and tightening economic sanctions that target businesses and banks that continue to cooperate with North Korea. To date, international sanctions have been watered down or poorly implemented by countries, such as China, which either seek to maintain a strategic relationship with North Korea or fear that sanctions could lead to its instability. But, that is precisely the point. Sanctions should signal that nuclear weapons could be the regime's undoing and not the ultimate guarantor of "the eternal future of the nation" in order to be effective.

Second, sanctions and economic pressure will be more effective in turning the North's nuclear ambitions if they are paired with a clear path to prosperity for its leadership to take. That path would likely need to include diplomatic incentives as well as detailed steps toward peaceful coexistence and opportunity for the regime to benefit—in terms of building an economically "strong and prosperous" nation—from halting its nuclear program or denuclearizing. Otherwise, it would have little incentive to do so. This could include some type of normalization of relations, although it is unclear that the North Korean regime is looking for better international relations, which would run counter to its anti-imperial partisan identity.

Third, information operations could be used to undermine the international and domestic legitimacy for a Kim regime that is bent on developing nuclear weapons. For instance, the United States could use radio broadcasts, leaflets, telecommunications, and so on, to spread information about the estimated costs of North Korea's nuclear program in contrast to the condition of ordinary North Koreans, including its human rights abuses, in contrast to the potential benefits of a "path to prosperity." Appealing to its historical identity and dignity of the ancient Korean nation, information operations could highlight the perverse priorities of the regime. After every nuclear test, missile launch, or other provocation, the United States and its allies should emphasize the narrative that such actions are a sign of weakness not strength of an increasingly desperate regime with no record of progress or success outside of nuclear capabilities.

Fourth, crises and tensions often serve to strengthen the North Korean internal narrative of being under attack by outsiders and the "sole defender" against US imperialism. Overreacting and hyping the threat from North Korea each time it conducts a nuclear or missile test can heighten the symbolic value of its nuclear program for domestic audiences. The United States and its allies should respond in a measured but concrete manner. Rather than looking reactionary, for instance, they should articulate well in advance how their military postures will respond should North Korea continue on its current path in order to convey that continued nuclear developments will not buy Pyongyang strategic advantage. The types of actions the United States and its allies could take include increasing trilateral security cooperation between the United States, South Korea, and Japan; modifying basing and prepositioning of regional assets to better fight under the nuclear shadow on the peninsula; enhancing intelligence, surveillance and reconnaissance capabilities and operations; building up quick response stealth aircraft and regional conventional prompt strike capabilities; increasing anti-submarine warfare assets and operations; and ramping up regional and homeland missile defenses. By telegraphing these types of actions in advance, the United States and its allies signal a willingness to pace the North Korean threat and incentivize restraint by Pyongyang.

Since North Korea appears bent on developing and deploying an operational nuclear weapons capability, the actions above may slow but are unlikely to stop it from its current course. If that is the case, US interests presumably would be better served by some North Korean decisions regarding doctrine and operations over others. To avoid encouraging

North Korean adoption of risky doctrinal and command and control arrangements, US military measures would need to balance resolve with its own restraint and assurances. The goal would be to convey that any additional US military measures needed to protect the United States and its allies against North Korea's growing nuclear threat are defensive in nature. How to do that is difficult, as it requires overcoming the quintessential security dilemma in international politics. Indeed, it is unclear whether North Korea would ever trust that US intentions are purely defensive. Anything that exacerbates North Korean concerns that the United States is preparing a decapitation or disarming first-strike will incentivize Pyongyang to disperse its weapons and pre-delegate launch authority. Such arrangements would increase the risk of nuclear conflict. At the same time, overemphasizing the defensive nature of US military measures might convince North Korea's leadership that nuclear weapons in fact secure the regime from US military coercion. As a result, it has less incentive to curb its nuclear ambitions.

Lastly, US policy also should consider an information campaign aimed at disrupting command and control arrangements should North Korea take steps to disperse its nuclear forces and delegate launch authority to lower-echelon commanders. The United States could conduct an information campaign aimed at exploiting any divisions in civil–military relations. For instance, it could communicate to military commanders and political leaders that, should conflict come, any and all individuals responsible for carrying out any part of a nuclear-use order will be held personally accountable. On the other hand, those who do not carry out those orders would receive amnesty and an opportunity to pursue a normal life in postwar Korea. An information campaign could also be used to raise questions about the surety, security and authority to complicate command and control related decisions. Conducting successful information operations against a hard target such as North Korea, however, would be very difficult.

NOTES

1. Joel Wit and Sun Young Ahn, "North Korea's Nuclear Futures: Technology and Strategy," US-Korea Institute at SAIS, February 2015, http://38north.org/wp-content/uploads/2015/02/NKNF-NK-Nuclear-Futures-Wit-0215.pdf

2. Kim Jong Un at the March 31, 2013, plenary meeting of the Central Committee of the Workers' Party of Korea, Korean Central Broadcasting Station (in Korean) April 1, 2013, http://www.ncnk.org/resources/news-items/kimjong-uns-speeches-and-public-statements-1/KJU_CentralCommittee_KWP.pdf

3. Scott D. Sagan, "The Origins of Military Doctrine and Command and Control Systems," in Peter R. Lavoy, Scott D. Sagan, and James J. Wirtz (eds.), *Planning the Unthinkable: How New Powers will Use Nuclear, Biological, and Chemical Weapons* (Ithaca, NY: Cornell University Press, 2000), pp. 16–46.

4. Joseph S. Bermudez, Jr., "North Korea and the Political Uses of Strategic Culture," in Jeannie L. Johnson, Kerry M. Kartchner, and Jeffrey A. Larsen (eds.), *Strategic Culture and Weapons of Mass Destruction: Culturally Based Insights into Comparative National Security Policymaking* (New York: Palgrave Macmillan, 2009), p. 191.

5. Don Oberdorfer and Robert Carlin, *The Two Koreas: A Contemporary History* (New York: Basic Books, 2014), p. 17.

6. Quoted in Ken E. Gause, "The Role and Influence of the Party Apparatus," in Kyung-Ae Park and Scott Snyder (eds.), *North Korea in Transition: Politics, Economy, and Society* (New York: Rowman & Littlefield Publishers, Inc., 2013), p. 22.

7. Hazel Smith, *North Korea: Markets and Military Rule* (Cambridge: Cambridge University Press, 2015), p. 65.

8. For discussion on this debate, see Ken E. Gause, *North Korean House of Cards: Leadership Dynamics under Kim Jong Un* (Washington, DC: Committee for Human Rights in North Korea, 2015).

9. Vipin Narang, "What Does It Take to Deter? Regional Power Nuclear Postures and International Conflict," *Journal of Conflict Resolution* 57(3), 2012, pp. 478–508.

10. Bruce Cummings, Korea's Place in the Sun: A Modern History (New York: W.W. Norton & Company, Inc., 2005), p. 414.

11. Korean Central News Agency, broadcast March 13, 1998, *BBC Worldwide Monitoring*, March 14, 1998. Referenced in Michael J. Seth, *A History of Korea: From Antiquity to the Present* (New York: Rowman & Littlefield Publishers, Inc., 2011), p. 443.

12. Seth, *A History of Korea*, p. 443.

13. Smith, *North Korea: Markets and Military Rule*, p. 45.

14. Seth, *A History of Korea*, p. 444.

15. Stephen Haggard, "The Fourth Nuclear Test," Peterson Institute for International Economics, January 6, 2016, http://blogs.piie.com/nk/?p=14724

16. Quoted in Alexandre Y. Mansourov, "The Origins, Evolution, and Current Politics of the North Korean Nuclear Program," *The Nonproliferation Review* (Spring–Summer 1995), p. 29.

17. Chol U Kim, *Songun Politics of Kim Jong Il* (Pyongyang: Foreign Languages Publishing House, 2008), p. 6.

18. Stephan Haggard, "The Fourth Nuclear Test: The Orders," Peterson Institute for International Economics, January 7, 2016, http://blogs.piie.com/nk/?p=14725

19. Haggard, "The Fourth Nuclear Test."

20. Peter Hayes, "The DPRK's Nuclear Constitution," NAPSNet *Policy Forum*, June 13, 2012, http://nautilus.org/napsnet/napsnet-policy-forum/the-dprks-nuclear-constitution/#axzz2jhUXzEj8

21. Tatiana Gabroussenko, "The North Korean Philosophy of Foreigners," in Rudiger Frank, et al. (eds.), *Korea 2012: Politics, Economy, and Society* (Boston: Brill, 2012), p. 245.

22. Gi-wook Shin, *Ethnic Nationalism in Korea: Genealogy, Politics, and Legacy* (Stanford: Stanford University Press, 2006), p. 93.

23. Chung-in Moon and Ildo Hwang, "Identity, Supreme Dignity, and North Korea's External Behavior: A Cultural/Ideational Perspective," *Korea Observer*, Vol. 45, No. 1 (Spring 2014), p. 10.

24. Hwang Jang Yop, "The Problems of Human Rights in North Korea (III)," *KEYS*, Summer 2002 (vol. 9), http://www.dailynk.com/english/keys/2002/9/04.php

25. "Law on Consolidating Position of Nuclear Weapons State," KCNA, April 1, 2013.

26. *Korea Today*, Editorial, "Make This a Year of Brilliant Victory," No. 3, 2004.

27. Smith, *North Korea: Markets and Military Rule*, pp. 120–130.

28. Bruce Cumings, "The Corporate State in North Korea" in Hagen Koo, ed., *State and Society in Contemporary Korea* (Ithaca, NY: Cornell University Press, 1993), 199.

29. "North Korean leader urges 'guerrilla-style' sports tactics," AFP, March 25, 2015, http://sports.yahoo.com/news/north-korean-leader-urges-guerrilla-style-sports-tactics-032650302.html

30. Scott Snyder, *Negotiating on the Edge: North Korean Negotiating Behavior* (Washington, DC: United States Institute of Peace Press, 1999), pp. 21–25.

31. Ibid., p. 22.

32. Joseph S. Bermudez, Jr., "North Korea's Development of a Nuclear Weapons Strategy," US-Korea Institute at SAIS, February 2015, http://38north.org/wp-content/uploads/2015/08/NKNF_Nuclear-Weapons-Strategy_Bermudez.pdf

33. Supreme Command Korean People's Army, "Press Statement," *The Pyongyang Times*, November 26, 2011, p. 1. Quoted in Smith, *North Korea: Markets and Military Rule*, p. 242.

34. Geoffry Blainey argues that optimism about victory in war is often the product of "moods which cannot be grounded in fact" and which "permeate what appear to be rational assessments of the relative military strength of two contending powers." It is the "process by which nations evade reality." Geoffry Blainey, *The Causes of War* (New York: Free Press, 1973), p. 54.

35. Shane Smith, "Implications for US Extended Deterrence and Assurance in East Asia," US-Korea Institute at SAIS, November 2015, http://38north. org/wp-content/uploads/2015/11/NKNF-Smith-Extended-Deterrence-Assurance.pdf

36. Betram D. Wolfe, "The Durability of Despotism in the Soviet System," *The Russian Review* Vol 17, No. 2 (April 1958), p. 92.

37. Oberdorfer and Carlin, *The Two Koreas: A Contemporary History*, p. 17.

38. Adam Cathcart, "'Thrice-Cursed Acts of Treachery'? Parsing North Korea's Report on the Execution of Kim Jong Un's Uncle: An annotated guide to one of the most grandiose news bulletins ever released," *The Atlantic*, December 13, 2013, www.theatlantic.com/international/archive/2013/12/-thrice-cursed-acts-of-treachery-parsing-north-koreas-report-on-the-execution-of-kim-jong-uns-uncle/282339/

39. Alexandre Mansourov, "The Rise and Fall of General Hyon Yong Chol," *38 North*, July 14, 2015, http://38north.org/2015/07/amansourov071415/#_ftn1

40. Michael Madden, "The Education of Choe Ryong Hae," *38 North*, November 24, 2015, http://38north.org/2015/11/mmadden112415/

41. Bermudez, Jr., "North Korea and the Political Uses of Strategic Culture."

42. Benjamin Buch and Scott Sagan, "Our Red Lines and Theirs: New Information Reveals Why Sadaam Hussein Never Used Chemical Weapons in the Iraq War," *Foreign Policy*, December 13, 2013.

43. Julian Ryall, "North Korea plan to attack US mainland revealed in photographs," *The Telegraph*, March 29, 2013, http://www.telegraph.co.uk/news/worldnews/asia/northkorea/9960933/North-Korea-plan-to-attack-US-mainland-revealed-in-photographs.html

44. "Musharraf moved nuclear weapons in Kargil war," *The Nation*, July 6, 2006, https://web.archive.org/web/20071223045736/http://www.nation.com.pk/daily/july-2006/6/index16.php

45. Nicholas Eberstadt, "The Most Dangerous Country," *The National Interest* Vol 57 (Fall 1999), pp. 51–52.

46. Alexandre Mansourov, "Kim Jong Un's Nuclear Doctrine and Strategy: What Everyone Needs to Know," *Nautilus Peace and Security Network*,

December 16, 2014, http://nautilus.org/napsnet/napsnet-special-reports/kim-jong-uns-nuclear-doctrine-and-strategy-what-everyone-needs-to-know/

47. Office of the Secretary of Defense, *Military and Security Developments Involving the Democratic People's Republic: A Report to Congress Pursuant to the National Defense Authorization Act of 2012*, 15 February 2013, http://www.defense.gov/pubs/report_to_congress_on_military_and_security_developments_involving_the_dprk.pdf

48. John S. Park, "Nuclear Ambition and Tension on the Korean Peninsula," in Ashley J. Tellis, Abraham M. Denmark, and Travis Tanner (eds.), *Asia in the Second Nuclear Age* (Washington, DC: The National Bureau of Asian Research, 2013), p. 169.

49. "Report on Plenary Meeting of WPK Central Committee," *KCNA*, March 31, 2013.

50. "Rodong Sinmun on DPRK's legitimate right to self-defence," KCNA, December 20, 2002, http://www.kcna.co.jp/index-e.htm

51. "DPRK FM on Its Stand to Suspend Its Participation in Six-party Talks for Indefinite Period," KCNA, February 10, 2005, http://www.kcna.co.jp/index-e.htm

52. "DPRK Foreign Ministry Clarifies Stand on New Measure to Bolster War Deterrent," KCNA, February 10, 2006, http://www.kcna.co.jp/index-e.htm

53. Marc Santora and Choe Sang-hun, "North Korean Propaganda Video Imagines a Brighter World, Without Manhattan," The New York Times, February 5, 2013, http://thelede.blogs.nytimes.com/2013/02/05/north-korea-propaganda-video-uses-call-of-duty-and-we-are-the-world-to-imagine-a-brighter-world-without-manhattan/?_r=0

CHAPTER 9

Conclusion: Using Strategic Culture to Explain Real-World Decisionmaking

Jeffrey A. Larsen

INTRODUCTION

Decisionmaking by political leaders of a nation, state, nonstate actor, or any other political entity is naturally influenced by value preferences. These values are the accumulation of a lifetime of learning, both active and passive, by that decisionmaker of his or her personal culture. Strategic culture can be thought of as an even larger set of influences. The editors of this book and some of its authors were also participants in an earlier publication on strategic culture: *Strategic Culture and Weapons of Mass Destruction: Culturally Based Insights into Comparative National Security Policymaking.* In a well-crafted definition of strategic culture in that volume they stated that "strategic culture is that set of shared beliefs, assumptions, and modes of behavior, derived from common experiences and accepted narratives (both oral and written) that shape collective identity and relationships to other groups, and which determine appropriate ends and means for achieving security objectives."[1]

That 2009 book was an effort to explain political decisions by nation-states and violent nonstate actors to acquire, proliferate, and potentially use weapons of mass destruction (WMD), and whether to abide by international norms. The book examined eight important states and one

J. A. Larsen (✉)
NATO Defense College, Rome, Italy

© The Author(s) 2018
J. L. Johnson et al. (eds.), *Crossing Nuclear Thresholds,*
Initiatives in Strategic Studies: Issues and Policies,
https://doi.org/10.1007/978-3-319-72670-0_9

251

nonstate actor that were central figures in the international security environment at the time. The project was in many ways a response to factors that had brought consideration of strategic culture back to the forefront of international relations and security: the attacks of 9/11 and the post-9/11 security environment, and calls to develop and establish new frameworks to guide policymaking in the post-Cold War era. Surely, it was thought just a decade ago, these shocks represented unusual and system-altering challenges to the existing system that were unlikely to be replicated any time soon.

CHANGES IN THE PAST DECADE

So what has changed in the decade since that book was written? Nearly everything—or so it sometimes seems. The narratives in many states are being rewritten, and occasionally acted upon; for the West the shocks just keep on coming. To wit:

- The return of Russia, a nuclear-armed great power adversary challenging Europe, and its acquisition by force of neighboring territory that it considered a part of its own sphere of strategic influence.
- The continued growth of China as a regional power and global economic colossus, with potential military power that it is testing in East Asia (especially the South China Sea) through spurious territorial demands and military actions.
- The continued disrespect shown by North Korea toward norms of international behavior, including development of its nuclear weapons and ballistic missile programs, its threats against the United States, South Korea, and Japan, and its belligerent and erratic public relations statements and military testing and exercises.
- Social and political collapse in multiple countries of the Middle East and North Africa, including civil wars in Syria and Libya, an ongoing Arab-Israeli conflict being led at the moment by state-sponsored terrorist groups, and the unresolved status of Palestine. These disputes are based on strategic cultures informed by religious differences.
- The rise of culturally inspired terrorism in the Middle East, most particularly in recent years the emergence of the Islamic State, which purports to represent a pure and extreme interpretation of Islam and the teachings of the Koran. The fact that its efforts are brutal, and that every nation on earth, including the Islamic states in which it

operates, has condemned the group, does not lessen the fact of its ideological grounding in a particular strategic culture perspective.

- The growth of culturally inspired independence movements in Britain, Belgium, Spain, and other states that were previously thought to be immune to such centrifugal forces.
- The rise of populism throughout the Western world. The growing political divisions within the United States and France, for example, reflect alternative views of the world within each country, based on different backgrounds and perspectives: in short, varying political cultures.

Strategic culture has a role to play in explaining, understanding, and possibly predicting the ramifications of all of these challenges to the international status quo. Of course, strategic culture alone is typically a necessary but insufficient explanatory tool for such matters, but at the same time it is nearly always inseparably part of the problem, the explanation, and any solution. This is what makes the concept so challenging: it is messy and amorphous, not easy to grasp like meta-concepts such as realism with its emphasis on more easily measured elements of power, or liberalism which assumes the goodness of humankind; instead, culture reflects the multilayered reality of life and each person's background. This milieu plays a role in decisions as innocuous as what type of bed one prefers to sleep on or what she eats for breakfast, to whether to launch a nuclear attack on a neighboring state. It is a learned set of preferences which determine behavior to a considerable extent. It is the background clutter we all must deal with no matter how rational we think our behavior is or our decisions are. This makes it more challenging than most theoretical or methodological approaches, as numerous authors have shown. But that intellectual challenge makes it no less vital to understanding ourselves, our friends, and our adversaries.

Let us look more closely at one of the above examples to see why we need strategic culture analysts. Since at least 2008, and most evidently since 2014, Russia has violated or ignored multiple norms of international behavior to which it had previously subscribed, including the UN Charter, the Helsinki Process, the 1994 Budapest Agreement, and others, including multiple arms control agreements. It is in violation of at least one international arms control treaty (INF), it continues to undertake a major nuclear weapons modernization program that may include arms build-ups in violation of another strategic nuclear arms control treaty (New Strategic Arms Reduction Treaty), and it is threatening neighbors with nuclear saber rattling and snap exercises. This behavior is undoubtedly driven to some extent by rational calculations and *realpolitik*, but it also reflects the underlying reality of Russian strategic culture. The problem for the West is that the field of Russian area studies, experts who can decipher and explain Russian strategic culture and identify its preferences and likely decisions, has been seriously neglected for a generation. As a result there are few experts left who can reliably explain what Moscow or its leaders are thinking, and nearly no one who can combine that capability with a lifetime of diplomatic or military experience. As but one example, in determining how best to respond to President Putin's challenges along Russia's Western borders—which abut NATO's borders, in many places—a logical question to ask is how the Alliance should respond. The answer is not easy, for cultural reasons. If Mr. Putin is an opportunist, seeking weaknesses in Western economic or military arrangements that he can exploit, the West should respond strongly, perhaps by forward deploying military forces along the border to meet strength with strength. But if the president is merely reflecting traditional Russian paranoia about its security, and if his administration truly believes its country is threatened by NATO or EU enlargement, then his military actions take on a different hue. In that case the deployment of additional Western military forces along the border is the last thing NATO should do; instead, it should focus on diplomacy and dialogue to reduce the level of Russian angst. Differing analyses, therefore, lead to different policy prescriptions that are both based on strategic culture, but which are substantially at odds with one another. Without good cultural analysts to help explain what is really going on, the West does not know which path is preferable.

STRATEGIC CULTURE AS A THEORY AND AS A METHODOLOGY

What does all of this uncertainty and instability mean for students and practitioners of strategic culture as a methodological approach to understanding the world? That is the purpose of this book. It focuses on a narrow slice of international relations to show the value of an approach grounded in strategic culture: identifying and explaining thresholds for nuclear decisions, and determining US foreign policy actions that might influence such decision points.

It may be instructive to recall the aspects that can be considered a part of strategic culture. Strategic culture can include such physical attributes as geography, climate, natural resources, technology, and generational change; political factors like historical experience, elite beliefs, and military organizations; and social/cultural aspects such as myths, symbols, and defining texts.[2] All of this becomes part of what many cultural theorists call the narrative, the basis on which decisions are made. And yet, as Colin Gray reminds us, culture matters deeply, but it is not all that matters.[3] Strategic culture must take its place alongside other explanatory variables when assessing a decision, or a threshold for decision.

The first book in this series included case studies of eight nation-states and one nonstate actor in an attempt to determine how strategic culture played a role in determining whether a political entity would choose to acquire, proliferate, or use WMD, and whether it would adhere to international rules and norms that proscribe such activities. This book continues that examination with six cases, four of which are new and two that are updated or extended from the earlier volume. The goal of the research that produced this volume was to look more closely at nuclear thresholds, those interstices where a state or nonstate actor has the opportunity to choose one path or another—one leading to further advancing its progress toward becoming a nuclear state, or to share or possibly even use its nuclear capabilities, and the other moving away from such aspirations. The secondary effort of the project was to then identify potential levers for US foreign policy in order to influence those decision points—the goal being to persuade the other party to choose the path toward reduced emphasis on nuclear weapons.

Traditional nuclear literature has treated nuclear problems by "type" and has developed a number of labels in order to effectively do so (i.e., counterproliferation, deterrence). By contrast, this volume provides an innovative approach to framing nuclear concerns. Rather than addressing them by type, the authors address serial decision points in a state's journey toward becoming a nuclear power. "Nuclear thresholds" are near to medium term actions which are both plausible and critical in that they have potential for significant impact in the international security environment. These may include nuclear proliferation concerns, but also actions as varied as unilateral military action to protect one's nuclear monopoly, or tactical nuclear use in violation of long-standing nuclear-taboo norms. Because these have the potential to occur simultaneously, there is value in treating these cases as complex and interconnected aspects of a global nuclear field. This approach is more reflective of the reality faced by policymakers and challenges the community of nuclear scholars to think in terms of the strategic complexity of such a dynamic environment, for example, the repercussions of attempting to influence the nuclear behavior of a long-standing "friend" of the United States (e.g., Saudi Arabia) at the same time as it is dealing in a different way with a long-standing adversary (such as Iran).

The book uses a new methodological approach developed by Jeannie Johnson and Marilyn Maines for the US intelligence community that they call the Cultural Topography Analytic Framework (CTAF). As explained in Chap. 2, the CTAF method draws from Grounded Theory,[4] an approach tested within anthropology and often unfamiliar to political scientists. Its approach is inductive rather than deductive. The CTAF process seeks to explain "why things which happened were to be expected," and then project probabilities for future iterations.[5] A deductive model which seeks causal connections—why an event *must* have happened—is an overly deterministic tool for capturing and explaining cultural influence. Humans act as willful agents, absorbing but also impacting the cultures around them. The result is a cultural context which flexes and bends, requiring a hermeneutical approach—the art of interpretation—rather than a positivist pursuit of natural laws.

The CTAF is designed to serve foreign and security policy decisionmakers by defining the range of probable behaviors pursued by a foreign actor in order to enhance efforts at planning, anticipate backlash to US policies, identify actors and issue areas within another polity most open to US influence, and craft tailored strategies accordingly. In this, the book's method invites a more nuanced approach to security policy than traditional realpolitik. True, it is possible that realism could anticipate many of the nuclear decisions taken by the states under consideration in our volume. The realist assumption of states as "black boxes" of similar motivation and trajectory is inhibiting, however, for policymakers who wish to explore options beyond the often blunt traditional toolsets used to influence the behavior of other actors on the world stage. This book, on the other hand, supplies the data required for a more carefully crafted set of strategic tools. By opening the box of state structure and examining its decisionmaking norms, its perceptions of acceptable mechanisms for exerting influence, its regard for the United States as a partner, its sense of identity and entitlement vis-à-vis nuclear arms, and cultural narratives regarding nuclear use, the analyst using CTAF can be better prepared to devise tailored and effective strategies for dealing with nuclear thresholds faced by other states, including potential adversaries. The variety of "inducements" each author identifies as salient for the particular regimes they study, and the distinct and regime-specific policy recommendations they offer, are a testament to the utility of a culturally informed approach to US nuclear strategy.

STRATEGIC CULTURE DOES MATTER

Each case study examines its country in terms of identity, norms, values, and perceptual lens in order to offer culturally based insights into their behavior and intentions. From this, each chapter makes recommendations for US foreign policy that were tailored for use with that actor. The focus on nuclear thresholds is a new and fresh approach to understanding nuclear decisionmaking.

Nuclear policy and decisionmaking have a long and rich pedigree created by some of the most brilliant minds of the last 70 years. As mentioned, most previous analyses have focused on nuclear challenges by type—deterrence policy, missile defenses, command and control, nuclear use, and so on—or by more general national studies of adversaries. This book takes a new and different approach, addressing the range of complex and dynamic nuclear challenges US policymakers are likely to face in the near to medium term, while taking into account the dynamic nature of such decisions, and the risk and potential dangers inherent in decisions involving nuclear matters. Its focus is on nuclear "thresholds," those critical nodal periods when an actor must decide "yes" or "no" on a decision of consequence for nuclear acquisition, proliferation, or use, and whether to violate extant norms and agreements. This is a refreshing approach to the realm of study known as strategic affairs.

Several themes emerged in the case studies in the book. For example, in those actors who have or are likely to make "go" decisions at various nuclear thresholds, there was a common perception of a strong sense of national pride and feelings of entitlement to being a nuclear player on the international scene. These were based on that state's commonly shared narrative—its strategic culture. In addition, many of these decision points were influenced by a perceptual lens colored by that actor's threat perceptions; a "go" decision was often related to the fear a state or nonstate actor had relative to one of its (often nuclear-armed) more powerful neighbors.

The Ukrainian sense of identity is Western-leaning and dedicated to basic international norms of nonproliferation, which predisposed its leaders to abandon plans for retaining Soviet-era nuclear weapons and to join the Nuclear Nonproliferation Treaty. This reflected a sense of restraint by Ukraine. Yet there is an underlying longing to return to those early post-Cold War years when Ukraine had more importance on the international scene, a situation that some believed was due in part to the existence of Soviet nuclear weapons on Ukrainian soil. One issue for the West will be how to maintain a feeling of restraint on Kiev's part.

Russia is an enigma.[6] The obvious trademarks of its strategic culture, however, are easy to identify: national pride, belief in its role as the keeper of the true Christian faith, its view of Russian civilization as unique and superior to that of the West. At the same time, it is afraid of outsiders, of invasion, and of the military, economic, and social aspects of the enlargement of European culture. The latter concerns require strong military forces, including modern nuclear weapons and the means for their delivery.

Israel's sense of identity as a law-abiding democratic nation with civilian control of the military, and limited power for the prime minister, has been reflected in its choosing on repeated occasions not to attack Iran's nuclear program. Israel's strategic culture gives it a real sense of entitlement to whatever forces will secure the Jewish state, including (presumably, if not openly confirmed) its nuclear arsenal. This is one part of its "peace through strength" policy.

Iran's identity as the vanguard of the Shi'ite worldview, with its sense of entitlement to nuclear power, makes it an untrustworthy actor in the international scene. While many in the West would prefer not to keep it as the adversary it has been for nearly 40 years, its own actions, based on its own strategic culture, keep it as one.

North Korea's identity is based on its self-perception as a bastion of racial purity, descended from the glorious emperors of the past, and the Kim regime's identity as the leader of a besieged country. The leader's comments and the propaganda coming from this backward country is so absurd as to be laughable, were it not for their dramatic improvements in nuclear weapons and delivery means in recent years. The combination of a strategic culture that believes in its own superiority and its role in regional leadership, combined with a lack of commitment to international norms, all mixed with modern weaponry, makes for a dangerous concoction.

Saudi Arabia's self-identity is to serve as the guardian of Islam's holiest sites, an identity and role that cannot be yielded to Iranian Shi'ite apostates. Despite its latent capabilities, however, the Saudis do not appear to be a serious contender for nuclear weapons capabilities, in part because they do not have the strategic cultural affinity to do so.

PRACTICAL MATTERS: A CHECKLIST OF POLICY RESPONSES TO NUCLEAR THRESHOLDS

Understanding the cultural factors involved in nuclear decisionmaking can enhance one's analysis of a state or nonstate actor, including the decisions it is likely to make at one of the nuclear thresholds. Decisions as to whether to cross one of those thresholds may be swayed to some extent by foreign policy and diplomatic, military, or economic factors. This in turn relies on improved understanding of the decisionmaking process of those states of concern. Such knowledge can lead to an improved ability to craft creative strategies to influence the process in other states.

The following checklist, developed by one of this book's co-editors, Marilyn Maines, represents an attempt to break out the many decision points or steps along the road to a nuclear weapons capability that fall within each of six categories.[7] Once these decision points have been successfully identified, the CTAF approach can be applied to each of the individual decision points with the goal of discerning and evaluating the impact of the key cultural factors on each of the individual thresholds. This effort will help policymakers determine the right way to influence a state's decisionmaking.

Nuclear Decision Thresholds

Thresholds Related to Compliance or Noncompliance with International Nonproliferation Regimes and Norms

Normally, the threshold of deciding whether to adhere to or violate commitments already undertaken, or commitments contemplated, could occur at any point in a nuclear development program. At this stage, the nation-state or nonstate group may not have decided whether it is pursuing a basic nuclear science and technology (S&T) capability for general knowledge, undertaking an effort for peaceful applications of nuclear power, or if it intends to progress to a nuclear weapons research and development effort. Many of the initial steps within this category may be taken with full adherence to the NPT. Crossing this threshold, however, ultimately involves deciding whether to cheat or violate existing arms control or treaty agreements, or to break commitments to international nonproliferation norms and attempt to procure a nuclear weapon or nuclear weapons capability. This threshold could include the following associated sub-thresholds:

- Whether to explore or pursue nuclear research and S&T capability.
- Whether to develop a cadre of qualified nuclear scientists.
- Whether to approach a sympathetic nuclear-capable state for assistance in training and/or to make efforts to incorporate scientists within other country's training and research programs.
- Whether to establish basic nuclear research laboratories and institutes.
- Whether to make initial resource investment in technology required to lay the foundations for a future nuclear program.
- Whether to begin uranium prospecting and exploration in country, or, if no uranium deposits exist, to acquire uranium from another nation-state.
- Whether to openly acknowledge interest in a nuclear program for basic S&T or peaceful applications of nuclear power.
- Whether the pursuit of nuclear weapons capability, once taken, will be open or covert.
- Who to include in the initial organizational structure for a nuclear program, including:

  - The role of nation-state leadership in nuclear program decisions.
  - The role of civilian nuclear authority within the nuclear program.
  - The role of military organizations within the nuclear program.

Acquisition of Nuclear Weapons or Nuclear Weapons Capability
This is the second stage of decisionmaking within the nuclear weapons development process in which a nation-state or nonstate group moves forward with the development of a nuclear weapons research and development and/or production capability and constructs indigenous production facilities. For each basic production capability or set of facilities, the nation-state or group must decide whether to acquire the capability on its own or to seek assistance from a sympathetic state or supplier for some part of the material or technology needed. Also at each decision point the state or nonstate group must decide if this production capability will be pursued openly or covertly. This threshold could be composed of the following sub-thresholds and decision points:

- Whether to begin uranium mining and processing.

  - Development of in-country mining sites if natural resources are available.

- Acquisition of uranium ore from outside source if there are no in-country deposits.
- Decision to build uranium ore refining and processing facilities for ore processing and production of yellow cake and green salt.

- Whether to build an initial nuclear research reactor.

  - Use own scientific capabilities and resources.
  - Seek assistance in construction from a sympathetic nuclear-capable nation-state.

- Whether to pursue uranium enrichment capability.

  - Type of enrichment process to be used: centrifuge, gaseous diffusion, laser isotope separation, or other more experimental process.
  - Build pilot plant or laboratory scale enrichment capability.
  - Construction of full-scale uranium enrichment facility.

- Whether to pursue plutonium production capability.

  - Use small-scale withdrawal/reprocessing of fuel rods from nuclear research reactor (only for certain reactor types).
  - Construction of dedicated plutonium production reactor(s).
  - Build pilot plant or laboratory scale plutonium separation and reprocessing facility.

- Construction of full-scale plutonium reprocessing facility.

  - Whether to build/acquire related technology capabilities and facilities necessary for a nuclear fuel cycle.
  - Construction of a heavy water production plant.
  - Construction or development of rare earth metals, chemical production, and conventional high explosives capability.
  - Development of a technology base for sophisticated machine tools and technical instrumentation.

- Whether to construct nuclear weapons assembly facilities.

  - Use of small-scale pilot assembly facilities located at nuclear research sites.
  - Construction of full-scale nuclear weapons assembly facility.

- Whether to acquire nuclear weapons delivery capability.

- Acquisition of nuclear-capable ballistic missiles from a missile producing state.
- Development of an indigenous ballistic missile production program.
- Development of nontraditional delivery system(s).

- Whether to proceed with nuclear weapons testing.

  - Use of laboratory level, sub-critical and cold-testing methods only, no full-scale nuclear testing program.
  - Decision not to test device. A nation-state may be using an existing nuclear design that has already been tested or may decide not to test to avoid international censure.
  - Construction of a nuclear test site. This decision requires (i) identification of a geologically suitable, remote location; (ii) preparation of tunnels/adits and/or drilled shafts to detonate nuclear devices; and (iii) acquisition or development of nuclear test instrumentation and diagnostic capabilities.
  - Use of alternative nuclear testing options. This could include another state's test site, or testing in a concealed manner (space, underwater, etc.)

Nuclear Counterproliferation: Actively Deny Acquisition of Nuclear Weapons to Others Through Preemptive Attack or Use Covert Means to Denigrate Capability of Nuclear Weapons

What role do sociocultural factors play in formulating policies and initiatives to actively deny or counter the acquisition of nuclear weapons by neighboring states or to negatively affect or prevent use of existing nuclear weapons? This could involve the following sub-thresholds:

- Whether to preemptively attack another country's alleged nuclear weapons development facilities to deny them acquisition of the infrastructure for acquiring nuclear weapons of their own.
- Whether to take covert steps to denigrate another country's nuclear weapons capability or render them useless by technical means.

Proliferation and Transfer of Nuclear Weapons

How do sociocultural factors promote or inhibit tendencies or incentives to proliferate or transfer nuclear weapons? This is the stage of decision-making within the nuclear weapons development process in which a nation-state or nonstate group that has already developed a nuclear capability decides if it is willing to share this capability with other nation-states or groups. Nuclear-capable nation-states or groups will also have to decide on their willingness to share full nuclear capability or to limit assistance to individual capabilities within the nuclear fuel cycle. For each decision point within this stage, nation-states or groups will also have to decide if proliferation assistance is to be supplied openly or secretly. It could involve these additional issues:

- Whether to transfer or sell a complete nuclear weapon to another nation-state or group seeking to acquire nuclear capability.
- Whether to share nuclear weapons design information.
- Whether to supply nuclear weapons technology or provide assistance with key nuclear components or production capabilities that would substantially advance a nuclear program (e.g., provision of uranium, assistance with nuclear reactor design/construction, supply of centrifuge technology for uranium enrichment, supply of plutonium reprocessing technology).
- Whether to share nuclear weapons delivery system technology or to supply nuclear-capable ballistic missiles.
- Whether to provide technical experts or nuclear scientists working in country with nation-state or group seeking to acquire nuclear capability.
- Whether or not to supply nuclear proliferation support at an official state level, but to overlook rogue scientists or private efforts to sell or transfer nuclear technology or production related equipment.

Operational Deployment of Nuclear Weapons
How do sociocultural factors help determine whether to proceed with overt deployment of nuclear weapons, or to deploy covertly? This threshold is composed of the following additional issues:

- Whether to proceed with development and deployment of an operational nuclear weapons capability.
- Whether to overtly deploy or covertly deploy nuclear weapons.
- Decision to develop a command and control system for authorized release and use of nuclear weapons.
- Decision on storage and deployment of nuclear weapons.

- Military or civilian control of nuclear weapons storage facilities.
- Physical deployment of combat ready nuclear weapons
- Option for separate storage of certain nuclear weapons components with need for some final assembly before release/use.
- Proximity of nuclear weapons to nuclear delivery systems (e.g., use of mobile missile systems, storage at/nearby ballistic missile sites or on board nuclear-capable submarines).

Use of Nuclear Weapons

How do sociocultural factors influence decisions to use nuclear weapons, either in the sense of wielding nuclear weapons for deterrence and coercive purposes or in the sense of actually conducting attacks with nuclear weapons? This is the ultimate stage of nuclear decisionmaking within the nuclear weapons development process in which a nation-state decides what nuclear weapons it will produce and how it will deploy or use its weapons. In this stage, a nuclear program is institutionalized, and cultural factors play a significant role in determining a state's nuclear doctrine. Strategic decisions must be made on use of nuclear weapons for deterrence and coercive purposes, use of nuclear weapons as a key symbol to obtain global status, and formulation of actual command and control doctrines on nuclear weapons use. Whether the state will adopt approaches that view nuclear weapons only as a last resort, adopt a "no first use" doctrine, or develop a more aggressive doctrine—such as preemptive nuclear strike, or use of conventional weapons or WMD within a region to deny nuclear capability to other regional rivals—become key threshold decisions is this stage.

- Whether to develop an explicit or tacit nuclear doctrine or national policy.

  - Use of nuclear capability primarily for deterrence. This approach could include such doctrines as "no first use," presumption of nonuse, or "minimum credible deterrence" policies.
  - Use of nuclear capability for defense only. Nation-state or group publicly states that it will use nuclear weapons only in retaliation for nuclear, chemical, or biological attacks on national territory or deployed forces.

- First-strike use of nuclear capability as a preventative, preemptive measure to prevent another state or adversary from acquiring nuclear capability.

- Decisions related to the size (numbers), composition (mix of basing options), and posture (alert status) of the nuclear arsenal. How many weapons, what types will be produced to achieve a desired level of nuclear capability or strategic assurance, and how will they be postured?

CONCLUSION

Strategic culture can serve as a valuable supplemental approach to achieve better understanding of another state and the factors that will play into its decisionmaking at various nuclear threshold points. Such an approach can supplement traditional methods, but using a cultural lens allows the analyst to cast a wider net for information than simply thinking in terms of realism or some other international relations theory. Focusing on nuclear thresholds can help avoid the proverbial stovepipe of information that is based solely on a particular aspect or type of nuclear weapons study. It also allows a country to better determine the decisions another state is likely to make when it comes up to a nuclear threshold, thereby allowing the first state to best influence the state facing that decision point. The cultural toppography analytic framework model is an effective way of conducting such research; it shows what can be done and how to do it. The case studies in this book showed how CTAF can be applied to real-world situations, and the checklist in this final chapter provides a rudimentary set of questions for the analyst interested in how another states will deal with a "go/no go" decision.

NOTES

1. Jeannie L. Johnson, Kerry M. Kartchner, and Jeffrey A. Larsen, "Introduction," *Strategic Culture and Weapons of Mass Destruction: Culturally Based Insights into Comparative National Security Policymaking* (New York: Palgrave Macmillan, 2009), p. 9.
2. Jeffrey Lantis, "Strategic Culture: From Clausewitz to Constructivism," Ibid., pp. 39–41.
3. Colin Gray, "Out of the Wilderness: Prime Time for Strategic Culture," Ibid., p. 223.

4. Barney G. Glaser and Anselm L. Strauss, *The Discovery of Grounded Theory: Strategies for Qualitative Research* (Chicago: Aldine Publishing Company, 1967).

5. Georg Henrik von Wright, *Explanation and Understanding* (Ithaca: Cornell University Press, 1971), 14.

6. I won't repeat Churchill's famous and overused expression here, but he was right.

7. Ms. Maines developed this list specifically for use in the applying the CTAF methodology presented in Chap. 2.

Index[1]

---

[1] Note: Page numbers followed by 'n' refer to notes.

© The Author(s) 2018

J. L. Johnson et al. (eds.), *Crossing Nuclear Thresholds*, Initiatives in Strategic Studies: Issues and Policies, https://doi.org/10.1007/978-3-319-72670-0

CPSIA information can be obtained
at www.ICGtesting.com
Printed in the USA
LVHW020729050921
696998LV00015B/2025

9 783030 102470